UNDERSTANDING LEARNING DISABILITIES:

A PARENT GUIDE AND WORKBOOK

Third Edition, Revised and Expanded

FOR PARENTS, TEACHERS, PROFESSIONALS, ADVOCATES AND OTHERS WHO WORK
WITH, OR COME IN CONTACT WITH, INDIVIDUALS WITH LEARNING DISABILITIES

Produced by the Learning Disabilities Council

Richmond, Virginia

FUNDING PROVIDED BY THE JACKSON FOUNDATION

Edited by Mary Louise Trusdell and Inge W. Horowitz

York Press, Inc.
Timonium, Maryland, 21094

Understanding Learning Disabilities: A Parent Guide and Workbook was developed and written by members of the Learning Disabilities Council of Richmond, Virginia, as a resource for parents and others concerned about individuals with learning disabilities. Considerable care and effort have been exercised in gathering and verifying information in the Guide. However, neither the Learning Disabilities Council nor the publisher is responsible for changes, errors or omissions. Furthermore, the Learning Disabilities Council does not endorse individuals, consultants, schools, groups, or organizations. Neither do we endorse or recommend any specific treatments, therapies, approaches, or techniques We welcome the input and comments of those using the Guide.

First Edition 1989
Second Edition 1991
Third Edition 2002

Copyright 1989, 1991, 2002 by the Learning Disabilities Council, P.O. Box 8451, Richmond, Virginia 23226.

Library of Congress Cataloging-in-Publication Data

Understanding learning disabilities : a parent guide and workbook / [edited by] Mary Louise Trusdell, Inge W. Horowitz.—3rd ed., rev. and expanded.
    p. cm.
  Previous editions published by the Learning Disabilities Council.
  Includes bibliographical references.
  ISBN 0-912752-67-X (pbk.) — ISBN 0-912752-68-8 (3 ring binder)
   1.Learning disabled children--Education--Parent participation--Handbooks, manuals, etc. 2. Learning disabilities--Handbooks, manuals, etc. I. Trusdell, Mary Louise. II. Horowitz, Inge W. III. Learning Disabilities Council (Richmond, Va.)

LC4704.5.U53 2002
649'.15--dc21   2002019968

THE BOOK WAS MANUFACTURED IN THE UNITED STATES OF AMERICA.
Printing and Binding by Data Reproductions, Inc.

UNDERSTANDING LEARNING DISABILITIES:
A PARENT GUIDE AND WORKBOOK

Table of Contents

	Page
DEDICATION	xi
FOREWORD	xiii
ACKNOWLEDGMENTS	xv
HOW TO USE THIS BOOK	xvii
The Purpose of This Book	xvii
Reading the Book	xvii
Your Suggestions	xviii

CHAPTERS

1. LEARNING DISABILITIES: THE HIDDEN DISABILITY	1
Who Has Learning Disabilities?	1
What Learning Disabilities *Are*	1
What Learning Disabilities *Are Not*	2
The Hidden Disability	2
Characteristics of LD	2
What are Attention Deficit Disorder (ADD) and Attention Deficit/Hyperactivity Disorder (ADHD)?	3
Diagnosis of ADD and ADHD	4
What Causes ADD or ADHD?	4
Management of ADD and ADHD	5
What About Special Education?	5
Do You Outgrow ADD and ADHD?	5
Summary	6
Examples of Characteristics of Learning Disabilities	7
Workbook: Parent Observation Sheet	17

2. COPING AS A PARENT..19

    Causes of LD...19

    Reactions of Parents...19

    Feelings of Guilt..19

    Others' Reactions...19

    Importance of Having a Confidant..20

    Parent Support Groups..20

    Being an Advocate...For Your Child.....................................20

    Being an Advocate...For Other Individuals with LD.............21

    Structure..21

    Communication..22

    Taking Care of the Caretakers...22

    Summary..22

    Bill of Rights for Parents of Children with LD.....................23

3. HELPING YOUR CHILD AT HOME..25

    Self-Esteem...25

        Signs of Poor Self-esteem..25

        Suggestions for Improving Self-esteem............................25

        Home as Haven..26

    Extracurricular Activities..27

        Suggested Activities..27

        Resources...28

    Family Involvement...29

        Helping the Whole Family...29

        Helping the Child With LD Learn.....................................30

        Tutoring and Homework..31

    Discipline..32

        Parent's Response to the Child...33

        Child's Response...33

        Handling Anger...33

        Consistency...34

Punishment...34

Interpersonal Relationships...35

    The Family..35

    Other Children...35

Summary..37

Workbook: Self-Esteem..39

Workbook: Weekly Schedule..41

Workbook: Special Assignment: Homework Success...43

Workbook: Homework Suggestions...45

Workbook: Daily Homework Sheet..47

Workbook: Launching Better Behavior: Accentuate the Positive.............................49

Workbook: 13 Parent Rules for Responding to Angry Children...............................51

4. THE STUDENT WITH LEARNING DISABILITIES AT SCHOOL...........................53

   Part A: The PUBLIC School's Role in Referral, Evaluation, Eligiblity,

        and the IEP...53

Free Appropriate Public Education (FAPE)..53

Individuals With Disabilities Education Act (IDEA)...53

Referral...54

After the Referral..55

Evaluations..56

    Educational Evaluation..56

    Medical Evaluation...57

    Socio-Cultural Evaluation..57

    Psychological Evaluation...57

    Observation...57

The Eligibility Meeting..58

    Preliminary Team...58

    What does the IEP do? 58

    What's in the IEP Document? 58

Before the IEP Meeting..59

    Notification of IEP Meeting..59

Preparation for the Meeting...59

Suggestions to the Older Student...60

The IEP Team...60

The IEP Meeting...60

Factors to be Considered...60

Components of the IEP...61

Additional Pointers for Parents..63

How is Placement Decided? 63

What Types of Placements Are There? 64

Who Has Access to the IEP? 65

Caution: Before You Agree to the IEP... 65

When You Don't Agree With the School District ... .66

After the IEP and Placement *Have* Been Agreed to, Then What? 66

Reviewing and Revising the IEP...67

Part B: The PRIVATE School's Role in Referral, Evaluation, Eligibility,

and Service Plan Development...69

Referral and Evaluation...69

Eligibility...69

Services..69

Part C: The Parent's Role in Problem-Solving and Maintaining Records............................71

Avoiding Problems...71

Resolving Problems..73

Informal Meetings...73

Mediation...73

Maintaining a Filing System..73

The Importance of Records..74

Your First Step..74

Materials Needed...74

Further Suggestions for Notebook...75

Use of Workbook Pages...76

Part D: Another Avenue for Services: Section 504......77

   What is Section 504? 77

   Section 504 Definition of a Disability......77

   A School's Obligations Under Section 504......77

   Resolving Disagreements Related to Section 504......78

   Chapter Summary 79

   The Identification → Evaluation → Placement Process......82

   Workbook: Make It Happen with Positive Parent Advocacy......85

   Workbook: Tracking the Special Education Process......87

   Workbook: How to Use the Form, "My Child's Test Results"......89

   Workbook: My Child's Test Results - 1......91

   Workbook: My Child's Test Results - 2......93

   Workbook: IEP Planning Forms for Parents......95

   Workbook: Telephone/Meeting Log......109

   Workbook: Table of Contents for Documents......111

5. THE YOUNG ADULT......113

   Independence Through Self-Advocacy......113

      With Parents' and Teachers' Help… 113

      Self-Advocacy......113

   Transition Planning While in School......114

   Laws Protecting Students After High School......115

      Americans With Disabilities Act (ADA) 115

      Section 504 of the Rehabilitation Act......115

   College for Students with Learning Disabilities......116

      Getting Ready For College......116

      Standardized Admission Tests (SATs) 117

      What Are the College Options? 117

      What Makes A College Student Successful? 117

      What to Look For In A College......118

      Services That May Be Available......118

      How Else Can Parents Help? 118

Vocational Education and Jobs..119

    Vocational Assessment...119

    Training and Employment Resources......................................120

    Jobs, Paid and Volunteer..121

Social Aspects and Success...121

    Social Awareness..122

    Giftedness and Perseverance...122

Summary..123

Workbook: Checklist: Planning For the Future..125

Workbook: Questions to Ask Before Applying to a College.........................127

6. **ADULTS WITH LEARNING DISABILITIES**...................................131

Characteristics of Adults with LD...131

The Workplace..132

    ADA and Section 504...132

    To Disclose or Not...133

    "Shall I Take the Job?" 133

Relationships..133

    Suggestions for Adults with LD..134

    Suggestions for the Partner of an Adult with LD.....................134

Self-Esteem..134

Success...135

Summary...136

Workbook: Could I Have a Learning Disability?..137

7. **ASSISTIVE TECHNOLOGY**...139

What is Assistive Technology?..139

How Can Assistive Technology Devices Help a Child or Adult

    with Learning Disabilities?...140

What Kinds of Technologies are Out There? 140

Cautions and Other Comments..142

    Skills Needed by Students...142

Information Needed by Teachers..142

Technical Devices at College..142

Technical Devices on the Job...142

On-Line Resources for More Information..142

Resources for More Information..144

Summary...145

8. GIFTED, WITH LEARNING DISABILITIES...................................147

Traits of Gifted Children with LD..147

Examples of LD/Giftedness..148

Incidence..148

ADD with LD/Giftedness..148

The School's Response to LD/Giftedness..149

Summary...150

APPENDICES...151

A - Definitions of Learning Disabilities...153

B - Explanation of Resource Pages:...155

    B-1: NCLD's Resource List..157

    B-2: Additional Resources..175

    B-3: Agencies by State...179

C - What if Your Child Requires Disciplinary Action by the School?..............181

D - How is an LD Classroom Different from a Regular Education Classroom?...183

    How is Accommodation Different from Remediation?............................183

E - Get Your Child Ready for Work..187

F - College, Vocational, and Transitional Resources...................................193

G - The GED Test...195

H - Tips for Workplace Success..197

PERSONAL STORIES...199

The Lifelong Impact of a Label...201

One Man's Battle Against Dyslexia..203

One Person's Path to Literacy..206

It's Never Too Late..208

A Brother's Perspective..211

Jonathan's Story..214

ADDITIONAL READING..219

Publications of Learning Disabilities Association of America...............................220

Publications of International Dyslexia Association..227

GLOSSARY OF LEARNING DISABILITIES TERMS................................231

ENDNOTES...243

BIBLIOGRAPHY..249

SUGGESTED CHANGES AND ADDITIONS TO THIS BOOK

DEDICATION

This book is dedicated to all individuals with learning

disabilities and their families, in hopes that it will

make each day a little better.

Foreword

I understand the challenges and frustrations faced by individuals with learning disabilities and their families. Whether the person with learning disabilities is a young child, an adolescent, or an adult, the environment in which he or she lives and works places demands that seem overwhelming at times.

As an adult with a learning disability and a professional in this field, I can empathize with the struggles faced by parents as well as their children. As parents, you need to realize that your child's learning disability can be viewed as a weakness in a sea of strengths and that there is always hope. There are ways that you and others can assist your child to reach his or her potential. But all this takes time, commitment, resources -- and information.

This commitment to assist individuals, families, and professionals is espoused by groups such as The Learning Disabilities Council. The council was initially formed as a coalition of civic, business, and educational organizations, in Richmond, Va., to aid the community in understanding the needs of individuals with learning disabilities. Additionally, this group was formed because there was no single organization to provide the help or information which parents and others so desperately needed.

Your first instinct, as a parent of a child with a learning disability, is to do all you can to help your child. This includes finding as much information as you can about learning disabilities. There perhaps have been times that you have felt helpless and not sure where to turn, finding that there was no one publication with all the information you needed. In 1987, the Learning Disabilities Council realized this need for one publication that contained comprehensive information on learning disabilities. As a result, *Understanding Learning Disabilities: A Parent Guide and Workbook* was created, and published in 1989, first for a local and then, in 1991, for a national audience.

Assembled by parents and professionals in the field, this book addresses issues from early childhood through adulthood. Besides containing current information on learning disabilities, it has invaluable suggestions, guidelines, resources, and worksheets, not only for parents but also for teachers, professionals, advocates, and others who work with or come in contact with individuals with learning disabilities.

In 1990, this publication was recognized by the National Center for Learning Disabilities (NCLD) as one of its first recipients of NCLD's National Replication Award. This award allowed the book to reach a national audience. This current edition reflects what is known today about learning disabilities and the federal laws and regulations to assist individuals with learning disabilities in realizing their potential.

It is important to remember that while there may be challenges, frustrations, and disappointments at times, your child *can* reach his or her potential. Most important, your child needs your continuous support, understanding, and love, along with your increasing knowledge about learning disabilities as well as the help of informed teachers. We must all work together to ensure that no child or adult is left behind or falls through the cracks because, along the way, there was no one who really cared and understood your child's learning disability.

Harley A. Tomey, III
February, 2002

Harley Tomey was president of the Learning Disabilities Council of Richmond, Virginia, at the time the first edition of the book was started in 1987. Currently, he is an educational specialist in learning disabilities with the Virginia Department of Education, and President of The International Dyslexia Association.

Acknowledgments

This is the third time that the Learning Disabilities Council of Richmond, Va. has undertaken an edition of UNDERSTANDING LEARNING DISABILITIES: A PARENT GUIDE AND WORKBOOK.

The first edition of the book, published in 1989, was conceived as a local project, and was written entirely by volunteer members of the Council, both parents and professionals. The original Writing Committee was composed of:

Elaine S. Ackman	Inge W. Horowitz
Robin S. Barton	Betty Randle
Missy Ritsch Chase	Jody L. Sands
Gweniviere L. C. Hancock	Martha C. Yeatts
Ruth Harris	

Presidents of the Council during this period were Harley A. Tomey, III (1987-88) and Sally C. Elliott (1988-89). Writers/Editors were Mary Louise Trusdell and Linda S. Williams, then Executive Director. The Memorial Foundation for Children of Richmond, Va.; Crestar Bank; CSX Corporation; and Cadmus Communications underwrote the endeavor.

By 1991, enthusiastic response to the book from parents across the country had prompted the production of a second edition. A grant from the National Center for Learning Disabilities (NCLD) enabled the Council to update and reprint the book, making it applicable to parents throughout the United States.

Revision and production of the second edition were under the supervision of Linda S. Williams, as Executive Director, with Peter W. D. Wright, Esq., as legal consultant. Members of the Learning Disabilities Council who oversaw the administration of the project were:

Maria C. Butler	Carol Harris, President
Missy Ritsch Chase	Jack F. Torza

In the years following 1991, changing priorities concerning learning disabilities, as well as new laws and regulations, encouraged the Board of the Council to seek funding and undertake, in the year 2000, another revision – this time more complete and extensive. Margaret P. Weiss, Ph.D., was engaged to write early drafts, following which Inge W. Horowitz and Mary Louise Trusdell were invited to complete this third edition.

A number of people have been most helpful in this undertaking, particularly members of the Learning Disabilities Council Board of Directors. They are:

Candace P. David	Deborah L. Ramer
Patricia W. DeOrio	Scott H. Ramer
Nancy St.C. Finch	Whitney P. Sears
Paul J. Gerber	Harley A. Tomey, III
Robin L. Hawks, President	Jack F. Torza
Inge W. Horowitz	Julie DeO. Wingfield
Edie McRee-Whiteman	

The L.D. Council is greatly indebted to reviewers of specific chapters and/or appendices, who gave generously of their knowledge and time. They are:

Linda McKelvy Chik	Jane T. Nott
Nancy St.C. Finch	Sheila C. Price
Paul J. Gerber, Ph.D.	Harley A. Tomey, III
Robin L. Hegner, Esq.	Priscilla L. Vail
Robert MacGillivray	Richard Wanderman

Others have made valuable suggestions about various sections and chapters. They are:

Carol G. Fruhwald	Susan B. Spielberg, Esq.
Barbara P. Guyer, Ed.D.	Evelyn R. Tower
Shannon L. Lavinus	

We are appreciative of the accurate technical support provided by typists Agnes Fischer, Anne Farmer, and Tia Kimbro, as well as computer experts Alexander L. and Alla Kogan, Harold Horowitz, and Sayako Earles. Alison Griffin has donated her many skills as the principal proofreader, while Bruce R. Simon, Library Associate of the Richmond Public Library, responded graciously to all of our queries about endnotes and the bibliography. Amiable and conscientious Wesley E. Foxwell was the Graphic Designer.

Undergirding the development of this third edition has been the financial support of the Jackson Foundation of Richmond, Va., an essential element in its production. We are particularly grateful to the Executive Director, Patricia M. Asch, whose personal interest has been unflagging, and vital to sustaining this project. We are indebted to Anne R. Fischer for arranging this contact, and to Edie McRee-Whiteman and Deborah L. Ramer for writing the grant with the Foundation.

We are grateful to both Jack Torza, Vice President of the Learning Disabilities Council, who has brought to this project wise counsel and skillful management of all the business negotiations, and to Scott Ramer, the Council's Treasurer, for his efficient handling of the finances. The editors feel keenly their good fortune in having the opportunity to work with Elinor L. Hartwig of York Press, Inc. She has provided unfailing encouragement and flexibility. We have also been blessed with the generosity of our husbands, R. W. Trusdell and Harold Horowitz, who have been willing to run errands when called upon, read sections of the book for clarity, and even become Chief Cooks and Bottlewashers when our work sessions lasted past dinner time.

Mary Louise Trusdell

Inge W. Horowitz

March, 2002

Mary Louise Trusdell has served as: public school LD teacher; founder and director of the Specific Language Disability Department at a Country Day School in Georgia; director of a private school for secondary-level dyslexics; director of a VI-G federal LD program in rural Virginia; and for ten years, as Supervisor of Programs for the Learning Disabled for the Virginia Department of Education. She earned her B. A. degree as an English major; her M.Ed. degree from the University of Virginia is in learning disabilities.

Inge W. Horowitz retired after nearly four decades from careers in Pediatric Occupational Therapy and Special Education. During the last twenty-five years, she served as Educational Consultant with the Virginia Department of Education. She is currently the acting Executive Director of the Learning Disabilities Council. In her roles as mother and grandmother, she has personally experienced the impact of L.D. She earned her B.S. degree in Occupational Therapy and M.Ed. degree in Special Education from Virginia Commonwealth University.

HOW TO USE THIS BOOK

This book is expressly intended for parents of children and adolescents who may have or who are already identified as having a learning disability (LD). There is also guidance for adults who have been dealing with LD all their lives, and for adults who have just become aware that learning disabilities may be at the root of the difficulties they've faced.

Another audience is made up of teachers and other professionals who have come into contact with individuals with learning disabilities. Many have told us during the years since the book was first published in 1989 that they, too, have found it an excellent resource.

THE PURPOSE OF THIS BOOK

Since no one book can hope to answer all questions, this guide has been designed to be a working tool, comprehensive in its own right, but one that can also grow as parents and others gather information. When used as suggested, the book will serve as a...

- source of information
- "how to" guidebook
- workbook
- reference
- guide to a filing system.

READING THE BOOK

For all parents, we recommend briefly skimming the Table of Contents and then flipping through the book to obtain a quick overview of the seven chapters.

If you're new to the subject of learning disabilities, you may decide to then turn back to the first chapter and work through the book, chapter by chapter. However, if you've had some experience in dealing with the subject, you may instead want to skim chapters, reading in depth those of particular importance to you at this time.

Adults with LD will probably want to turn first to Chapter 6. But they will probably also find the background material in Chapters 1, 5, 7, and 8 of special interest. Workbook pages at the end of certain chapters are differentiated by a triangle at the upper right-hand corner. These are designed to be completed after reading the accompanying chapter.

In completing the activities on the workbook pages, parents have an opportunity to translate the theoretical material presented in the chapter into practical information about their own child. Completing the workbook pages will also indicate how well one understands the concepts presented — relative to the needs of one's own child.

Also included are generous appendices, personal histories, a list of additional resources, glossaries of terms, and a list of references.

The format of this book has been specifically designed to encourage its readers to use the guide on an ongoing basis, instead of just reading it through once and putting it away on a bookshelf. The suggestions in Chapter 4 will help to personalize the guide so that it does indeed become a working tool.

YOUR SUGGESTIONS

As you use this guide, you are encouraged to note additions and changes that you feel would make it more useful to parents. Your suggestions to the L.D. Council will be most welcome. Simply complete the form in the back of this book and mail it to:

Learning Disabilities Council
P.O. Box 8451
Richmond, Virginia 23226
(804) 748-5012

Chapter 1 — LEARNING DISABILITIES: THE HIDDEN DISABILITY

Many more people are aware of learning disabilities in our society today than there were in the 1960s, when the term originated. There have always been children and young adults with symptoms of what we now call learning disabilities, but they have not always received the correct diagnosis and help. This chapter describes what learning disabilities are and what they are not.[1] In addition, ADD and ADHD and their relationship to LD are discussed.

WHO HAS LEARNING DISABILITIES?

An individual with a learning disability may be:

- Male or female
- Of any race
- Of any social level
- Of any economic level
- Of any age.

WHAT LEARNING DISABILITIES **ARE**

Learning disabilities are:

- Sometimes inherited or sometimes acquired following neurological injury;

- Different in each individual; can affect those with any level of intelligence, including genius;

- May affect learning, behavior, and social skills.

- Difficulties in acquiring, remembering, organizing, recalling, or expressing information;

- Problems with reading, comprehension, writing, speaking, listening, and/or calculating. Rarely would a person show all the characteristics listed below; instead, there will be problems in one or more of the following areas:

Reading — difficulty in:
- remembering the printed word or symbol
- sounding out words
- reading with adequate speed
- understanding what has been read

Writing and Spelling:
- poor penmanship
- bizarre spelling
- poor written composition

Speaking — difficulty in:
- making certain speech sounds
- remembering names of things
- organizing and sequencing ideas for verbal expression
- speaking rhythmically

Listening — difficulty in:
- remembering directions
- understanding rapid speech
- interpreting what is heard

Calculating — problems in:
- remembering math facts such as multiplication tables
- sequencing steps (as in long division), arithmetic processes
- distinguishing math signs correctly (e.g., + - x ÷ < >)

Some people use other terms when referring to learning disabilities, such as:

- Perceptual handicaps
- Dyslexia
- Minimal brain dysfunction
- Diverse learner
- Dyscalculia
- Dysgraphia
- Auditory or visual processing disabilities
- Developmental aphasia.

WHAT LEARNING DISABILITIES ARE NOT

Learning disabilities are NOT problems primarily CAUSED by:

- Visual, hearing, or motor impairments
- Mental retardation
- Emotional/behavioral disorders
- Environmental, cultural, or economic disadvantages
- Inappropriate instruction

NOTE: Sometimes a person can have learning disabilities along with other handicapping conditions. For example, learning disabilities are not caused by emotional/behavioral disorders but a child may have both a learning disability AND an emotional/behavioral disorder. (See Appendix A for the definition of learning disabilities included in the Individuals with Disabilities Education Act, used by the public schools, and the definition given by the National Joint Committee on Learning Disabilities.)

THE HIDDEN DISABILITY

Because a learning disability is usually not obvious in a person's outward physical appearance, some people are skeptical that it even exists. They may describe individuals with learning disabilities as:

- Lazy: "I know he could do better if he'd just work harder."
- Careless: "He can do it right; I know he can. He's so smart, but he just rushes through and makes careless mistakes."
- Doesn't try: "When he takes his time and really puts forth some effort, he can do the work. But most of the time, he just doesn't want to try hard enough."
- Unmotivated: "He couldn't care less about school. In fact, he isn't really interested in learning. He's just one of those unmotivated kids."

Learning disabilities can lead to:

Frustration —Your child may look like everyone else but have difficulty doing what everyone else does.[2]
Confusion —Your child may seem far ahead of others in some things but may be surprisingly inept in other skills. You may notice that he or she does not seem to acquire or remember day-to-day bits of information which others "naturally" seem to know.
Lack of confidence "Students with learning disabilities may say, "What is wrong with me? I can't do anything right.""

CHARACTERISTICS OF LD

As a parent, your most important role is to gather as much information about your child as you can, from home and from school. Look over table I, "Characteristics of Learning Disabilities," in Chapter 1. These are not all of the characteristics, but are those most frequently found. Then, use the Workbook page, "Parent Observation Sheet," at the end of this chapter, to make notes for your meetings with teachers and others. This will be useful later on to note changes in your child's development.

Keep in mind that every one of us has our own learning strengths and weaknesses. As you look at the examples in table I, you may find a description or two that even sounds like something you do! To a certain extent, we all have some of the characteristics associated with learning disabilities. The difference is in the number of characteristics that are demonstrated and the degree they deviate from what is considered "normal." When the number and degree cause severe problems in the person's life (academically, vocationally, or socially), that person may be considered to have learning disabilities.

> NOTE: Throughout the book you will find individuals with learning disabilities referred to as *he* and *she* and *him* and *her*. Our desire is to be inclusive, since both males and females are represented in the world's population of people with learning disabilities.

WHAT ARE ATTENTION DEFICIT DISORDER (ADD) AND ATTENTION DEFICIT/HYPERACTIVITY DISORDER (ADHD)?

Much has been written in recent years about ADD and ADHD. These are medical terms referring to related difficulties. Even though some professionals in the field believe these are basically the same condition, with almost identical characteristics, others believe that individuals with these characteristics but who are not hyperactive can be more accurately diagnosed as having ADD.[3]

"People with ADD are often noted for their inconsistencies.... They can have difficulty remembering simple things, yet have 'steel trap' memories for complex issues...."[4] Typically they *may*...

- have problems with following through on instructions,
- have difficulty paying close attention to details (focusing attention and then maintaining focus),
- be disorganized,
- have poor handwriting,
- miss details,
- have trouble starting tasks or following through with tasks that require planning or long-term effort,
- be easily distracted,
- lose or forget important things.

BUT not all people with ADD have all these difficulties, nor have them all of the time.

A person with ADHD will have some of the above characteristics, but will also display some of the following. They might...

- feel restless, often fidgeting with hands or feet, or squirming,
- run or climb excessively,

- talk excessively,
- blurt out answers before hearing the whole question,
- have difficulty awaiting his or her turn.

While LD is not the same as ADD or ADHD, it can co-exist with either of them. A glance at the examples of LD characteristics listed in table I gives evidence of this pairing in some individuals:

- Preschool (Motor):
  May be much more active or much less active than other children;
- (General):
  May have a short attention span, be impulsive, and/or easily distracted.

DIAGNOSIS OF ADD AND ADHD

For a person to be diagnosed as having ADD or ADHD, the behaviors have to be apparent over time (at least 6 months). They also have to be severe enough that they are creating a definite handicap in at least two aspects of the person's life (such as school, work, home, or social settings). They must also interfere with the probability that the person will reach his or her potential.[5]

Comprehensive evaluations must be administered. These include a complete individual and family history, ability tests, achievement tests, and a collection of observations from people who are close to the person being assessed.[6]

It is also important to uncover any co-existing conditions such as LD, behavior disorders, or any other problem that could be causing symptoms that look similar to those of ADD or ADHD.[7]

WHAT CAUSES ADD OR ADHD?

"ADHD is **NOT** caused by poor parenting, family problems, poor teachers or schools, too much TV, food allergies, or excess sugar. One early theory was that attention disorders were caused by minor head injuries or damage to the brain, and thus for many years ADHD was called 'minimal brain damage' or 'minimal brain dysfunction.' The vast majority of people with ADHD have no history of head injury or evidence of brain damage, however. Another theory which is still heard in the media was that refined sugar and food additives make children hyperactive and inattentive. Scientists at the National Institutes of Health (NIH) concluded that this may apply to only about 5 percent of children with ADHD, mostly either very young children or children with food allergies.

"ADHD IS very likely caused by biological factors which influence neurotransmitter activity in certain parts of the brain, and which have a strong genetic basis. Studies at NIMH [National Institutes of Mental Health] using a PET (positron emission tomography) scanner to observe the brain at work have shown a link between a person's ability to pay continued attention and the level of activity in the brain. Specifically, researchers measured the level of glucose used by the areas of the brain that inhibit impulses and control attention. In people with ADHD, the brain areas that control attention used less glucose, indicating that they were less active. It appears from this research that a lower level of activity in some parts of the brain may cause inattention and other ADHD symptoms.

"There is a great deal of evidence that ADHD runs in families, which is suggestive of genetic factors. If one person in a family is diagnosed with ADHD there is a 25% to 35% probability that any other family member also has ADHD, compared to a 4% to 6% probability for someone in the general population."[8]

MANAGEMENT OF ADD AND ADHD

The most effective management for ADD and ADHD may include a combination of...
- medication (when necessary),
- therapy or counseling,
- educational adjustments.

Medication is used to help normalize brain activity. The most commonly used are Ritalin, Dexedrine, and Adderall. But there are many other medications available, to be used at a physician's discretion.

Therapy is often helpful in modifying certain behaviors, and in dealing with the emotional effects of ADD and ADHD. Some individuals may also need help in developing coping skills. This may include suggestions for organizing, studying and time management. Furthermore, guidance in rearranging the physical setting may bring about greater success.[9]

In making *educational adjustments*, teachers — as well as parents — may need special training. After all, teachers are the managers of life at school, while parents manage life at home, and both must deal with a child's possible loss of confidence and negative perceptions about himself, based on repeated frustration and failure. Teachers will find excellent suggestions on the Internet at www.add.org/content/school.htm.[10] Parents would benefit greatly by accessing www.add.org/content/abc/basic.htm. A teenager may find helpful articles at the same site: www.add.org/content/teens1.htm.

WHAT ABOUT SPECIAL EDUCATION?

Once a child is diagnosed with ADD or ADHD, this does not mean that he or she automatically qualifies for special education services from the public schools. The U.S. Office of Education requires that the school must determine that "the ADD is a chronic or acute health problem that results in limited alertness, which adversely affects educational performance." In this case, students with ADD or ADHD qualify for special education services under the category of Other Health Impaired (OHI). If the student does not qualify for special education under OHI, he or she may qualify for special services under Section 504 of the Rehabilitation Act — which is discussed in Chapter 4.

DO YOU OUTGROW ADD AND ADHD?

ADD and ADHD, like LD, are lifespan conditions, so people do not outgrow them. However, the symptoms of hyperactivity can diminish with maturity, so it may appear that a student no longer needs accommodations, or should discontinue treatment. But such a decision should be made only after careful review.[11]

As for coping skills, about half the children diagnosed with ADD are able, in time, to compensate quite well without medication.

But the other half will continue to require medication, a structured environment, and accommodations in order to work at full potential as adults. They may benefit from attending adult LD support group meetings. (For help in locating a group, access www.add.org/content/group1.htm)[12]

SUMMARY

Learning disabilities are hidden disabilities that can affect any age child or adult. The characteristics of learning disabilities are varied, but most children with LD are very good in some things and not nearly so good in others. Learning disabilities may be diagnosed at early ages but they continue through adulthood.

ADD and ADHD are attentional disorders. Students with these conditions may have problems focusing in class, completing school assignments, acting impulsively, or a combination of all of these. They may be eligible for special education. They may also need medication and therapy. As adults, they may find a support group helpful. Some students with LD also have attentional disorders.

Table I

Examples of Characteristics of Learning Disabilities [13]

An individual need not demonstrate all of the following characteristics to have a learning disability. Rather, he or she will exhibit a cluster of difficulties to such a degree as to cause real problems in daily living or learning.

Area	Characteristics		
	Preschool	School Age	Adult
Language	• May be slow in learning to talk • May continue using baby talk and substituting similar sounds in words past the expected age (e.g., "wuv" for "love" or "fink" for "think") • May forget the names of things; can describe the object, its use, etc., but cannot think of the name • May have difficulty learning letter names and the sounds that go with them • May confuse the order of sounds in words (e.g., "pasghetti" for "spaghetti" or "aminals" for "animals")	• May have great difficulty learning to read, write, or spell • In reading, may have difficulty learning phonics, segmenting words into sounds, or blending sounds into words • May read very slowly; may omit and substitute words while reading orally; may not understand what is read • May make spelling errors which are not even close to proper spelling; may include all the letters in a word, but in the wrong order; may spell the word correctly one time and then wrong several minutes later • May have trouble retrieving words from memory	• May still have difficulty saying longer words, confusing the order of sounds in words or phrases (e.g., "episcopal," "statistical," "crisp biscuits") • May avoid reading, spelling, and writing whenever possible; may never read for pleasure • May have difficulty getting a job using his capabilities because is unable to complete a job application correctly • May read slowly or inaccurately, making it difficult to understand what is read

Table I - continued

Area	Characteristics		
	Preschool	School Age	Adult
Processing	• May confuse words which sound the same: pin-pen, quiet-quite • May be unable to focus on what is being said by parent if radio or TV is audible in the background	• May be confused by worksheets or pages crowded with print; may read "stilt" for "slit," "cover" for "clover," etc.; may lose place while reading • May be unable to focus on what teacher is saying if other students are talking in background, or an air conditioner or heater is making background noise • May make letter/number/word reversals (b-d, m-w, 6-9, was-saw) in reading and/or writing	• May have difficulty reading the newspaper, following small print, columns, maps, etc. • May have difficulty focusing on what employer is saying if office or factory machines are audible in background • May have trouble following a sewing pattern, construction diagram, etc • May have difficulty dialing phone numbers, reading addresses or route numbers; may reverse numbers in checkbook
Spatial-Temporal Orientation	• May have difficulty learning and understanding left-right, up-down, before-after, first-last, yesterday-tomorrow, etc. • May have difficulty gauging the edge of table in setting things down, causing frequent spills; may bump into objects when walking • May have difficulty telling a series of events in proper sequence, such as retelling a story or relating a TV show	• May work quickly, completing work in a rush, but poorly; or may work slowly, with many incomplete assignments • May have difficulty in planning time in order to complete long-term assignments; may wait until last minute to study for tests • May have difficulty arranging work on paper — it may be cramped into small space or spread all over page • May have difficulty lining up numbers of math problems; may try to subtract the top number from bottom number, etc.	• May have difficulty following a schedule, planning time, being on time for appointments and deadlines; may overestimate what can be accomplished in a given amount of time • May get lost easily, whether driving or trying to locate a room in a large building; may have difficulty following directions from maps (north, south, east, west, left, right) • May have difficulty balancing a checkbook; doesn't "line up" numbers vertically, one under the other, or may subtract the top number from the bottom number

Table 1 - continued

Area	Characteristics		
	Preschool	School Age	Adult
Problem Solving/Math	• May have difficulty perceiving the relationship between actions and possible results or consequences (e.g., if you run with your cup of juice, it will spill on your shirt)	• May have difficulty learning the steps needed in more complicated math processes (multiplication, division, algebraic equations) • After listening to part of a story, may have difficulty predicting what will happen next	• May have difficulty with brainstorming (i.e., thinking of different ways to do the same things); may see only one way to do something
Motor	• May be clumsy, awkward, accident-prone • May have difficulty buttoning, tying, using scissors, catching or hitting a ball • May be much more active or much less active than other children • May have difficulty learning to write the numerals or letters	• May do poorly in sports requiring eye-hand coordination, such as tennis or baseball • May have difficulty learning to write; handwriting may be cramped or illegible • May be able to present information verbally but cannot "get it down on paper," or may take an excessive amount of time to do so • May have difficulty copying from book or board, omitting letters or entire words	• May avoid hobbies, such as making models, woodworking, needlework, that use fine motor skills • May avoid writing whenever possible, preferring to dictate information for someone else to write down
Memory	• Seems to take a long time to learn information that others pick up quickly (alphabet, days of week, colors, holidays, etc.) • May have difficulty providing information about self or family (age, birthday, number of brothers and sisters, etc.) • May lose train of thought; can't remember the topic of conversation	• May forget books needed for homework or forget to take completed homework to school • May have trouble following oral directions or steps when several are given at one time • May have difficulty with rote memorization of spelling words, math facts, history dates, etc. • May have difficulty remembering sequences (steps in long division, alphabet, etc.)	• May have difficulty learning new procedures and techniques at work if established routine is interrupted • May forget dates with friends or errands planned • May still lose train of thought in conversation; can't remember topic of conversation, if interrupted; may still have difficulty with multiplication tables, dates

Table I - continued

Area	Characteristics		
	Preschool	School Age	Adult
Organization	• Bedroom, school area, cubbies may look like "disaster area," with belongings everywhere • May have difficulty perceiving patterns (blocks, beads, pegboards) • When given general directions (e.g., "Get dressed."), may not know where or how to begin • May not understand rules of games	• School desk and locker may be a "mess" — papers and books everywhere • Even if reading is not a problem, may have difficulty in understanding relationships between concepts and ideas (three branches of government and checks and balances; speed and velocity) • Notebooks and notes may be incomplete, disorganized — student may not be able to decide what is important to write down and what is not	• Conversations may seem disjointed • May have difficulty telling or understanding jokes • May constantly misplace belongings at work or home; seems bright, but like an "absent-minded professor"
Behavior/ Social Skills	• May exhibit sudden mood swings, such as bursts of rage when frustrated • May have difficulty taking turns or following rules of game	• May have difficulty assessing own classroom performance; may think test grade will be high but then is disappointed • May have difficulty making friends, or friends may be much younger; teacher may say, "appears immature" • May have difficulty in social conversations (unable to stay on the topic or find the right words)	• May have difficulty interpreting body language, facial expressions, tone of voice, etc., leading to poor job performance and poor social relationships

Table I - continued

Area	Characteristics
General	• May demonstrate uneven learning abilities, doing well in some things but very poorly in others • May be able to learn information presented in one way but not another: may learn what is seen but not what is heard; may remember what is practiced by writing but not by reciting orally; may have difficulty with abstract ideas presented orally, if the concept is not presented in a concrete or observable form • May have a short attention span, be impulsive, and/or easily distracted

Parent Observation Sheet

Instructions

To help prepare for school meetings and share your knowledge of your child, review the characteristics in table I in this chapter and use the observation sheet below to record information. Use this checklist to provide input for all teacher conferences and meetings in the Special Education Process. (These steps are described in detail in Chapter 4, "The Student with Learning Disabilities at School.") Try to jot down how often the various behaviors occur, too. When the number and degree of characteristics cause severe problems in a child's life, that child may have a learning disability. **Remember:** Your observations are important in helping the school determine if learning problems do exist.

- **Language**

    Reading
    Does your child have trouble...
    ___sounding out words?
    ___remembering sight vocabulary (what, where, was, etc.)?
    ___recalling what has been read?
    ___other :_____
    ___other :_____

    How often does this happen?

    _____

    Writing
    Does your child have trouble...
    ___copying?
    ___writing in manuscript or cursive?
    ___other :_____
    ___other :_____

    How often does this happen?

    _____

    Spelling
    Does your child have trouble...
    ___memorizing spelling words?
    ___spelling these words correctly in sentences and paragraphs?
    ___other :_____
    ___other :_____

    How often does this happen?

    _____

    Listening
    Does your child have trouble...
    ___following directions?
    ___understanding what you say?
    ___other :_____
    ___other :_____

    How often does this happen?

    _____

- **Processing**

    Does your child have trouble...
    ___confusing words that sound similar?
    ___focusing on what you say if other noises are in the background?
    ___other :_____
    ___other :_____

    How often does this happen?

    _____

- **Spatial-Temporal Orientation**

    Does your child have trouble...
    ___arranging and spacing work on paper?
    ___learning left from right?
    ___other :_____
    ___other :_____

    How often does this happen?

    _____

- **Problem Solving**

Does your child have trouble...

___predicting what will happen after hearing part of a story?
___figuring out different ways to accomplish a task?
___other :_____
___other :_____

How often does this happen?

_____

- **Math**

Does your child have trouble...
___remembering math facts?
___confusing math signs (+ - < > etc.)?
___following a sequence of steps (as in long division)?
___other :_____
___other :_____

How often does this happen?

_____

- **Motor**

Does your child have trouble...
___copying from the board?
___getting information down on paper?
___in sports, seeming to be awkward?
___coloring, using scissors?
___other :_____

How often does this happen?

_____

- **Memory**

Does your child have trouble...
___following a series of oral directions?
___retaining spelling words, math facts, history dates?
___other :_____
___other :_____

How often does this happen?

_____

- **Organization**

Does your child have trouble...
___losing or misplacing things?
___turning in school assignments on time?
___keeping school desk, notebook, and other belongings in order?
___understanding concepts in social studies and grammar?
___other :_____
___other :_____

How often does this happen?

_____

- **Behavior/Social Skills**

Does your child have trouble...
___focusing attention on one thing?
___interpreting body language, facial expressions?

How often does this happen?

_____

_____

Chapter 2 — COPING AS A PARENT:

Mediator, Advocate, Referee, Planner, Negotiator, Supporter!

Exasperated...puzzled...uncertain...frantic...exhausted...helpless...sad...mad... hopeful. These are the feelings of the mother or father or sibling of a child with a learning disability. He can be bewildering. He sometimes drains parents and teachers. When they are with such a child, adults who are otherwise competent may feel helpless and inadequate. Parents may feel very alone as they sense that friends and other family members do not understand what they are experiencing with their child.[1] Parenting a child with a learning disability adds stress to any family, but it *can* be dealt with positively. This chapter discusses causes of LD, normal human reactions to it, and ways parents can help.

CAUSES OF LD

Evidence is building to suggest that learning disabilities may be inherent in some children's biological make-up. However, at this point in the on-going research, we just can't always be sure how or why it happens. You may want to check your local library or the library of a nearby college or university, as well as on-line, for reports about the most recent findings.

In the library, go to the Card Catalog (which is usually on a computer these days), and key in Learning Disabilities: Causes. This will give you names of books on this subject. You may find more recent information in magazines. They will be listed under Journals.

On the Internet, go to these sites:
- www.interdys.org
- www.idanatl.org
- www.ncld.org

REACTIONS OF PARENTS

There are a number of reactions to finding out that your child has a learning disability: denial...flight...isolation... guilt...anger...blame...fear...envy... bargaining...depression...mourning... acceptance...hope.

It's OKAY to react in these ways! This is YOUR CHILD those people are talking about! Give yourself and others involved permission to work through these emotions. It may take others more or less time than you and they may process this information differently. That's okay. When you can, get ready to help your child.

FEELINGS OF GUILT

Try to overcome any guilt feelings you may have. It is useless to take or place blame. You, no doubt, have always done your best with the information you have had at the time. Dwelling on the past will not help; just use your past experiences to guide present and future decisions.

OTHERS' REACTIONS

Don't forget that siblings and grandparents and aunts and uncles and cousins and close friends will react in varying ways to your child's learning disability. It's not a good idea to hide things from them. The best way for them to deal with it is to talk about it — with you, if possible, after you've gained a good understanding about LD. The important point to make is that *it is nobody's fault*, and the person with LD does not *intentionally* display the characteristics of learning disabilities. Your child with a learning disability will also be going through a variety of emotions. Talk to her about it. What does she think? How does she want to handle it? It is important to help her identify her strengths. Talk with your child about whom to tell and whom not to tell. Let him know what you're comfortable with, who may need to know; and LISTEN to what your child has to say. He may be feeling he's unworthy of love — that he can't do anything right. Chapter 3 discusses ways to help your child deal with such self-esteem issues.

IMPORTANCE OF HAVING A CONFIDANT

Having a confidant may help. Being able to talk with someone — one's spouse, a family member, or a close friend — who is a good listener and has an interest in your child may provide support and comfort. If this is unsatisfactory to you, it might be wise to seek the professional help of a licensed professional counselor, a school psychologist or licensed clinical psychologist, or a licensed clinical social worker. (See the glossary for definitions of these professionals.)

PARENT SUPPORT GROUPS

It is very important to educate yourself and to look for some help. Various national organizations for parents have small branches all over the country. You can find a list of some of these organizations in Appendix B. They have regular meetings and newsletters. It is important and helpful to seek out your local group, attend meetings, and become active, if you can.

These groups also have Web sites with discussion groups and information. LDOnline is a Web site devoted exclusively to learning disabilities and it provides a

wealth of information on every aspect of LD, even first-person accounts and discussion groups.

Talk with other parents in your community who have children with learning disabilities. They may know of local resources that could help you and your family.

BEING AN ADVOCATE...

...For Your Child

The child with LD needs an advocate. **You know your child better than anyone else**. Learn as much as you can about your youngster's strengths and weaknesses, unique learning style, and special needs. If, in spite of your love, interest, and knowledge, you feel inadequate for the task of advocacy, find someone who will champion your child for you, possibly a teacher, a coach, a counselor, an educational consultant, a psychologist (again, refer to the glossary), or one of the groups listed in Appendix B, under Legal Issues.

If you do decide to undertake the role of advocate for your child, it should be with the realization that this is not a skill you will learn and then use for just a year or two. Parents of children with LD need to acknowledge that they will be the person (usually the only person) who has the overall picture of their child's disability, not only at a single point in time but throughout the years. You will find yourself playing the role of facilitator, coordinator, and overseer — no matter how good your child's school program and no matter how competent the professionals working with your child.

It's much better to undertake the job realizing that it's a long-term commitment that will demand the best of your skills and energy than to approach the situation with the idea that your responsibility will be to find the right school and the right teacher, and, that done, you will be able to relax while others take over.

The "light at the end of the tunnel" will approach as you gradually teach your youngster to be his or her own advocate. Some of the greatest gifts parents can give their teenagers with LD as they move through the upper grades are the confidence and skills to speak up in order to secure the accommodations needed: more time to complete a test, shorter assignments, help in taking lecture notes, etc.

It's a fine line the parent must learn to walk, between providing enough support so their teenager doesn't flounder, and teaching the student "learned helplessness," a situation certainly to be avoided.

BEING AN ADVOCATE . . .

. . . For Other Individuals with LD

At some point, you may recognize that the difficulties which you have faced or are facing with your child are similar to those faced by other parents whose children are learning disabled. Perhaps problems exist within the system — possibly a school or a school system or legislation, etc. — which affect many individuals with LD, but are beyond the grasp of one parent to change.

You may wish to join other parents and professionals to advocate for specific policy changes in a given system. For example, you may feel there is a need for regular classroom teachers to receive additional training and support to enable them to integrate children with varying needs, including learning disabilities, into the regular classroom. This type of system-wide change is not something that

one parent can hope to accomplish alone. However, by joining groups such as your school system's Special Education Advisory Committee or the local affiliates of the Learning Disabilities Association of America (see Appendix B), you can begin to advocate for systemic policy changes affecting all learning disabled individuals.

Some parents may find this type of advocacy overwhelming while their own child seems to require so much of their attention. Other parents find it stimulating and rejuvenating.

STRUCTURE

Maintaining structure in the home makes things smoother and easier for all members of the family. Life runs more smoothly, too, if both parents can agree on strategies for handling discipline. (See "Family Involvement" and "Discipline" in Chapter 3.)

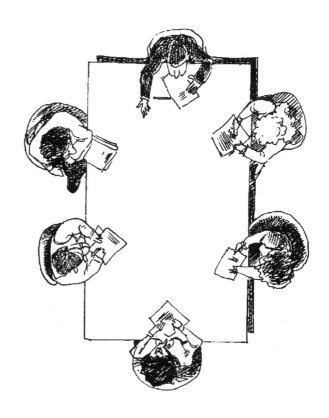

COMMUNICATION

When you feel bad about an unfortunate incident, your child probably feels worse and needs love and acceptance. Make a conscious effort to keep the lines of communication open. Listen carefully to what your youngster says and be aware of the signals given through body language and actions. Let your child know what makes you feel happy. Try to prepare him or her for the consequences of impulsive and inappropriate actions.

TAKING CARE OF THE CARETAKERS

Find time to be alone. You need time to relax and think. If possible, make time for your favorite relaxation technique, whether it's listening to quiet music, soaking in a hot tub, or curling up with a good book.

Set aside a time to engage in your favorite hobby without interruption (if possible!). In addition, make an effort to get away with your spouse or a close friend for some time together. If it's inconvenient or too costly to get a baby-sitter for that time, try to arrange for another parent with whom you can reciprocate to keep your child or children for the weekend.

Try to maintain a sense of humor. It can be a great release when tensions build. It can enable you to help your child examine the hurts and reduce the pain. Humor is a great therapist!

Live one day at a time and focus on the positive aspects of your life and on each small success of your child. (You might want to keep handy the "Bill of Rights for Parents of Children with LD" on the next page.)

SUMMARY

The diagnosis of a learning disability affects everyone in the family. Reactions to the diagnosis will be different for each person and will probably change over time. It is essential for parents and children to communicate with one another about their feelings and their understanding of LD. It is important for parents to find sources of support and to take a break from school and disability issues on a regular basis. And it's vital to keep a sense of humor!

Bill of Rights for Parents of
Children with LD

Freedom To ...

Feel that you have done the best you can.

Enjoy life as intensely as possible.

Let your child have his or her own privacy.

Have hostile thoughts once in a while without feeling guilty.

Enjoy being alone at times.

Feel free to take a break. Say to friends, "I'm not talking about my child's problems today."

Lie once in a while: Say, "Everything is fine."

Feel free to tell your child you don't like certain things he does (even though you've been told to offer much praise). Always reassure him that you love him, despite not liking some of his behavior.

Tell people about your child's progress and achievements with a real sense of pride. (And be sure he sometimes hears you make these positive comments.)

Have your own hobbies and interests.

Warning: Parents who do not allow themselves to enjoy almost all of these freedoms at one time or another are in trouble. Martyrs are seldom appreciated by anybody.

*Adapted from **A Survival Guide for People Who Have Handicaps** by S. Gordon.*

Chapter 3 — HELPING YOUR CHILD AT HOME

If your child has a learning disability or, if after reading Chapter One you suspect that your child may have a learning disability, you are no doubt wondering what will make life better for him or her. It is important to recognize the significance of activities outside of the school day and out of the school environment. Furthermore, it is in the home and family that you, the parent, can have a direct, immediate impact. This chapter deals with issues of self-esteem, extracurricular activities, family involvement, discipline, and interpersonal relationships.

SELF-ESTEEM

Self-esteem can affect every aspect of a child's life. It is not always built on what people say about a child; rather, it develops when a child realizes he has achieved success in various aspects of his life.

Signs of Poor Self-Esteem

Does your child show any of the following traits?

- Can't accept being wrong; it is always someone else's fault;
- Blames self excessively for inadequacies: "I knew I wouldn't do it right!";
- At the opposite extreme, is satisfied with inadequate performance;
- Shows excessive need for acceptance; has a great desire to please authority figures;
- Is self-conscious, always minimizing accomplishments;
- Either has difficulty in accepting responsibility or accepts too much responsibility (is constantly trying to prove self);
- Is overly dependent;
- Can't believe that he is as intelligent as others because he performs worse than they do in school;
- Has difficulty in making decisions and is insecure about own ideas.

If you see these traits in your child, he or she

may be having difficulty with self-esteem — with feeling worthy. These difficulties can come from any aspect of your child's life.

A feeling of self-worth affects our thinking processes, our emotions, desires, values, and goals; it underlies our every behavior. Children with low self-esteem often suffer from feelings of frustration and helplessness. They may feel angry and depressed. Children with high self-esteem feel confident and effective. They interact with their environment assertively and make decisions easily.[1]

Suggestions for Improving Self-Esteem

Self-esteem begins to develop early. Therefore, long before the child starts school, it is important for parents and other family members to provide experiences and promote attitudes that build a child's feeling of being a worthy person.

How do we accomplish this? How do we promote our children's feelings of self-worth? Some suggestions are:

- *Speak openly and honestly with your child.* Acknowledge problems but accentuate the positives. Help him or her understand that trouble at school does not mean failure in life.
- *Listen to your child.* Communication is a two-way process so let your child know that you don't have all the answers but that you want to understand.
- *Communicate your love without words, too.* Touch is a real human need.
- *Maintain a sense of humor.* The incident that sent you through the roof today will probably be a hilarious family story in years to come.
- *Allow autonomy, independence, and self-reliance to grow.* Give your child time to be alone and to take on responsibility without always stepping in to help. This establishes the connection between one's own actions and one's own comfort or happiness.
- *Help your child experience success.* Sometimes a youngster will need guidance in learning a task or skill. In providing the guidance, build on your child's strengths and competencies so success will follow. Break tasks down into small steps. It is important that excessive frustration and failure be avoided. Acknowledge your child's **efforts** towards a goal, not just the **achievement** of a goal.
- *Allow your child to experience **some** frustration.* Too much protection will not allow your child to develop coping strategies or to find self-worth in struggle. However, it is important that excessive frustration and failure be avoided! A child needs to develop the concept of himself as a person who can fail without losing self-confidence and self-respect.
- *Help your child set realistic goals.* Children with self-esteem difficulties often set goals too high or too low, and then these become self-fulfilling prophecies.
- *Help your child talk through experiences and describe feelings and frustrations.* This promotes self-awareness and self-control, because understanding which feeling is being experienced is the first step toward dealing with it.
- *Talk to your child about his/her learning disability.* Make sure your child understands how it affects a person. Give your child opportunities to practice with you in order to become comfortable in explaining the difficulty to others.

Home as Haven

In leading a child with LD to an honest acceptance and understanding of his or her own disability, parents must be sure that they and any other family members do not get in the habit of making comments which would encourage a feeling of guilt or shame for something for which the youngster is not to blame. **The youngster's home should be the one place in the world where understanding and encouragement can always be found.** Unless all members of the family work toward this goal, the child may develop strong feelings of guilt and worthlessness.

Convincing a child that he or she is not stupid is always a long process. It cannot be accomplished by a speech that is made only once. Day by day things happen that make these youngsters feel dumb, such as forgetting to finish chores assigned at home; or always being the last one chosen for a team in the neighborhood ball game because of clumsiness in catching and hitting the ball.

Very often, your child will come home with embarrassing stories or tales of woe such as these:

- I said *ass* instead of *ask* in front of the whole class today! The teacher made me go to the principal.
- I studied hard for that test and flunked it. Why should I even try?
- I couldn't read the book so I threw it in the trash. My teacher caught me, and now I have to pay for the book.

As such situations arise, the child will need help getting over the hurt feelings, anger, and embarrassment. There will be a need to have someone calmly help the youngster figure out which LD symptoms caused the problem, how that particular problem is different from really being generally "dense," and how to avoid letting the problem lead to another bad situation in the future.[2]

> **The importance of self-esteem in a child's life can hardly be overemphasized. It is the mainspring that launches every child toward success or failure as a human being. Because children begin to generate their own ideas of their self-worth during the early years, it is important that we know how to nurture and support this process.[3] (See Workbook page, "Self Esteem.")**

EXTRACURRICULAR ACTIVITIES

Finding an area of competence outside of academic subjects provides a boost in self-esteem for a child who does not feel good about the way things are going in the classroom.

Suggested Activities
The student with learning disabilities may gain status among peers through, for example:
- collecting rocks or trading cards,
- becoming the neighborhood ornithologist,
- becoming a karate expert,
- excelling in music or art.

These are worth spending time on, even if it leaves somewhat less time for studying academic subjects.[4] The importance of helping your child gain a feeling of self-worth should not be minimized

As a parent, you know your child best. Let your child's interests guide you in helping to find activities in which he or she can succeed. If your child is physically strong and well coordinated, team sports such as football and basketball can be great. But not all children with LD have the eye-hand coordination needed to handle a ball and keep up with their peers in competitive team sports. In that case, they need opportunities to try such things as:
- Swimming
- Gymnastics
- Bowling
- Boating
- Climbing
- Hiking
- Karate
- Horseback riding
- Skiing
- Archery

- Fencing
- Sailing.

Swimming, especially, is a sport at which children with learning disabilities may excel, as no hand-eye coordination is required. In tennis and golf, it is usually possible to find other individuals at one's own level of skill with whom to play; however, the difficulty with hand-eye coordination may make tennis a poor choice. Children with LD who have the opportunity to ride horses and to sail often find these especially appealing.

Some children with LD become adept at games of strategy, such as chess, backgammon, checkers, bridge, or pinochle. Playing these well can be ego-strengthening and a source of lifetime pleasure.

Give your child opportunities to explore — to find those activities at which he or she can be successful. Don't become upset if your youngster tries one kind of extracurricular activity and then drops it and moves on to another. What is important is for each child to find that which brings the most satisfaction. As with all human beings, young people with learning disabilities like to do those things at which they can succeed, and they will want to continue to be involved in the activities which make them feel good about themselves.

Resources

Private or group instruction in voice, piano, band instruments, and all facets of dance is generally available in most communities, with categorical listings in the "yellow pages" of the local phone directory. Additional opportunities in these areas, as well as in art and drama, may be available

through the fine arts and performing arts departments of nearby colleges and universities. Likewise, museums often offer special workshops on topics of particular interest to children. In addition, a national program, *Very Special Arts*, promotes participation in all the arts by children with special needs. Their web site is www.vsarts.org and their phone is 1-800-933-8721.

For students with an interest in the outdoors, activities may be available through:
- 4-H clubs
- local garden clubs
- area parks or botanical gardens.

If your child has an interest in a special craft or in photography, the adult education department of your local schools may be helpful in identifying individuals who may be able to work with your child. Perhaps a friend or acquaintance would be willing to share a special hobby.

Boy Scouts and Girl Scouts offer an excellent outlet for the tremendous energy that many children with learning disabilities have. It structures their time and teaches them useful skills in an atmosphere that can be non-threatening. Look in the "white pages" of your phone book or check with area schools or churches to locate a group near you.

Opportunities to participate in organized sports activities generally abound. Check with your community recreation department, schools, and YMCA.

Summer camping may be another option to consider. You may wish to consult the directory of camps published by the

American Camping Association (1-800-428-CAMP). They have a free Summer Camp Answer Booklet for parents. They can also provide a phone number for reaching a regional office of the Camping Association that may be able to provide you with a directory of camps in your area. Their web site is www.acacamps.org.

FAMILY INVOLVEMENT

There are both practical and emotional issues with which a family must cope when a child has a learning disability. The educational decisions and special arrangements, the financial strain, the disappointments and frustrations all create pressures on the entire family.[5]

Helping the Whole Family

It is vital that the family find ways of demonstrating its acceptance of the child with learning disabilities and of working together. Of course, children will argue or find fault with one another. But the following suggestions may be helpful for you in maintaining a positive family environment.

- *Be firm, consistent, and explicit.*

Clear, concise, consistent expectations prevent confusion, insecurity, and misunderstanding. It may take a while to figure out what clear, concise, and consistent mean to your child but it's worth the effort. For example, "There are to be no other people in this house unless I am home" gives a clearer message to a child than "I would prefer that you not have other people in the house unless I'm home." Be consistent; repeat the instruction every time you leave home, and make no exceptions.[6]

- *Give all of your children a voice in major decision-making processes.*

If a very important decision must be made, give time to listen to your children's opinions and their reasons for them. Make sure they know that the final decision is not theirs but that you want to hear the how and why about what they think. It will encourage your children to think through any problem that arises.[7]

- *Assign chores around the house.*

This helps everyone feel a part of the family. It also teaches responsibility, fine motor control, sequencing, and memory skills. There are some things to remember about assigning chores for children with LD:

➢ Use reminders (lists on the refrigerator, pictures of chores, drawings of what needs to be done).
➢ Use charts with pencil nearby to let your child check off tasks when they are completed.
➢ Put in some contingency measures at the outset (when chores are to be completed and what happens if they are not).
➢ Check on the completed chore. If it's done incorrectly, find some positive aspect to praise and then, teach the child again how to do it.[8] Evaluate the child as an individual, not necessarily with expectations identical to those of other siblings.[9]

- *Establish a regular routine at home.*

Clearly established routines reduce confusion and anxiety for everyone. It is much "safer" when one knows what to expect. With the child's input, you may want to write a weekly schedule on a chart (see Workbook page, "Weekly Schedule").

For a young child, a schedule for school days might look something like the following:

School Day Schedule

6:30	Get up
	Dress
	Make bed
7:00	Breakfast
	Brush teeth
7:30	Leave for school
3:30	Return from school;
	snack
	Free time
5:15	Chores
5:45	Homework
6:30	Dinner
7:15	Complete homework
8:30	Bedtime[10]

The last three suggestions, which follow below, apply particularly to the young child with LD:

- *Be direct, brief, and supportive.*

Say what you expect in simple, easy terms, with a pleasant and encouraging tone of voice. Be as concrete as possible when you ask the youngster to do something.

For many who have trouble following directions, it is helpful to remind, "Look at my face while I speak." If you are not sure the child understands, ask him or her "gently" to repeat what you said. But if you are still not sure you've gotten through to your child, suggest a demonstration of what you asked for. Remember, be positive; support and direct, rather than criticize.[11]

- *Simplify; reduce stimulation.*

Simplify family routine. If mealtime is particularly stimulating in your home, your child with LD may react by becoming irritable. If this happens, the youngster may need an "escape route," perhaps being allowed to leave the table — not ordered to. Or to eat earlier than the rest of the family.

Your child's room should be a retreat, a place for relaxation. If a separate room is not possible, consider screening off a part of a room with a folding screen or tall piece of furniture.

To reduce clutter, keep as many possessions as possible on closet shelves or in drawers. For younger children, you may have to store some toys for a few weeks, then exchange them for the toys that have been out a while.[12]

- *Provide as few alternatives as possible in decision-making situations.*

Numerous choices can be confusing and overwhelming to a youngster with LD. Fewer alternatives presented usually bring about quicker and easier decisions.[13]

Helping the Child with LD Learn
- *Day-to-Day Experiences*

Parents can become very skilled at using day-to-day experiences in teaching their children order, logic, arithmetic, and language skills. In addition, the involvement of the child with LD in the life of the household gives him a feeling of competence that can help to counteract the sense of failure instilled by lack of success in the classroom.

Fractions can cease to be mystifying for many children when they learn in the family kitchen — through seeing and feeling — that oranges cut straight through once become two <u>halves</u>. And that, when the halves are then each cut straight through, the result is four <u>fourths</u> (or <u>quarters</u>), and the <u>quarters</u> can be made into eight <u>eights</u>. To reverse the procedure, when all eight of the eights are put together, they become <u>one whole</u> orange. The same principle can be demonstrated with the fourths and halves.

Playing "store" with items from the pantry, using play money, can teach not only money values but also counting by fives and tens. Trips to the real grocery store can be missions in planning, checking prices, asking for help from store clerks, and greeting other shoppers.

TUTORING AND HOMEWORK

As a parent, becoming a tutor for your child could bring an end to a wonderful relationship. The problem is that when the parent-child relationship is converted to a teacher-child relationship, both the parent and the child are too emotionally involved to remain objective and "neutral."[14] Then anger or frustration flares, and guilt and fear are not far behind. Everyone in the family suffers. On the other hand, most students with LD need help with homework from time to time. Here are some suggestions to help take the agony out of such a situation.

1. *As much as possible, avoid sitting down to work with your child with LD.* Set up a study place in his or her room or some other quiet part of the house where there is the least likelihood of being disturbed. Then when help is needed, if possible have the child come to someone for assistance, then return to the study area to work alone. If the learning disability is severe enough that this would not be practical, set up a study place near enough to the person helping so the youngster won't have to leave the desk or make someone come to it.

If you find you do have to sit down with your child, set limits before you start, based on your review of the work that must be completed that evening.[15] You might say, "You have ten social studies questions to answer? OK, I'll read the questions to you, then you answer as many as you can on the tape recorder, by yourself, while I'm fixing dinner. After dinner, you can write them down; then I'll go over what you've written. After that, you can make any changes that are needed, by yourself."

2. *Set time limits on homework and give some breaks.* Consult with your youngster's teacher or teachers concerning the amount of time that should be needed to complete the assigned homework. It could very well be that the amount of time suggested by the teacher won't be adequate for your child, depending upon the severity of the learning disability, the speed with which the child normally works, the amount of "drive" in the personality, and other factors. If so, you can help the child understand that reality says he or she is going to have to spend more time on homework than some of the others in the class.

However, if you find that your child is spending so much time on homework that there isn't an adequate amount of time for recreation and socializing, this should be discussed with the teacher. Perhaps some adjustment can be made in the **number** of problems assigned, or the **length** of the essay to be written. There's no reason that every child in the class should have an identical assignment, **as long as the appropriate learning of the concept or principle takes place**. Even so, you'll find that this is a difficult concept for some teachers to accept. Before approaching the teacher with this idea, you should have had sufficient conversations with the teacher that he or she understands how your child functions academically.

3. *Be aware that you may need to change the extent of help given.* Sometimes, because of habit, parents will continue to provide direct assistance to a child with a subject that is difficult even though the youngster has reached the point where it could be done alone. Perhaps only a quick check by the parent after the work is completed will suffice.[16]

4. *The person who provides help does not have to be one of the child's parents.* However, in choosing the best possible person, three qualifications must be considered:
    a. Most important, the helper must be able to work peacefully with the child. Sarcasm, harsh criticism, arguing, sulking, tears, or shouting mean that the wrong person has been chosen.
    b. College degrees or high school diplomas are not as important as empathy, ability to clarify confusing points, and intelligence.
    c. Anyone forced into the job is likely

to have the wrong attitude. Older siblings are often the worst possible choices.[17]
(See Workbook pages at the end of this chapter: "Special Assignment: Homework Success," "Homework Suggestions," and "Daily Homework Sheet.")

Staying away from the direct teaching or tutoring of your child helps to maintain your relationship. However, this DOES NOT mean to stay away from your child's education. It is vital that you maintain contact with the school and teachers and follow up on your child's progress.

DISCIPLINE

Though it is not often described as such, discipline is the glue that either holds a family together or tears it apart. The interaction cycle between parent and child can be either positive or negative. If the cycle is negative, it is not impossible to change.

Parent's Response to the Child
In some families, an interaction cycle develops between parent and child with LD

that is negative: the child's behavior elicits a negative response from the parent, and in turn the parent's negative feedback elicits further negative behavior from the child. If you are in this cycle, step back and examine your stance and emotions. You are the adult and the only one that can break this cycle.

The first step is to realize that your child is not "out to get you." Remember, the behaviors exhibited may be part of the learning disability. She may lack the inner controls needed to modify impulsive and "driven" behavior.[18]

Child's Response

The second step is to help the child accept responsibility for the behavior, understand what made it happen and why it is inappropriate, and work toward a solution. This will not happen if the first step has not taken place or if the child feels blamed or perceives your anger. It would be too painful for the child to accept responsibility in an atmosphere full of blame and punishment.

Some examples:

- Despite numerous warnings, John forgets to pour his milk slowly. He pours it too quickly and spills it all over the table and floor. Mom got mad before, but that did not help him pour his milk more slowly this time. Instead, Mom could try responding, "You forgot the rule about pouring too fast. What do you need to do to fix the problem?" Then, John and Mom together can come up with solutions such as an apology, wiping up the table and floor, and/or making contributions from his allowance toward replenishing the milk. Either way, John is now

learning to take responsibility for the problem and doing something about it, tending to relieve his guilt.[19]

- Even though Marie has made numerous attempts to "get it all together" for school, she is constantly leaving her notebook or textbook at home. Marie's father has decided that instead of the nagging that has been ineffective, he will help Marie establish a routine in the evenings: she will place all of her materials by the front door when she has finished her homework. They decide a checklist on her bedroom door will help her recall all of the things she needs to put by the door.

In summary, **remember to attack the situation — not the child.** (See Workbook page, "Launching Better Behavior: Accentuate the Positive.")

Handling Anger

Many children and young adults with LD feel anger about their difficulties. The child has a right to feel angry. How would you respond if you had a problem that made you look stupid and kept you from doing many of the things you wanted to do?

It is not just the anger itself that parents respond to most. It is what the child does with that anger that can cause trouble. The only way to get rid of it is to express it, but the child must learn to express it in a way that does no harm. This is something that the child or young adult with LD often must be taught. And guess who does the teaching?!

If your child's anger gets out of control, many parents successfully use Time Out, a method of removing the child from the situation and allowing time to cool off or calm down in the privacy of another room or area.

This isolation should not be viewed by either the child or the parent as punishment. If the order, "Go to your room!" is accompanied by the parent's anger, this may be interpreted by the child as rejection and punishment. Instead, instruct your child in a manner that communicates that this is the best place to be at this moment to relax, and to reflect on how to handle similar situations in the future. In other words, state what the inappropriate behavior was (not that the child is bad) and tell him or her to go to Time Out to cool off.

Remember that Time Out is to be used for relatively short periods of time — it is not meant to be a place where a child spends so much time that he or she finds something fun to do there!

If Your Child Fights a Lot:

➢ Express how you feel about your child's behavior but state that your love has not changed. Judge the behavior, not the child.

➢ Listen to your child's side of the story, but also have him or her play the role of the other person in order to feel the other person's feelings.

➢ Explore alternatives to aggressive behavior and role-play them.

➢ Establish a reward system, e.g., the child will earn a reward for a day without fighting.

Consistency

Most children and young adults are more manageable when their parents are consistent with discipline. But this is a hard task for you, the parent. So, the trick is to be as consistent as possible and not feel guilty when things don't go as planned. Do what you teach your child to do — go to another place, evaluate what has happened, and plan for next time. If you value a certain kind of behavior, don't just advocate it; use it yourself. Your child will likely copy or model your behavior.[20]

Punishment

When you punish, try to be fair, calm, and prompt. Do not delay punishment; delay can make the child uncertain about what he did wrong, and heighten his anxiety.[21]

1. Let the punishment fit the crime. Don't impose a major punishment for a minor "crime."
2. Don't punish the same behavior with different penalties at different times.
3. Avoid long sermons, talk, and logical reasoning.
4. Be direct and simple.
5. Don't demand verbal assurances that such a thing will never happen again.
6. Try to avoid punishments that are violent or lead to great excitement. Don't let your own feelings of anger and frustration distort the situation.
7. Make clear to the child that you dislike his actions, not him. The youngster needs an improved self-image, not to be degraded.
8. Avoid threats, bribes, or promises.

9. Avoid being too strict and then too forgiving (cold anger at one time and then loving embraces soon after).
10. Hold your temper if you want your child to learn that a temper can be held.[22]

(See Workbook page, "13 Parent Rules for Responding to Angry Children.")

INTERPERSONAL RELATIONSHIPS

Interpersonal relationships can be difficult for students with learning disabilities. They often have difficulty processing conversational language, picking up subtle social cues, and making quick decisions about how to act. Everyone in the family can help develop these skills.

The Family
Problems arise in all families, but often, families which have children with LD may experience problems that are more intense. The child may feel hated by siblings. Brothers and sisters may feel that their parents favor the child with LD because of the extra time and attention required to deal with problems related to the disability.[23]

Siblings are going to disagree and fight. Parents, however, must see to it that the child's disability is not allowed to become a special target for insults.[24] They must assert, "No one in this family is dumb or stupid!"

It is up to the parents to help all family members — not just siblings, but aunts, uncles, cousins, and grandparents — to understand the nature of learning disabilities and that the child is not being deliberately difficult.

Other Children
There are a number of things that parents can do to improve the way their child interacts with others:

- *Observe your child.*

   Try to figure out what your child does that is different from the children who have successful interpersonal relationships. As you observe, state to yourself what the specific behavior is.[25] For example, say, "Billy got mad, grabbed his football, and walked off when his side began to fall behind in a touch-football game," instead of "Billy won't share his belongings."

   You might find it worthwhile to keep a written record of your observations — not to confront Billy with, but to help you understand how Billy behaves differently, in general. Ask yourself, "What does my child do or not do that causes problems? When does this happen? Why? What are the possible motives?"[26]

- *Structure the environment for success.*

   Failures in peer relationships can frequently be avoided through careful planning. For example, when your youngster's friends have been invited over, have the snack ready (your child can help with this), and discuss ahead of time what game will be played or what activity would be most enjoyed. Also plan with your child the length of the visit, so the friends can leave before there is time for failures. Rehearse the *do's* and *don'ts* of being a good friend. If your child is going to have a party, encourage the child to help with the planning. Consider serving refreshments — either at your home or at a snack shop — and then taking the group to the movies or a special entertainment (e.g., an ice-skating show, or a basketball game). Rehearse the entire schedule beforehand so your child knows what to expect.

Some children with LD "roll with the punches" better than others. Some need preparation for an upcoming event. Change in schedule or environment is not easy for many of these children. Even such family events as dinner parties, vacations, and weekend visits by relatives or friends are handled better by the child affected if the youngster is prepared in advance and is told what to expect. Role-playing situations and making suggestions as to how to act or what to say might give the child greater confidence when facing a new situation or change in his routine.

- *Work out a signal system.*

Many children respond well to having a "secret" signal system or code word to help remind them to relax, slow down, take a deep breath. The signal can also be for, "It's time for your friends to go home," or "It's getting too loud." Make sure the signal (a wink or a finger on the nose) is obvious to your child. Train him or her to acknowledge it when you give it. The acknowledgment might be the same signal given back.

- *Replay the moment.*

After an unpleasant experience, it is worthwhile to work on the problem. But do not do it while either your child or you (or both) are still upset. Let your child problem-solve and role-play in order to arrive at an alternative behavior plan for the future. Make sure your child or young adult plays the role of the other

person so he may feel how the other person felt.

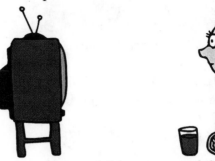

- *If your child or young adult isolates him- or herself:*

  ➤ Enroll your child in structured activities in which he or she feels successful (e.g., art lessons, Scouting, etc.).
  ➤ Help your child engage with peers by making suggestions: baking cookies, riding bikes, playing frisbee, hiking to the park, shooting baskets, gardening.
  ➤ Do not push your child too quickly. It is necessary to build confidence first. Success builds more success.
  ➤ Suggest ways to make new friends: Walk up to someone who is standing alone. Let the person talk about him- or herself. Look at the person and listen well. Rehearse conversation starters (e.g., "Tell me more!").

- *Praise your child's efforts.*

  ➤ Be sure to give positive feedback when you notice that your child or young adult is trying to make positive changes.[27]

SUMMARY

How a child feels about himself affects every aspect of his life; therefore, it is crucial that his family help him feel self-confident. This can be encouraged by the family in several ways. For example, through supporting his participation in extra-curricular activities in which he can gain some expertise; by allowing him to help the family to function more smoothly (e.g., by being responsible for doing some household chores); by arranging his after-school hours so he can gradually assume complete responsibility for doing his own homework; and by teaching him to respond to various situations with acceptable behavior.

The key is for the family to support, encourage, and appreciate each other. Your child with LD — as well as your other children — will then be able to reflect this strengthening kind of love. The greatest gift parents can give their children is a home life that teaches them they are valued and are contributing members of the family.[28]

Self-Esteem

Instructions: At the end of the day, sit down by yourself to think about your interactions with your child on this particular day. Using the checklist that follows, check off those statements which best describe your behaviors, and, in the same space, add the date you checked it.

Choose one or two items and make a conscious effort during the next day (or week) to act in such a way as to enhance your child's confidence. If necessary, jot yourself reminders on post-it notes and place them in visible places to help you remember. At the end of this time period, use the checklist and a different color pen to reassess your interaction. Then set new goals, select new items to emphasize, and repeat the process.

Use the checklist from time to time to check on how you're doing.

How Am I Doing?

Today, I ...	Yes, I did it	No, I forgot	I thought about it	I need to work on it
Told my child that I love him or her.				
Hugged him or her.				
Praised him or her. I said..._____				
Laughed **with** my child, not **at** my child.				
Asked my child to tell me one good thing that happened today.				
Gave my child special jobs to do (and praised my child for doing them).				
Spent time alone with my child.				
Allowed my child to do what he could for himself (dressing, planning, gathering school materials, etc.).				
Really listened to what my child said.				
Helped my child solve a problem rather than **telling** my child what was best to do.				
Made sure that my child was successful at something at home.				
Told someone else something positive about my child and made sure that my child heard me.				
Encouraged my child to let the teacher know when he or she was having trouble. (Caution: Do this sparingly. You do not want to encourage interventions that make your child feel inadequate.)				
Encouraged my child to participate in extracurricular activities in which he or she can succeed.				

WORKBOOK PAGE

Weekly Schedule

From _____ to _____
(Dates)

Time	Sunday	Monday	Tuesday	Wednesday	Thursday	Friday	Saturday

Special Assignment: Homework Success

Instructions: Before reading the next several pages, jot down problems or concerns you have noted about your child's homework and schoolwork.

_____

_____

_____

_____

_____

_____

_____

_____

_____

_____

_____

_____

_____

_____

Now look to the next page for suggestions to help make the homework experience less painful and more productive for you and your child.

Homework Suggestions

Problem	Solution
Homework is too difficult.	a). Before your child starts, make sure that he or she understands the concept and process. (Have your child do the first few math problems with you.) b) Ideally, assignments should be completed without help. If this does not seem possible, talk with the teacher; ask for suggestions.
Homework takes too long.	Talk with the teacher: • Ask how much time your child should spend and let the teacher know how much time he or she is actually spending. • Negotiate on an amount of time for your child to spend on homework. • Ask the teacher to accept reduced amount of work to be done in that time frame (fewer math problems, shorter writing assignment). • Ask the teacher to allow for modifications such as dictated assignments, using a computer, tape recorder, etc.

Lack of organization.	a) Provide a notebook with dividers and folders for each subject and a zippered bag for pencils, pens, and supplies.
	b) Give your student an assignment book or daily homework sheet which you and the teacher can initial (hard to do but effective — stick with it!). (See Daily Homework Sheet on next page.)
	c) Have your student make a weekly schedule. (Younger ones may need help.)
	  • List *all* after-school activities (meals, snacks, playtime, sports, phone calls, homework).
	  • Select a half-hour to be used for planning the week.
	  • Record everything.
	  • Divide long-term assignments among days.
	d) Leave books, notebooks, and other items needed for school in the same place each night. (Next to the front door is best; never wait until the next morning.)
	e) Develop checklists to remember necessary steps for packing bookbag at night, going to locker before school ends, etc. Laminate them and have your child mark them with dry erase pens.

Unpleasant scenes at home.	a) Decide on the best time to complete homework and stick with it. b) Provide a quiet uncluttered work place that is not also used for making model airplanes and other recreational activities. c) Decide on who should give assistance (parent, grandparent, older sibling, tutor, etc.). d) Provide incentives for completion. (Decide together how long he will work, and then set a kitchen timer. "When you have finished your homework, you may watch TV.") e) Don't require perfection. (Errors explain to the teacher that the skill needs more work at school.) Don't do your child's homework for him! f) Praise for a job well done!

WORKBOOK PAGE

Daily Homework Sheet

Name _____

Date _____

Class/Subject	Assignment	Assignment recorded correctly (teacher initials)	Assignment completed (parent initials)	Assignment turned in (teacher initials)

Launching Better Behavior: Accentuate the Positive

Instructions: Read through the descriptions below. Put a check mark next to the items that best describe how you discipline your child and handle bad behavior.

Are the techniques you are presently using positive or are they mostly negative?
Choose one or two areas in which you are presently using negative techniques and make a concerted effort in the next week to use the positive techniques described.
At the end of the week, review your progress and choose additional positive techniques to try.[29]

☺	Positives	☹	Negatives
	Use eye contact; speak directly to your child while he's looking at you.		Call from across the room.
	Speak in short, meaningful sentences.		Use a lot of words.
	Use positive instructions. ("Speak softly, please.")		Use negative instructions. ("Don't yell!")
	Give one direction at a time.		Expect too many things at once.
	Praise the behaviors you want to continue.		Always emphasize negative behaviors.
	Praise the specific job. ("That was a great job of setting the table.")		Just say "Good!"
	Be specific when speaking about an undesirable behavior.		Attack his personality or make him feel guilty.
	Make sure that your child knows the rules. Keep them simple and consistent. Ask him to repeat them.		Deal with a situation only after it has happened.
	Use incentives.		Make demands.
	Give choices when possible.		Make all the decisions.
	Let your child know what to expect. ("After you play for 30 minutes, it will be time to do homework.")		Surprise him. ("Come in this minute and do your homework!")
	Follow through with what you say.		Make empty promises or threats without acting on them.
	Model appropriate behavior.		Do one thing yourself but expect something else from your child.
	Let the punishment fit the crime.		Impose a major punishment for something minor.
	Remain calm when managing behavior.		Become angry.
	Try a little laughter. (Remember your sense of humor.)		Take life too seriously all the time.

13 Parent Rules for Responding to Angry Children

Children with learning disabilities are often angry at themselves, at you, and at school. They may act out. Parents should not make their children ashamed or guilty for their anger, but should teach their children to channel and redirect it to constructive uses. These "13 Parent Rules" are reminders of ways to do that![30]

- **Catch the child being good** (praise, praise, praise).

- **Ignore inappropriate behavior — unless it is dangerous.**

- **Provide physical outlets to get rid of energy** (swimming, gymnastics, etc.).

- **Use closeness and touching** (your hand and touch are calming).

- **Show affection.**

- **Ease tension through humor.**

- **Explain situations.**

- **Remove tough situations; control the environment.**

- Use (and keep!) **promises; use rewards.**

- **Say "No," but use punishment cautiously.**

- **Model appropriate behavior** (children learn what they see).

- **Don't criticize or compare behavior** (brothers and sisters aren't perfect either).

- **Avoid danger words and statements!**
  - Don't be stupid!
  - Your brother never did that!
  - When are you going to grow up!
  - I can't trust you!
  - Stop acting that way!
  - Can't you do anything right!
  - You're a mess!
  - How many times do I have to tell you!

Chapter 4 — THE STUDENT WITH LEARNING DISABILITES AT SCHOOL

This chapter is the most extensive in the book; it covers four kinds of vital information needed by parents of school-age children who are suspected of having learning disabilities, or who have been identified as having LD.

Part A **takes a parent step-by-step through the identification and placement process and the preparation of a plan to help the child in a public school, emphasizing the school's responsibilities.** ***Part B*** **cites the differences in the process for a private school student.**

Part C **delineates the parent's role and responsibilities in dealing with a school system, and suggests ways to become an effective advocate for a child.** ***Part D*** **provides a quick overview of Section 504 of the Rehabilitation Act of 1973, another avenue for protecting the rights of students — and adults — with disabilities.**[1]

Part A: The *PUBLIC* School's Role in Referral, Evaluation, Eligibility, and the IEP

Children with learning disabilities often have unique needs, both at home and at school. Your child may not have been identified as having a learning disability, yet you find yourself wondering if that could be the reason for his or her special needs. You may want the public school system to do an evaluation. Both the school and the parent(s) play roles in securing necessary services. The Individualized Education Program is the tool by which parents and teachers develop and monitor a student's program and progress when the student has been accepted into special education.

FREE APPROPRIATE PUBLIC EDUCATION (FAPE)

A free, appropriate public education is guaranteed by Public Law 101-476: the Individuals with Disabilities Education Act. When a student has been found eligible to receive special education, and in some cases related services, he or she is entitled to an appropriate education at public expense — thus a *free, appropriate public education*.

Special education provides specially designed instruction to meet the needs of individual students with disabilities, while *related services* are provided when needed for a student to benefit from special education.

INDIVIDUALS WITH DISABILITIES EDUCATION ACT (IDEA)

IDEA is the federal law that outlines both the special education process and the way students with disabilities are to receive services to meet their needs.

[There are two other laws that affect students with disabilities: Section 504 of the Rehabilitation Act of 1973 and the Americans with Disabilities Act (ADA). We describe Section 504 later in this chapter and ADA in Chapter 5.]

IDEA requires that all states and public schools follow certain processes. The individual states and school districts, however, develop their own procedures for putting these requirements into practice.

The U.S. Department of Education has established regulations to implement IDEA. The law and its regulations may be found on the Internet at www.ed.gov/offices/OSERS/IDEA. In turn, each state establishes its own regulations to implement IDEA.

As you get involved in special education, you should have a copy of your state's regulations, policies, and procedures. You may obtain this information by contacting your State Department of Education (see Appendix B-3). This information is available in print, audio cassette, and Braille.

Additionally, each state has a federally funded Parent Training and Information Center (PTI) (see Appendix B-3), and a Protection and Advocacy agency (see Appendix B-3). You should call the above agencies for any literature, pamphlets, and booklets they may have concerning your state's regulations as well as your and your child's rights.

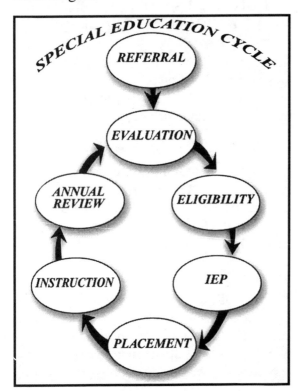

The foregoing "Special Education Cycle" graphic[2] is explained in more detail at the end of this chapter. (See the "Identification → Evaluation → Placement Process" flow chart.) You may also find helpful the Workbook page, "Tracking the Special Education Process," once you have received all your local and state information. It provides spaces where you can record your district's timelines and names of committee members.

You need to become familiar with your state's timelines, and with the terminology it uses for the various meetings involved in the special education process; these can vary from state to state. Having this information will help you feel more self-confident in meetings with school personnel.

It is also of central importance for parents to find out what the local procedures and criteria are concerning a student's eligibility for special education. Some states allow local school districts to make these decisions themselves. Ask for any guidelines and criteria that your school uses to determine (1) whether your child has a learning disability, and (2) if so, if the child is eligible for special education and related services.

REFERRAL

In most cases, teachers will initiate a conference with you about your child's school performance and any concerns they may have. If you have questions, you are free at any time to contact the teacher or the school to discuss your child's performance.

At conferences or meetings, you, your child's teachers, and others can brainstorm ideas about ways to help your child be more successful in school. In all cases, you, as the parent, should negotiate a follow-up meeting to determine how the new ideas are working.

However, if at any time during this process you suspect that your child has a learning disability and is in need of special education and related services, you can make a referral. This referral should be made to the school principal or special education coordinator.

It is necessary to make the referral in writing. It should be dated, and you should keep a copy for your files. Your written referral should include these five components:

1. That you are requesting "an *evaluation to determine if my child has a learning disability and is eligible for special education and related services.*" (It is advisable to use these words exactly as shown here because they trigger the referral process for special education.)
2. Why you think your child has a learning disability;
3. How you feel it is affecting his or her school performance;
4. What has been done by you, the parent, or by the school to address these concerns;
5. Samples or examples of your child's work that demonstrate these concerns.

AFTER THE REFERRAL

Upon receipt of the referral, school district personnel will review your child's records, current assessments, the classroom situation, information provided by you, and current classroom progress.

Based upon this review, the school *must* respond in writing to your request for an evaluation.

If the school district **refuses** your request for evaluation, they must tell you:
- They are refusing your request;
- Why they are refusing your request;
- What other options they considered;
- What information and procedures they used to make the decision;
- Your right to appeal this decision.

Along with this refusal, the school district may recommend:

a) Further meetings with a specialist, the classroom teacher or teachers, or persons outside of the school system who may be working with your child;

b) That the classroom teacher try some strategies that have not been used before. The district should put in writing when it will meet with you and the teachers to determine whether the new strategies are working.

If the school district **agrees** to your request for an evaluation, then you will be part of a team. The team will decide what additional information is needed in order to determine if your child has a learning disability.

This preliminary team will include:

1. You (the parent)
2. At least one of your child's general education teachers
3. A teacher who specializes in the area of suspected disability (i.e., a teacher of students with learning disabilities)
4. A representative of the school district who is qualified to provide, or supervise the provision of, special education, is

knowledgeable about the general curriculum and the availability of resources

5. Someone who can interpret what the testing means about classroom instruction

6. Anyone else that the district or you feel is necessary and has knowledge or expertise regarding your child

7. Your son or daughter, at your discretion.

This team will first review existing evaluations of your child. It will include information provided by you, as well as current classroom assessments and observations.

Based on this review and input from you, the team will, next, identify the additional information needed to determine:

- Whether your child has a learning disability;
- Your child's current educational performance levels and educational needs;
- Whether your child needs special education and related services;
- Whether there are any modifications or accommodations needed to help your child meet his or her goals and participate in the general education curriculum.

Before the school district can conduct any initial evaluations to obtain this additional information, they must have your written consent.

EVALUATIONS

In order to satisfy the definition of a learning disability in IDEA (see Appendix A), there are a number of components that **may** be addressed in a formal evaluation. These include:

- an educational evaluation
- a medical evaluation

- a socio-cultural evaluation
- a psychological evaluation
- an observation in the classroom
- other tests, as deemed necessary.

If the school wants to have any of the above evaluations made, it will be done at no cost to the parent.

Educational Evaluation

This evaluation will include, but is not limited to, assessment of basic academic skill areas such as reading, writing, and mathematics. The school may also gather information about your child or young adult's performance in areas such as concept formation, memory, auditory perception, fine and gross motor development, and language processing. Information may include the following:

- Grades
- Report cards
- Standardized tests
- Teacher-made tests
- Criterion-referenced tests
- History of educational experiences (when started first grade, attendance, grades repeated, etc.)
- Description of current class performance and work habits
- Description of student's strengths
- Description of peer and adult relationships
- Description of successful and unsuccessful interventions tried previously
- Description of educational needs that

cannot be met in regular classroom setting

The person who completes the educational evaluation will submit a written report containing all of the information used. You are to receive a copy of this report.

Medical Evaluation

The medical evaluation should identify any physiological factors that might interfere with the learning process. A medical and developmental history should be obtained, with note made of any condition or current medication that might affect classroom performance. Although gross vision and hearing screening may have revealed no major problems, subtle difficulties may be caught with more comprehensive testing. You must receive a written report.

Socio-Cultural Evaluation

This evaluation generally consists of interviews with, or checklists and rating scales from, parents, guardians, or other caregivers. It may include an interview with the child. Information is gathered about any history of developmental lag, family learning problems, and any other evidence that indicates that the learning problems are not due primarily to environmental, cultural, or economic disadvantage. Such information may be obtained by a professional who is typically referred to as the school social worker. You must receive a written report.

Psychological Evaluation

This evaluation is performed by a psychologist and usually includes individual tests of intellectual functioning, assessments of the child's behavior and personality, and other tests as appropriate. You must receive a written report.

The written report should include a statement of intellectual potential, verbal and performance standard scores, and scaled subtest scores (if available), as well as interpretation of this information.

Observation

The federal regulations requiring observation of the student who is suspected of having a learning disability read as follows:

> At least one team member other than the child's regular teacher shall observe the child's academic performance in the regular classroom setting. In the case of a child of less than school age, or out of school, a team member shall observe the child in an environment appropriate for a child of that age.

The results of the observation are presented in a written report that includes data on the length of the observation, the behavior noted during the observation which is relevant to a diagnosis of learning disabilities, and the relationship of that behavior to the student's academic functioning. You must receive a written report.

Other

When indicated, assessment of speech, language, gross and fine motor abilities, etc., should also be made. You must receive a written report of any of these other evaluations that are made.

THE ELIGIBILITY MEETING

Preliminary Team
Generally, within a certain number of days of the receipt of your request for evaluation, all parts of your child's comprehensive evaluation must be completed and a preliminary team of qualified professionals, as well as you, the parent, must meet. (The requirement that this be done within a certain time limit varies by state.)

This team must consider all information collected during the evaluations and then present it to you at an eligibility meeting. You should receive a copy of the minutes, along with copies of all of the reports.

Before you attend the meeting, see the Workbook page "How to Use the Form 'My Child's Test Results,'" which is at the end of this chapter. Also prior to the meeting, ask school personnel to review and explain your child's evaluation to you. While not required, this will help you to be a better participant as a member of the team that determines eligibility.

This is an important meeting for you and your child. *Make sure you understand what the other members of the team are saying about your child and make sure they hear what you are saying. If you do not understand scores or terms presented by a team member,* ASK THE PERSON TO EXPLAIN IT!

This team, at this stage, must make two decisions:
1. Does the student have a learning disability? If the answer is "yes," then the next question, according to the law, is:
2. Does the student, by reason thereof (i.e., of the disability) need special education and related services?

If the answer to the second question is "no," then your child is not eligible for special education and related services as a student with a learning disability. If the answer to the second question is "yes," then your child is eligible for special education and related services.

The next step is for an Individualized Education Program (IEP) Team to meet and develop an IEP for your child. This team must meet for this purpose within **30 calendar days** *from the date that eligibility was determined.*

What does the IEP do?
The IEP (Individualized Education Program) document outlines goals that are prioritized, and services that are described in detail, to help the student with a disability achieve success in school and in transition to life after school. The IEP is the heart of special education.

What's in the IEP Document?
1. Your child's present level of educational performance in all areas;
2. Measurable goals for each area, including benchmarks and objectives;
3. Special education and related services to be provided with supplementary aids, modifications, and supports needed;
4. A description of how the child's disability affects involvement and progress in the general education curriculum and extracurricular activities;
5. An explanation of the extent, if any, the child will *not* participate with students who do not have disabilities, in regular class and other activities;
6. By age 14, transition planning to prepare a child for life following graduation;
7. Dates for beginning the services, location, planned length of the services, and modifications;
8. Extended school year services, if required;

9. How progress will be measured and how parents will be regularly informed;
10. Information regarding the child's participation in local and statewide assessments, including needed modifications, if any.

BEFORE THE IEP MEETING

Notification of IEP Meeting

The school district must notify you, orally or in writing, of the IEP meeting. This notice must include:

- The purpose of the meeting
- Time and location of the meeting
- Who will attend
- Your and the school district's right to invite others to attend
- Statement that your child will be invited when transition services are to be discussed
- Names of any agency which will be asked to send a representative when transition services are to be discussed.

The time and place of the meeting must be mutually agreed upon. You and the school district may use alternative forms of meeting, such as e-mail or conference calls. More than one meeting may be required to complete the IEP.

It is VERY IMPORTANT for you, the parent, to participate in developing the IEP. After all, what you know about your child is essential to the development of the IEP. However, if you decide not to participate, the school district can conduct the IEP meeting without you.

Preparation for the Meeting

It is important that you and your child invest time in preparing for the IEP meeting. This is an excellent time for you and your child to discuss some of the topics suggested below. Use the Workbook pages at the end of this chapter, "IEP Planning Forms for Parents,"

to help you.

For Parents:
1. Think of yourself as the parent "information specialist" and develop a written agenda of information about your child that you will want to share with the IEP team, and items you will want addressed during the development of your child's IEP. Your personal notebook, described in Part C of this chapter, will be of tremendous help to you in becoming an "information specialist." You should find the "Parent Observation Sheet" at the end of Chapter 1 useful.

2. Contact your child's school, if this is your initial IEP meeting, to help you understand the process, the issues that will be discussed, and your rights and responsibilities. Ask for a copy of the IEP form they will use.

3. Ask someone to attend the meeting with you, if that will put you more at ease. That person can make notes of the proceeding if you wish.

For Parent and Student Together:
4. With your child, examine the long-range vision of your child; discuss what your child wants to do when he or she leaves school, or in the next 3 years.

5. What do you and your child expect him to learn this year? Consider what annual goals would help your child accomplish his long-range plans.

6. Explore together how much your child should participate in regular education programs, in light of your child's learning style and special education needs.

7. Determine together the extent to which

your student will be involved in the IEP meeting. Emphasize that this is his or her life that people are making decisions about. Older students, especially, should be involved in the process to the greatest degree possible.

Suggestions to the Older Student: (at least by age 14):

• Think about what you want to learn this year.

• Talk to your parents and teachers about what you want to do when you leave school.

• Ask for assistance from your teachers and parents to prepare you to participate actively in your IEP meeting so that you will be able to understand the process, present your concerns and educational needs, ask questions, and make decisions.

• Practice telling people about your hopes and desires, especially as they relate to life after high school.

THE IEP TEAM

(NOTE: This is different from the Preliminary Team described under "The Eligibility Meeting," earlier in this chapter.)

As the parent and a full partner on the IEP team, you have a right and a responsibility to help the school team to develop your child's IEP. The basic IEP team includes:
• You, the parent(s);
• At least one of your child's regular education teachers;
• At least one special education teacher who is knowledgeable about learning disabilities;
• A representative of your school district who...
   1. is qualified to provide or supervise the provision of special education
   2. is knowledgeable about the general education curriculum

   3. is knowledgeable about the availability of resources within the school district;
• A person who can explain the kind of instruction your child needs, based upon the result of his or her evaluations. This may be an additional person or one of the other team members (but not you or your child, of course);
• Any other persons with knowledge or special expertise regarding the child whom you or the school district choose to invite;
• Your child, if appropriate.

NOTE: Transition services *must* be discussed at the IEP meeting *at least* by the time your child has reached age 14. When transition services are to be discussed at an IEP meeting, *your child must be invited to attend.* If your child does not attend, the school district must assure that the preferences and interests of your child are considered at the meeting.

The federal regulations further state that, by the time your child reaches age 16, the school district shall invite representatives of other agencies, as well. For example, a representative of the Department of Rehabilitative Services (DRS), or any other agency that is likely to provide or pay for transition services will be invited.

THE IEP MEETING

Factors to be Considered
IDEA federal regulations require the IEP team to consider and discuss at the meeting the following factors pertaining to the student:

• Strengths of the student;
• Concerns of the parent(s) for enhancing the student's education;
• Results of most recent evaluation(s);
• Results of the student's performance on

any state- or district-wide assessment;
- Behavior-changing strategies, if needed;
- Language needs, if any, resulting from limited English proficiency when these needs relate to the student's IEP;
- Instruction in Braille, if needed;
- The communication needs of the student;
- The student's language and communication mode in the case of students with hearing impairments;
- Assistive technology devices and services, if needed;
- Transfer of rights to the student at the age of majority.

COMPONENTS OF THE IEP

IDEA requires that each IEP contain the following:

1. *Present level of performance:*
   This includes up-to-date information about your child's or young adult's...
   - strengths, especially in those areas causing the most concern;
   - specific areas of concern and how the disability affects your child's involvement and progress in the general curriculum;
   - performance in both academic and non-academic areas (as appropriate);
   - learning style;
   - response to techniques and/or materials that have been tried previously.

This information should be based on a variety of diagnostic procedures. You should not accept statements which are not documented.

2. *A statement concerning transition beyond school:*
   This should be done by the time the student is 14 years old, as determined by the IEP team. It must be updated annually. The statement focuses on the student's courses of study — such as participation in advanced placement courses or vocational programs.

Beginning at age 16 or younger, as determined by the IEP team, the statement focuses on the student's goals and dreams for post-secondary employment, education, and adult living.

3. *Measurable annual goals:*
   These reflect answers to the question, "What do we want the student to be able to do in a year's time?" The goals...
   - are based on the major areas of concern identified in the student's Present Level of Educational Performance section of the IEP;
   - are stated in terms of behavior that can be observed and measured;
   - address the skills the student needs in order to participate and progress in the general education curriculum;
   - are realistic in terms of the student's physical and cognitive abilities;
   - are prioritized on the basis of the student's age and amount of time left in school;
   - are prioritized according to the student's needs, including his or her ability to live independently.

Finally, there must be a statement about the means* the school district will use to inform you regularly of...
(a) your child's progress toward the annual goals, and
(b) whether — to what extent — the progress made is sufficient to enable your child to achieve the goals by the end of the year.

*These means could be through report cards, but they must be sent to you <u>at least</u> as often as reports are sent to parents of nondisabled students in your child's school.

4. *Short-term objectives or benchmarks:*
Each annual goal must have short-term objectives or benchmarks, or both. These objectives of the IEP:

- are based on annual goals relative to the present level of educational performance;
- are a sequence of skills/steps or milestones;
- are stated in observable behavioral, measurable terms; and
- answer the questions:
  (a) Who will achieve…
  (b) What skill or behavior…
  (c) How (in what manner or at what level)?
  (d) Where (in what setting or under what conditions)?
  (e) When (by what ending date)?

Note: The objectives or benchmarks are in no way intended to be as detailed as lesson plans.

5. *A statement of the special education or related services to be provided:*
When deciding upon special education and related services needed, it is important for the IEP team to determine what will be most apt to help the student…

- advance appropriately toward attaining each of the measurable, annual IEP goals;
- be involved and progress in the general curriculum and participate in extracurricular and other nonacademic activities; and
- be educated and participate with other children with and without disabilities.

The team's discussions may cover:
- Related services;
- Supplementary aids and services

such as Talking Books to be provided to the student, or on behalf of the student;

- Program modifications and accommodations that are needed for the student to:
  1. advance appropriately toward the IEP goals
  2. be involved in the general curriculum and make progress in it
  3. participate in other school activities.
- Supports for school personnel;
- Assistive technology services and devices;
- Transition services;
- Extended school year (ESY);

Next, relative to these services and modifications, the IEP team will need to:

- Determine the beginning and ending dates as well as the frequency, location, and duration of these services and modifications; and
- Provide an explanation of the extent, if any, to which the student will be participating only with other disabled students, in academic, non-academic, and extra-curricular activities.

6. *A statement regarding the administering of state- or district-wide achievement tests:*
The IEP team decides whether it is appropriate for the child to take the test (or any part of it). If it is, the team will list any modifications needed. If it is not appropriate, the IEP team will state why that assessment is not appropriate for that child, and how the child *will* be assessed.

NOTE: If your child's behavior adversely affects either his learning or the learning of other students, it would be good practice for the IEP to identify the problem behavior, as well as strategies and positive supports the school will use to address the behavior. If a suspension is proposed, the law requires that a Functional Behavioral Assessment of your child be conducted. For further information concerning disciplinary action, see Appendix C, "What If Your Child Requires Disciplinary Action By the School?"

Additional Pointers for Parents
There are a few things to remember as you help to develop the IEP for your child or young adult:

1. *There is no "right" set of services for all students with LD. You and your school should look at your child's strengths and weaknesses and make a program that fits his or her needs.*
2. *The IEP, with its annual goals, objectives/benchmarks, and services, outlines the program for your child. The classrooms where your child receives instruction are not the "program."*
3. *When developing the IEP, the goals and objectives/benchmarks, ALWAYS come first. Only after the goals and objectives/benchmarks are described should the "where" of services be part of the discussion.*
4. *A student's program/IEP should be developed on the basis of what the student needs, not what services are presently available in the school system. The intent of the law is that school systems must either provide appropriate services or provide the funds needed to secure them elsewhere.*

If your child is approaching or is in high school, there are a number of questions that you should ask when negotiating the IEP:
- *What course requirements must my child meet to get a diploma?*

- *Will the program outlined in the IEP allow my child to get a diploma?*
- *What tests must my child take and pass in order to get a diploma?*
- *Does the IEP list the modifications/accommodations that will be needed to enable my child to participate in these tests?*
- *If my child cannot meet the requirements for a diploma, what other options are available?*

HOW IS PLACEMENT DECIDED?

Once the goals and objectives are outlined and agreed upon for the IEP, a team must decide your child's placement — how services will be provided to your son or daughter. This team is made up of you, the parent(s), as well as others who know about your child and what the evaluation results mean, and what types of placements are appropriate. In some states, the IEP team serves as the group making the placement decision. In other states this decision may be made by another group of people. In all cases, the parents have the right to be members of the group that decides the educational placement of the child.

Placement decisions must be made according to IDEA's least restrictive environment requirements — commonly known as LRE. (IDEA stands for Individuals with Disabilities Education Act. See Glossary.) These requirements state that, to the maximum extent appropriate, children with disabilities must be educated with children who do not have disabilities.

The law also clearly states that special classes, separate schools, or other removal of children with disabilities from the regular educational environment are allowed only if the nature or severity of the child's disability is such that education in regular classes **with** *the use of supplementary aids and services* cannot be achieved satisfactorily.

Depending on the needs of the child, his or her IEP may be carried out in one or more of a continuum of options. For example, we'll say that Jose has a severe learning disability that causes him to read considerably below the level of his peers in 8th grade. Therefore, while he participates in the regular 8th grade English classroom with modifications, accommodations and supports, he receives reading instruction in the special education classroom.

Or Marie has a learning disability that makes it difficult for her to learn when the 10th grade history teacher uses lecture as the primary mode of teaching. To reduce this problem, the teacher gives Marie an outline of the lecture before class begins. (In fact, this practice will also help the other, non-handicapped students in the class.)

Both of these students are receiving special education services based on their individual needs.

WHAT TYPES OF PLACEMENTS ARE THERE?

Although different states and school systems may have different names for the programs they provide for students with learning disabilities, most services fall within the models described below.

- Collaborative Consultation
  In this model, frequently called a "consultation model," the student with learning disabilities continues to receive all instruction in a regular classroom. The LD teacher consults with the classroom teacher on a regular basis, monitoring the student's progress, making suggestions as to how to adapt materials and assignments, etc.

- Co-Teaching
  The student participates in the general education classroom. The special educator and general educator teach the class together, both involved in planning and delivering instruction.

- Special Class (part-time) *
  This is often called a "Resource Room." In this model the student with learning disabilities leaves the regular classroom for a certain period of time for instruction in specific areas. This is done with a special educator, usually in a small group setting, in a separate room. In order for this to be successful, the regular classroom and special education teachers must work closely together to coordinate instruction.

- Special Class (full-time) *
  The student spends the majority of his or her day in a separate classroom with a smaller group of students who receive intensive instruction from a special educator in areas of need. The students may spend a portion of their day in regular classrooms, but most of their instruction occurs in this special class.

- Special Day School *
  The student spends the entire day in a separate school that is designed to provide the intensive instruction that the student needs for learning disabilities. Although some public school systems do have special schools devoted entirely to the education of learning disabled students, it is more common to find this model in private schools.

- Residential School *
  Residential schools for LD students offer a 24-hour environment in which the student attends school and lives with other students, at least during the school week.

- Hospitals and Institutions

These models are the most restrictive settings for a student. In general, they would be chosen only if a child had severe medical and/or emotional problems, as well as learning disabilities.

- Homebound Instruction
  Homebound instruction is usually used for short, temporary periods of time when a student cannot attend school. In this situation, a teacher comes to the home and provides instruction there.

It is important for parents to remember that federal and state laws mandate that public school systems provide a continuum of services. If a school system does not have certain levels of service within its own system, and if it is determined that your child with LD needs a level of service not provided, then the school district must either start providing the service or seek the needed services outside of its system, and must pay any tuition and transportation costs.

* Four of the above placements are marked with asterisks. Each of these describes a setting which, in some cases, is called a Learning Disabilities Classroom. Appendix D describes how this type of learning environment is different from a regular education classroom.

WHO HAS ACCESS TO THE IEP?

When the IEP has been written, parents must receive a copy at no cost to themselves. IDEA also stresses that everyone who will be involved in *implementing* the IEP must have access to the document. This includes the child's …

- regular education teacher(s);
- special education teacher(s);
- related service provider(s) (for example, speech therapist); or

- any other service provider (such as a paraprofessional) who will be responsible for a part of the child's education.

As the parent, it is your job to find out <u>who among school personnel</u> is in charge of making sure that each person on the above lists knows his or her specific responsibilities for carrying out the student's IEP appropriately. This includes the specific accommodations, modifications, and supports that the child must receive, according to the IEP.

<u>CAUTION</u>: ***Before you agree to the IEP…***

Parents should carefully review the IEP. Do not agree to the IEP until you have studied it thoroughly and understand it. You should be aware that you have the right to have someone (another parent or professional) accompany you to the IEP meeting. You may also take home your copy of the IEP before agreeing to it and consult with other professionals and knowledgeable parents.

The IEP is a legal document, protecting your child's right to an appropriate education. The school district must provide the special education and related services set forth in the agreed-upon IEP. However, IDEA does not require the school district or teacher to be held accountable if the child does not achieve the growth projected in the goals, benchmarks, or objectives, as long as the school district has provided the IEP services and has made a good faith effort to assist the child in achieving the goals, benchmarks, and objectives. You may wish to contact a local parent group, Parent Information and Training Center, or representative from your state protection and advocacy agency, if you have questions or concerns (see Appendix

B).

WHEN YOU DON'T AGREE WITH THE SCHOOL DISTRICT...

There are times when you, the parent(s), may not agree with the school's recommendations about your child's education. Under the law, you have the right to challenge decisions about your child's eligibility, evaluation, placement, and the services that the school provides to your child. If you disagree with the school's actions — or refusal to take action — in these matters, you have the right to pursue a number of options. You may do the following:

- *Request an independent educational evaluation.* You have the right to this evaluation at school district expense if you disagree with an evaluation obtained by the school district. An independent educational evaluation is an evaluation conducted by a qualified professional who is not employed by the school district. Upon your request, the school district must either pay for the independent evaluation or initiate a Due Process hearing to show that the school district's evaluation is appropriate.

- *Try to reach an agreement.* You can talk with school officials about your concerns and try to reach an agreement. Sometimes the agreement can be temporary. For example, you and the school can agree to try a plan of instruction or a placement for a certain period of time and see how your student does. For resolving disputes prior to Due Process, you may request mediation, or the school may offer mediation.

- *Ask for mediation.* During mediation, you and school personnel sit down with a qualified mediator who is not involved in the disagreement and try to reach an agreement. Your state will pay the cost of this. Discussions during mediation proceedings are confidential.

- *Ask for Due Process.* During a Due Process hearing, you, as parent(s), and school personnel appear before an impartial hearing officer and present both sides of the story. The hearing officer decides how to solve the problem, and must make a decision within 45 days after the request for a hearing is made. (Note: Mediation must be available at least at the time a Due Process hearing is requested.)

- *File a complaint with the state education agency.* To file a complaint, generally parents write directly to their State Department of Education and say what part of IDEA they believe the school has violated. The agency must resolve the complaint within 60 calendar days. An extension of that time limit is permitted only if exceptional circumstances exist with respect to the complaint. (Also, see "Resolving Problems" in Part C of this chapter.)

AFTER THE IEP AND PLACEMENT *HAVE* BEEN AGREED TO, THEN WHAT?

Once you agree to the IEP, you are, in effect, giving permission for your child to receive the services designated. The school district is required to provide ONLY those services specifically stated in the IEP, so you must be sure they are included if they are needed. Parents should be aware that school districts are not required to provide the best services for a student, only those that allow the child to benefit.

But there's the cue: you want to be sure your student IS benefiting from the placement.

The following suggest ways of monitoring his or her progress:

1. Examine the papers which reflect the work your child does at school. Determine whether your child's level of accomplishment correlates with the goals and objectives of his IEP. For example, if testing has revealed deficits in reading comprehension and subsequent goals for the improvement of reading comprehension were included on the IEP, then classwork should reflect this focus. If you do not find a correlation between IEP objectives and classwork, request a meeting with the teacher and/or IEP team to clarify the situation.

2. Make sure you receive reports at least as often as students who are not disabled. The manner of reporting to you will have been described in your child's IEP. Ask for frequent feedback. If your child is not making progress, request an IEP meeting to consider possible revisions. If your child is making progress in the LD class but not in the regular classroom, ask that the IEP team meet to ascertain whether additional accommodations within the regular classroom are needed or whether additional time is needed in the LD class. Remember the importance of balancing accommodation and remediation (see Appendix D).

3. Be aware that sometimes students with other disabilities (emotional disturbance, mental retardation, etc.) may be placed in special classes with students with LD. Such a classroom situation puts great demands upon the teacher. If your child is in such a setting, be especially careful to monitor progress to be certain that your youngster's needs are being met. If they are not, ask that the IEP team meet

again.

A well-written IEP is the tool by which parents and teachers develop and monitor a student's progress. If you have concerns that the IEP is not meeting your child's needs, you may request that the IEP team be reconvened to review the IEP at any time.

REVIEWING AND REVISING THE IEP

IDEA requires the IEP team to review the IEP at least once a year. One purpose of this review is to see whether your child is achieving his or her annual goals. The team must revise the individualized education program, if necessary, to address:

- your student's progress or lack of expected progress toward the annual goals and in the general curriculum;
- information gathered through any reevaluation of your child;
- information about the child that you share with the school;
- information about your child that the school shares (for example, insights from the teacher, based on his or her observation of the child or the child's classwork);
- your child's anticipated needs; or
- other matters.

Although the IDEA requires this IEP review at least once a year, in fact the team may review and revise the IEP more often. Either you as parent(s) or the school can ask to hold an IEP meeting to revise the IEP. For example, your student may not be making progress toward the IEP goals, and you or the teacher(s) may become concerned. On the other hand, your student may have met most or all of the goals in the IEP and new ones need to be written. In either case, the IEP team would meet to revise the IEP.

At least every three years, the school district has to determine whether the student is still eligible for services. This involves a reevaluation by the school district. The reevaluation might turn out to be very simple or highly involved.

The team which originally received the referral about your child's eligibility will again make this decision.

Part B: The *PRIVATE* School's Role in Referral, Evaluation, Eligibility, and Service Plan Development

If your child is enrolled in a private school and you suspect a learning disability, your request for services from the school district in which you reside will be similar to that for <u>public</u> school children. School districts are required to identify all students with disabilities who live in their district and who are in need of special education and related services.

REFERRAL AND EVALUATION

If you are the parent of a child in a private school and you become concerned about his academic progress, you should write the Director of Special Education of your local school district. State your concern and request a formal evaluation of your child by the public schools. The purpose will be to determine his or her eligibility for special education and related services. According to federal and state law, your child, while attending a private school, is entitled to this evaluation by the public schools at no charge.

There are private testing agencies which parents may decide to use. You should recognize, however, that this is your choice and that schools are required only to <u>consider</u> this information, along with the information they have accumulated.

ELIGIBILITY

Once the child has been evaluated, eligibility proceedings take place as described in Part A of this chapter. If it is determined that your child has a learning disability, the public school system is required to offer appropriate services, programs, and placement. If your child attends a private school full-time, he is entitled to a *Service Plan*, not an IEP. (A Service Plan describes specific special education services and related services that the local school division will provide for the student.)

SERVICES

As a parent, you may choose to accept the services offered by the public schools or you may choose to continue your child in private school placement. Should you choose to continue the private school placement, the public school system is NOT obligated to <u>pay for</u> your child's education at the private school, as long as an appropriate program is available at the public school.

The public school IS required to <u>provide</u> special education and related services to meet your child's unique educational needs even though he or she attends a private school. Such services may be provided through arrangements such as dual enrollment, educational television, and the use of mobile educational services and equipment.

These services may be different from those provided for children actually attending the public school if the differences are necessary to meet the special needs of the private school child. However, these services must be comparable in quality, scope, and opportunity for participation with non-handicapped children to those provided to students in the public schools. The local school system maintains administrative control of these services, as governed by your child's Service Plan. The amount and type of services are based on a federal funding formula — a very complicated formula!

There is another option for parents: You have the right to simply refuse the services that are offered by the school district, and keep your child in the private school, using only the services offered there.

Disagreements may arise during these various steps. These can be handled by negotiation, mediation, or Due Process. (See Part A of this chapter for details of these processes.)

Part C: The Parent's Role in Problem Solving and Maintaining Records

Problems may arise in your dealings with your school district. Suggestions for solving such problems are in this Part C. As you apply these suggestions, you will find that prior documentation of your son's or daughter's school experiences will greatly enhance your efforts. A detailed outline for organizing such documents, "Maintaining a Filing System," makes up the latter section of this part. It also includes suggestions for using the workbook pages.

AVOIDING PROBLEMS

Until your child becomes mature enough to become his or her own advocate, you, the parent, must assume that role. You play a vital part in shaping your child's school experiences; therefore, you should begin preparations early in your youngster's school career.

There are several things you can do to avoid problems at school:

- One of the first things you can do is to join your school's PTA and attend as many meetings as possible. In this way you will get to know the principal and the teachers in a non-threatening setting. If possible, volunteer to be a room parent, or to accompany your child's class on field trips, so that you can form positive relationships, and the problems that may arise do not constitute your only involvement with the school.

- Read about other children with problems similar to those of your student. Learn as much as you can about the ways in which other parents have handled them.

- Gain an understanding of your child's strengths and weaknesses. Ask questions of any professionals who have worked with him. They can help you to understand the professionals' interpretation of test scores, to understand the way in which your child learns, and to be aware of special services he may require.

As you gain knowledge about your youngster as well as the school and its staff, you will increase your self-confidence. It will enable you to approach the school with assurance.

- Be pleasant and let your attitude reflect your desire to make positive contributions to the decisions being made.

- Try to build a good working relationship with the teacher and any of the other professionals who demonstrate empathy and understanding of your role as the principal monitor and important decision-maker for your child. Most teachers are very dedicated and hard working. You should try to work with them, not against them, if at all possible. Making life miserable for the teacher is not a ticket to a better education for your child. The best path to a better education is joint decision making, mutual respect and teamwork — with you as a vital member of that team.[3]

- Participate in all meetings and activities concerning your child. When possible, both parents should participate. When appropriate, your son or daughter may also participate. (This is particularly important for teenage students.)

- In communicating with the school, you should use primarily written notes —

and be sure to keep a dated copy. Use telephone calls for only the least important issues. Your copy of your written communication is documentation for your files.

- Prepare for meetings by making a list of issues beforehand in the order of importance. In this way the points of primary concern to you and your child will be discussed first.

- Do not feel inadequate in the presence of professionals because of their credentials. Remember, this is **your** child, and you have known this child longer and more intimately than anyone else on the team.[4]

- Insist — politely — that the results of testing and evaluation be explained to you in clear, jargon-free terms and that you have copies for your own file.[5] Ask questions so that you and the school have the same understanding of terms. Listen to the views of all participants. Many times the solution to a problem is the combination of several ingredients — some previously unknown to you.

- Be as clear as possible in your own mind about what kinds of things you believe your child is ready to learn. Make sure that the others at the conference never forget that you are talking about a real child.

- Take some time beforehand to think about how to be assertive without "taking over" or antagonizing people. Meetings about a child's school needs are not intended to be hostile confrontations; they should provide the chance for honest examination of alternatives. It should be possible to iron out disagreements through persuasion and mutual understanding.[6]

- Express your concerns and ideas. From daily observation under all conditions, you can contribute much information about your child's strengths and weaknesses. You may know that your child becomes particularly lethargic right after lunch or has particular difficulty in following directions when not sitting near the front of the room. At the same time, you may be able to point out strengths your child possesses that the school was not aware of, such as having the ability to redesign and construct bicycles or play a musical instrument, or having a wealth of knowledge about animals. Providing an outlet for a child's special interest or ability will help create a more balanced day and may prevent boredom or behavior problems. Success in something can be a great morale booster.

You may have ideas or questions that no one else has brought up. Don't be reluctant to ask questions or make contributions to the discussion.[7]

As the year progresses, check on the effectiveness of the program designed for your child. If you have doubts, again ask questions and participate actively in finding causes for any lack of progress and in making adjustments to the educational plan.

Listen to your child; respect what he or she is saying. You need to know your youngster's reaction to schoolwork, to teachers, to classmates.[8] At the same time, be aware that there may be two sides to the picture. You need to keep an open mind to viewing **both** sides. It is useful for you to be able to state the other point of view, even if you do not accept it; in putting into words the view opposite to your own, you can be better assured that you thoroughly understand it.

If you assume that someone else will surely say or do something if your child's or young adult's problems are serious, you may be sadly disappointed. It is the parent who must move past the pain, the guilt, and the anger to help his child. It is okay to ask for help. It doesn't mean you are a bad parent. You waited because you didn't know what else to do. Now, go ahead. Ask for service. Ask for clarification. Ask for information. Seek the answers. Don't accept "wait and see."[9]

RESOLVING PROBLEMS

Even when parents and public school officials work together cooperatively toward what each sees as an appropriate education for a student with learning disabilities, they sometimes find themselves unable to agree.

It is best however, to avoid formal hearings and court actions if at all possible. They can be costly in terms of time, money, and physical and emotional well being. It is wiser to use these procedures only as a last resort.

When you have a major concern about the identification, evaluation, or the program in which your child has been placed, try at least one more time to work with school personnel. You may find it necessary to become somewhat more assertive at this point.[10]

Informal Meetings
First, meet informally with your child's teacher or teachers and the school principal. Examples of concerns that might prompt you to ask for a conference are: (1) your child seems bored, restless or angry in the resource room and you think the youngster needs a more challenging program; (2) you have moved into a new home so that your child now needs transportation, and you'd like that written into the I.E.P., or (3) you

feel your child is in an improper educational setting.

If that process fails, IDEA makes available the avenue of mediation. (See Part A of this chapter for detailed information about IDEA.)

Mediation
Mediation is a process by which you or the school invite a third, impartial party to hear both sides of your argument in an informal fashion. The mediator then helps you and the district come up with solutions.

The procedures for getting a mediator vary by district but most states have a list of qualified mediators from whom you and the district may choose. The mediation process is voluntary for both you and the school and is not to be used to delay decisions or Due Process hearings.[11] It can be very beneficial in that the two parties, the teacher/school and you, learn to work together as you will have to do to help your child anyway.

MAINTAINING A FILING SYSTEM

One ingredient that is essential in your working successfully with the school district is documentation to back up your point of view. This may include test results, your notes from conferences with school personnel, samples of your child's classroom work, etc. You may already have a drawer full of such information, accumulated over the years of your child's development and school experiences. It is vital that you organize and safeguard this material so it is quickly available when needed. Continue reading below for suggestions in organizing what you have already accumulated — and what you will very probably add in the future.

The Importance of Records

Accurate and accessible records are needed at every step along the way — when your child enters a new school, is considered for special services, needs medical or mental health services, requires legal intervention in case of disagreement with the school system, or, in the post-school years, seeks rehabilitation, professional or career training services, or is the object of your estate planning. Furthermore, as a parent of a child diagnosed with a handicap, you may qualify for insurance and tax benefits for certain expenses. Claiming these will require reference to your file.

Your First Step

If you haven't done so already, you should secure a complete and entire copy of your child's cumulative and confidential file from the school system and from all agencies that have ever evaluated or worked with your child.

Materials Needed

Next, obtain a few materials you'll need to set up a file. They are:

- A large three-ring notebook (the bigger, the better; oversize binders are generally available at stationery or office supply stores)
- Notebook tab dividers (20)
- Pack of 3-hole notebook paper
- Notebook hole reinforcers
- Paper hole-puncher
- Post-it note pad
- Three hole punched pocket folders (3-5)

We suggest gathering all needed supplies as soon as possible. Getting organized now will save time and headaches later.

Listed below are suggestions for using each of the above items, to make your file functional.

Notebook — This will hold all records pertaining to your child's learning disability and educational progress. (See "Notebook Sections" below.)

Notebook tab dividers — We have described below seven notebook sections. You will need a divider for each section.

3-hole looseleaf notebook paper — You'll need a good supply!

Notebook hole reinforcers — Use these on all materials as you add them to your file. You'll be glad later.

Paper hole-puncher — Use a 3-hole punch in order to file in the notebook your child's significant records.

Post-it note pad — Never highlight or write on the documents (except for putting a date in the lower right corner). If you wish to call attention to particular passages, affix post-it notes with your comments.

3-hole punched pocket folders — Use these pocket folders to file irregularly sized items such as report cards, teacher notes, etc. Label each pocket clearly.

With your supplies in hand, you're now ready to set up your notebook file.
Notebook Sections
These are the suggested sections into which your notebook will be organized, using the tab dividers:

1. Telephone calls: This will give you a record of significant telephone conversations with

teachers and other professionals. Be sure to include the date, time, name of the person you talked with, the reason for the conversation, and any important points to remember, including any follow-up steps to be taken. (Use form, "Telephone/Meeting Log," at end of this chapter.)

2. Meetings: Keep a short written summary of each meeting you have with teachers and other professionals. (Use same form as for #1.)

3. Correspondence: Record all documents and correspondence received, as well as copies of letters which you have written about your child. (Use Workbook page, "Table of Contents for Documents.")

4. Reports of tests; notes about test results: These include medical test reports, significant birth and developmental history, visual exams, auditory evaluations, etc. They also cover psychological and educational test reports, as well as any notes you have made during conferences where your child's evaluations were interpreted. (Use same Workbook page as for #3.)

5. Official special education documents: Include referral, child study, eligibility, IEP, and all other official documents pertaining to your child's special education process and program. (Use same Workbook page as for #3.)

6. Report Cards: This covers official school and interim report cards, as well as written comments from all teachers, camp counselors, Sunday School teachers, tutors, etc. (Use same Workbook page as for #3.)

7. Samples of your child's classwork: Keep dated samples of your child's school papers, collected over a period of time, in a separate notebook. Make note of the subject for which the work was done (e.g., social studies, creative writing, science, etc.).

You will note that we have suggested you reserve many of the Workbook pages as master forms, from which to make copies as needed.

Further Suggestions for Notebook

- In maintaining the Table of Contents, each document should be entered with information about the date, person or evaluator or author, description of type of document, and brief summary or explanation. If author is unknown or not available, use name of the agency or school system. It is helpful to store this chronological list of documents on a word processor, if one is available, for ease in making insertions and changes.

- Date each item in the lower right-hand corner in pencil. Do this even if the date appears elsewhere on the document. This date will be used to keep and to locate documents in chronological order. In case of documents which span a period of time, such as report cards and telephone logs, use date of the last entry.

- Keep your notebook organized and up-to-date. Whenever you receive a new report, file it immediately. Don't succumb to the temptation to allow a stack of papers to accumulate that you hope to file later.

- As you come across helpful written material about learning disabilities, make a copy of the material, three-hole punch it, and file it in your notebook.

- Refer to your notebook often. Take it with you whenever you meet with a professional about your child. You will have an immediate, personalized resource to which you can refer. Yes, it will take time and effort to organize it in the manner described. However, once you have set it up in this manner, it will prove to be an invaluable tool to you and your child—and, in the long run, it will save you much time and frustration.

Use of Workbook Pages
The Workbook pages all have a dark triangle in the upper right hand corner. They are designed for you (or in some cases, your youngster) to complete. This gives you an opportunity to put to use the knowledge you've gained. You will probably want to keep your completed sheets in your notebook file.

> ### NOTE
> If the school requests your records, have extra copies of your chronological list of documents available for them so they can indicate which reports they want you to copy and provide to them.

Part D: Another Avenue for Services — Section 504

Section 504 of the Rehabilitation Act offers another means of protection for students — and adults — with disabilities. Differences between IDEA and Sec. 504 include: (1) the <u>requirements</u> for Section 504 are different, and (2) the Rehab Act is administered by the Office of Civil Rights instead of the Federal Department of Education.

Included in this section is information about qualifying for Section 504 services, the responsibilities of a school when a student has qualified, and your options if you don't agree with the decisions made by your school under Section 504 regulations.

WHAT IS SECTION 504?

Section 504 of the Rehabilitation Act was enacted by Congress in 1973 to eliminate discrimination against persons with disabilities, both in schools and in jobs. It is a civil rights act aimed at "leveling the playing field" because it is written specifically to protect the rights of individuals with disabilities in programs that receive federal funds (this would include all public schools).

How you qualify and what you are guaranteed is different from IDEA. Section 504 can provide services and protections to students with learning disabilities or attention problems who do not meet the criteria of IDEA.

SECTION 504 DEFINITION OF A DISABILITY

Unlike IDEA, Section 504 defines a disability as a physical or mental impairment which substantially limits one or more of a person's "major life activities." It also includes students who have a record of a disability (e.g., were identified LD under IDEA but no longer qualify), or are regarded by the community as having a learning disability.

For school-aged children, learning <u>is</u> a "major life activity," so problems or needs in a learning environment are covered under Section 504. If your child does

qualify under IDEA, he or she is still protected from discrimination in all classroom situations by Section 504.

This section of the Rehabilitation Act goes on to say that a physical or mental impairment could be "any mental or psychological disorder, such as mental retardation, organic brain syndrome, emotional or mental illness, and specific learning disabilities." There are no categories in Section 504; therefore, any child or young adult who qualifies as having one of the impairments listed above also qualifies for services under Section 504.

A SCHOOL'S OBLIGATIONS UNDER SECTION 504

If your child or young adult is protected under Section 504, the school must provide services (special education, general education, or related services) necessary to help your child receive educational opportunities that are as adequate as those of non-handicapped students.[12]

This can be and has been interpreted to mean many things, such as:

- That accommodations can be made in the general education classroom to help a student be successful by providing, for example:

  — Extended time on tests,
  — Help with note-taking from lectures,
  — Taped books,
  — Taping of classes,
  — Use of a keyboard to complete assignments;

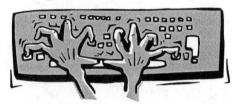

- That certain arrangements can be made so that classrooms and facilities are accessible to someone with problems such as:

  — Illegible handwriting,
  — Inability to copy accurately from the board,
  — Impaired auditory processing,
  — Attention Deficit Disorder;

- That special education services must be provided so a student can learn to read, in order to return to general education classes.

The procedures for Section 504 are not as clearly defined as for IDEA. That is, each school is required to set up its own procedures for identification, evaluation, and placement. Most schools have "504 Plans" that they develop to help teachers and parents understand exactly what types of services are needed. Be sure to *get a copy* of your school's procedures.

The school is always required to contact parents about any testing or evaluation of a child, including testing for Section 504 services. The school gathers information from many sources, and then a team that knows the child well makes the decision about whether or not there is a disability. This group also makes decisions about necessary services or accommodations. You should be an active member of this group.

The student must be placed with peers without disabilities as much as possible, just as is required by IDEA.

RESOLVING DISAGREEMENTS RELATED TO SECTION 504

If you do not agree with what the school has decided, the school is required to provide an impartial hearing for you. That means that you can present your case (with an attorney, if you feel it necessary) to an impartial hearing officer. That officer will then make a decision about what is best. The details of how that is set up (the grievance procedures) are left to the school.

Another option: You may file a complaint with your regional office of Civil Rights (OCR). (The Rehabilitation Act is administered by OCR, not the U.S. Office of Education.) The OCR will then investigate and issue findings. (See Appendix B-1, under Government Departments/Agencies.)

For general information on Section 504, contact your State Department of Education or the COPAA (Council of Parents, Attorneys, and Advocates, at www.copaa.com).

CHAPTER SUMMARY

There are many people involved in the determination of a student's learning disability and the planning of that student's program. The school's role is to evaluate students, to communicate with parents, and to plan and implement an appropriate program for each child with a disability. The parents' role is to actively participate in each step of the process, to gather and maintain information about their child, to try to resolve problems, and to monitor their child's program. Both IDEA and Section 504 guide these processes.

THE IDENTIFICATION → EVALUATION → PLACEMENT PROCESS

START HERE

Does your child have problems affecting performance in school? If "yes," there are **two options:**

If "Yes..." Meet with your child's teacher(s) to develop/review a classroom intervention plan.

The school implements plan and continues to review and modify.

If problems affecting your child's school performance persist and a disability is suspected, then...

However...

If "Yes..." Make a referral to school personnel for evaluation for special education. (Steps shown from this point follow IDEA guidelines.)

School district determines whether your child needs evaluation.

If "Yes..." A preliminary team, including you, the parents, decides what information must be gathered in order to determine eligibility for special education.

You are provided a written notice of the proposed evaluation. Your written consent is needed before school district can evaluate.

Evaluations are completed.

If "No..." You are provided a written notice of school's refusal to evaluate and your right to appeal the decision.

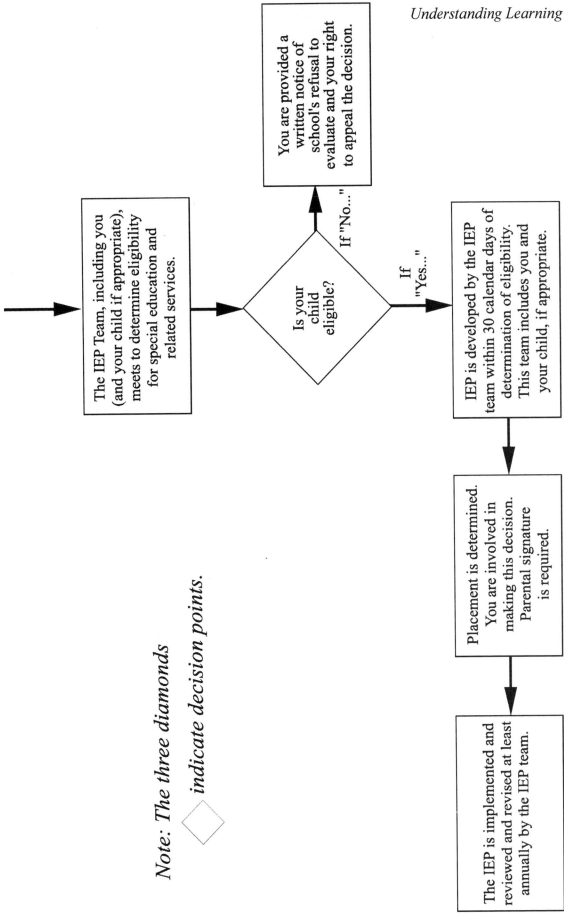

The IEP Team, including you (and your child if appropriate), meets to determine eligibility for special education and related services.

Is your child eligible?

If "No..." You are provided a written notice of school's refusal to evaluate and your right to appeal the decision.

If "Yes..." IEP is developed by the IEP team within 30 calendar days of determination of eligibility. This team includes you and your child, if appropriate.

Placement is determined. You are involved in making this decision. Parental signature is required.

The IEP is implemented and reviewed and revised at least annually by the IEP team.

Note: The three diamonds ◇ indicate decision points.

Make It Happen with Positive Parent Advocacy

— Getting Involved —

Have you...	Yes	No
Joined the PTA?		
Attended the PTA meetings? (Joining is only the first step!)		
Become a room volunteer? (Your child loves to have you at school.)		
Accompanied the class on a field trip? (Pack good walking shoes.)		
Volunteered to help with a special school project? (fundraisers, athletics, carnival)		
Attended special education advisory or school board meetings?		
Offered to do something special for the class or school?		
Complimented school personnel? (Everybody likes to hear nice things!)		
Joined a local learning disabilities organization?		

The more YES answers, the more you are on the road to positive, involved advocacy. Remember, your attitude and commitment to the overall school program demonstrate your support.

Tracking the Special Education Process

<u>Instructions</u>: Federal and state regulations stipulate the steps that must be followed in order to determine whether a child has a learning disability. They also establish time limits for each step. <u>Contact your state Department of Education for information about timelines</u>.* Use the following chart to track your child's progress through the procedure.

Referral for evaluation and possible special education services.	Date of Referral _____ Referral made by _____

* Days allowed by state ____

Child Study Committee meets to determine what should be done and if formal evaluation is needed.	Date of Meeting _____ Did you receive copy of decision? _____

IEP team (including the parent) meets to determine what testing or information it is necessary to gather.	

Parent gives permission for testing to be completed.	Date permission given for evaluation _____

Testing, observation, etc. completed.	

* Days allowed by state ____

IEP team meets as *eligibility committee* to review information and determine if child is eligible for special education.	Date of eligibility meeting _____ Did you receive copies of all reports? _____

* Days allowed by state ____

IEP team plans Individualized Education Plan.	Date of IEP meeting _____ Did you receive copies of the IEP? _____

Date services began for my child _____

How to Use the Form, "My Child's Test Results"

It is important that you, as a parent, fully understand the results of educational and psychological evaluations, as they will be the basis for decisions about your child's identification as LD and the types of services to be provided.

Any time your child is tested, whether by the public schools or by a private agency, it is most important that you meet with those individuals who completed the evaluations, so that they may review the test results with you.

Use the form which follows to help you organize and take notes at this meeting. Use it to help you ask questions. If you are concerned that you will have difficulty listening, asking questions and taking notes at the same time, ask your spouse, a friend, or parent advocate to take notes, using the form, while you ask questions. You might begin the meeting by showing the form to the professionals present and telling them you are going to use it to take notes during the meeting to help you better understand their test results.

As each professional discusses his test results, ask him to:

- Name the particular test given.

- Describe exactly what the test evaluates. Some tests have many different subtests that measure various skills; ask him to describe each. **Be certain to ask questions now if any terms or educational jargon are unclear.**

- Give an example of the types of questions on the test, what your child

had to do, etc. For instance, the evaluator may tell you that a particular test was given to test your child's spelling skills. You need to know whether your child had to actually write the correct spelling of words, indicate the correct spelling when given several choices, or spell the word aloud, etc.

- Describe how your child performed on this particular test or subtest when compared to other children of the same age and/or grade level. In other words, does your child seem to have a problem in the skills evaluated by this test when compared to others of the same age/grade?

- Describe how your child performed on this particular test or subtest, given his own particular ability or general intelligence level. Not all children have the same ability. It is important to know not just how your child compares to **other children** (the item discussed above), but also how he does on a particular skill compared to **his own ability**. In other words, is your child doing the best that we might expect on a particular skill, given his own ability, or is he doing more poorly than we would expect, given his ability.

(You may want to make several copies of the first page of the form so that you will have sufficient space for notes in case many tests were given.)

Once the evaluator has described the individual tests, use the questions on the last page of the form to help guide your discussion to pull all the information together. If the evaluator does not offer this information on his own, do not hesitate to ask the specific questions suggested.

Throughout your meetings and discussions about the test results, keep the following in mind:

- **Ask questions when you do not understand what is being said.** Without a thorough understanding of the test results, you will be unable to participate actively in planning and monitoring your child's educational program.

- **Do not pay attention to test scores reported as grade equivalents or age equivalents.** [e.g., if someone says your child tested on a 5.3 grade level (5th grade, 3rd month of school) or at a 7.4 year old level (7 years, 4 months old).] Due to the manner in which these scores are calculated, they are very easily misinterpreted. In fact, many professionals and professional organizations no longer use grade or age equivalents at all.

As soon as possible after the meeting, review your notes. If you have any questions about the terminology, refer to the glossary of this handbook. If you still have questions, contact the evaluator to clarify them. Once you are certain that you understand your notes, file them with a copy of the actual evaluation. Use this information to help plan for the IEP and/or if you plan to contest the school's recommendations.

Note: If you child has already been tested and you have already met with the evaluator(s) to review the test results, complete the forms which follow by yourself, referring to a copy of the evaluations. If you are unable to do this, you do not have a good understanding of the test results. **Request another meeting; use the forms and ask questions.**

My Child's Test Results — 1*

Summary of _____ _____
               (Name of Psychological or Educational Test)   (Child's Name)

Evaluation Review for _____

Date Tests Administered _____

Name of Evaluator _____

Date of Review Meeting _____

Individuals Present _____

Test Results:

Name of Test	What Does It Test?	Example	How Did My Child Do Compared to Others Same Age/Grade Level?	How Did My Child Do Compared to Own Ability/General Intelligence Level

* *Suggestion:* Reserve this to use as a master form from which to make copies as needed.

My Child's Test Results — 2

Summary of _____
(Name of Psychological or Educational Test)

Date Tests Administered _____

Date of Review Meeting _____

Evaluation Review for _____
(Child's Name)

Name of Evaluator _____

Individuals Present _____

Conclusions:

1. What are my child's specific <u>weaknesses</u> compared to others of the same age/grade level?

2. What are my child's individual <u>weaknesses</u> compared to his own ability/general intelligence level? Are these weaknesses different from those noted in questions #1?

3. What are my child's specific <u>strengths</u> compared to others of the same age/grade level?

4. What are my child's individual <u>strengths</u> compared to his ability/general intelligence level?

5. What are the recommendations based on these test results?

6. Is there a need for further testing? Are there any remaining questions about my child?

7. Do the test results indicate that my child is learning disabled? Why or why not?

8. According to the test results, how will my child probably progress in the present classroom placement? Can we anticipate that he/she will do well or poorly?

9. Do the test results indicate a need for special help? If so, in what?

WORKBOOK PAGE

IEP PLANNING FORMS FOR PARENTS*

The three sections of this form are to be used at different times in the IEP process:

   I. For you to think about before the IEP meeting;

   II. Questions to ask at the IEP meeting. (You may want to ask a friend to go along to jot down the school's answers.)

   III. Points for you to review after the IEP meeting, but BEFORE YOU SIGN THE IEP document.

I. You may want to jot down notes concerning the following, <u>before</u> you go to the IEP meeting:

- At least one week before the IEP meeting, request copies of reports of all evaluations of your child (except for ones you already have). Also ask for a draft copy of the IEP, if one has been completed. (Note the dates you requested these items.)

- In thinking about your child and his/her comprehensive educational needs, list any specific things you want the school to provide that you feel might be overlooked (e.g., specific interests).

- List any concerns your child has expressed that you believe should be considered in writing the IEP. (Include your child at IEP meetings when appropriate.)

Suggestion: Reserve this to use as a master form from which to make copies as needed.

II. Put a check by any of the following questions you may want to ask <u>at</u> the IEP meeting; then use the space provided to jot down the school's answers.

_____ • "What are my child's specific areas of <u>strength</u>?"

_____

_____

_____

_____

_____

_____

_____ • "What are my child's specific areas of <u>weakness</u>?"

_____

_____

_____

_____

_____

_____

• "What do you believe is of highest priority at this time (e.g., reading,
_____   written work, math, spelling, etc.)?"

_____

_____

_____

_____

_____

(If your child has a reading problem):

- "Since my child is reading below level, how can I ever expect him/her to pass other school subjects?"

_____

_____

_____

_____

_____

_____

- "Where will the specialized instruction take place — will it be at this school?"

_____

_____

_____

_____

_____

- "How many other students will be with my child and what are their needs?"

_____

_____

_____

_____

_____

- "What regular classes will be missed while my child is with the LD teacher?"

- "What is the maximum number of students an LD teacher may have in an LD classroom in this state?"

- "What is the maximum number of students on the caseload of an LD Resource Teacher in this state?"

_____ • "What will my child's daily schedule be, in general?"

_____

_____

_____

_____

_____

_____

• "Will some of the methods and instructional materials used in the LD classroom be different from those the regular teachers use? If so, _____ please explain the differences."

_____

_____

_____

_____

_____

• "What is it about how my child learns that makes these different _____ methods or materials better?"

_____

_____

_____

_____

_____

_____

- "How will my child's regular classroom activities relate to the LD program?"

_____

_____

_____

_____

_____

_____

- "With so many teachers, who is going to coordinate what is happening in my child's school day?"

_____

_____

_____

_____

_____

_____

- "How soon will I know if the program is working? If I have concerns about whether the program is working, can I suggest changes in the program or can I remove my child from the program?"

_____

_____

_____

_____

_____

_____

_____

_____

- "If this were your child, would you consider the program we have discussed one that would meet his/her needs?"

_____

_____

_____

_____

_____

_____

- "What can I do at home to help?"

_____

_____

_____

_____

_____

- "In looking toward the future, can I expect my child to pass minimum competency tests?"

_____

_____

_____

_____

_____

_____ • "If my child can't read the tests, will special help be provided?"

_____

_____

_____

_____

_____

_____

*Parts of this form have been adapted, with permission of the authors, from **Learning Disabilities: Understanding Concepts, Characteristics and Issues**, by C. Houck and C. Geller.*

III. After the IEP meeting but <u>before you sign the IEP document</u>, use this checklist to review the contents of the IEP. <u>Your response to each item should be "yes."</u> If you can't answer "yes," clarify that item with school professionals before signing the IEP.

A. PRESENT LEVELS OF EDUCATIONAL PERFORMANCE

_____ • Is there <u>up-to-date</u> information about my child's present level of performance?

_____ • If standardized tests were used to document skill levels, have I been given test names, dates administered, and standardized test scores?

_____ • If teacher observation is used to document skill levels, are specific descriptions of what my student can (or can't) do, under what circumstances, included, as well as the date(s) observed?

B. ANNUAL GOALS AND SHORT-TERM OBJECTIVES OR BENCHMARKS

_____ • Are there annual goals included for <u>every</u> identified area of weakness?

_____ • For each annual goal, are there short-term, specific objectives that, taken together, outline the sequence of steps needed to achieve the annual goal?

_____ • Are the short-term objectives specific (i.e., do they state what my child will do or learn, and how we will know if he has learned it?)?

(Key words: percent accuracy, _____ *number* out of _____ *number* correct, _____ *number* out of _____ *number* attempts, etc.)

Example of poorly written objective: "Johnny will learn the alphabet."

Example of specific, behavioral objective: "When shown flash cards with individual letters of the alphabet, Johnny will (a) say the name of the letter and (b) provide the sound of the letter with 100 percent accuracy on 3 out of 4 attempts."

_____ • Does the IEP state how often I will receive information concerning my child's progress toward specific objectives?

C. SPECIFIC EDUCATIONAL SERVICES

- Are the number of hours per day, and the subject/content areas covered in the *special education* program, designated?

_____

- Are the number of hours per day, and the subject/content areas in the *regular education* program, designated?

_____

_____ • Is the location at which services will be provided designated?

_____ • Is the provision of transportation to any alternate location designated?

Concerning state-required testing:
- Does the IEP say my child will take the test at the same time as regular education students?

_____

— If "yes," are any needed <u>accommodations</u> included in the IEP?

— If "no," is there a statement in the IEP about <u>exemption</u> from testing?

- Are any related services designated, if they are needed for my child to benefit from special education (i.e., counseling, physical, occupational or speech therapy, etc.)?

_____

- If my child has qualified for special accommodations, have these been listed? (They could be oral tests, longer time to complete assignments, availability of calculator, etc.)

_____

- If my child is receiving services under IDEA, is there any one individual at the school designated to coordinate my child's services?

_____

- If my student has a Sec. 504 Plan, is the 504 Coordinator specifically designated?

_____

- Are projected dates for the start of services and anticipated duration of services included?

_____

D. ANNUAL REVIEW

- Is a date included (at least once a school year) indicating when the IEP Committee will meet again to examine my child's progress relative to the IEP?

_____

_____ • Is there a statement indicating how progress will be evaluated?

• Will the same methods/tests administered to assess levels of educational performance be re-administered for the sake of comparison? (Alternate forms of the tests should be used for retesting.)
_____

E. TRANSITION SERVICES

• If my student is 14 years of age or older, are transition plans, with specific goals and objectives, included to help move from the school environment to the "real world"?
_____

• If my student is 14 years of age or older, is there a description of which other agencies, besides the school, will assist with transition services and what exactly they will do?
_____

F. MISCELLANEOUS

• Are the names and signatures of all individuals participating in the development of the IEP included?
_____

*Adapted, with permission of the authors, from **Learning Disabilities: Understanding Concepts, Characteristics and Issues** by Houck, C. and C. Geller (Englewood Cliffs: Prentice-Hall, Inc. 1984).*

Telephone / Meeting Log *

Instructions

Keeping track of your communications is easier if you make notes immediately
following the conversation. Take a few minutes each time to record your
calls and meetings. Do this for **every** phone call or meeting.

Date/Time	Conversation/Visit With...	Reason (Subject/Substance)	Important Points and Follow-up Steps

* Suggestion: Reserve this to use as a master form from which to make copies as needed.

Table of Contents for Documents *

Instructions

Organize material in chronological order. File the most recent reports in the front of this section. To help keep track of the reports and keep your file in order, put the author's name and date of the report in the lower right hand corner of the report. Then fill out and file this form in front of the reports.

Date	Person/ Evaluator/Author	Description	Summary or Explanation

* *Suggestion: Reserve this to use as a master form from which to make copies as needed.*

Chapter 5 — THE YOUNG ADULT

**Self-Advocacy, Transition Planning, ADA and Section 504, College,
Vocational Education and Jobs, Social Skills, Success**

The goal of most parents is to help their child become an independent, self-determining adult. While it would be comforting to believe that learning disabilities can be "cured," or that they will "disappear" once a student leaves high school, thereby making this goal easily met, we know that is not based in reality. Most professionals recognize that a learning disability remains across the lifespan. The good news, however, is that there are federal, state, and community resources available to ease the transition from high school. For success, parents and students with disabilities should be involved in planning for this transition early, certainly by the middle grades.

INDEPENDENCE THROUGH SELF-ADVOCACY

It is important to emphasize that, regardless of a student's specific post-secondary goals, the high school program should help the student become more independent. Parents and teachers alike must work toward decreasing the student's dependence on others while helping him learn the skills to advocate for himself. This is not something that will happen overnight, nor will it happen "automatically" — it must be taught.

With Parents' and Teachers' Help...
With parents' and teachers' help, the older student with learning disabilities must learn to:
- evaluate his own strengths and weaknesses and be able to describe his learning disability to others;
- identify the strategies that help him to work around his disability;
- identify any accommodations he may need to succeed in his different classes;
- gradually assume responsibility for seeking those accommodations from classroom teachers, rather than depending solely upon the initiation of his parents or a teacher;
- be an active participant in all IEP and other meetings relative to planning his

future.

The need to overtly teach the LD student these skills which allow him to exercise his independence cannot be over-stated. To do otherwise, either consciously or not, perpetuates the cycle of "learned helplessness" which, in turn, can result in a young adult being much too dependent on others.

Self-Advocacy
Self-advocacy is the ability to speak on one's own behalf. It means knowing:
- how to approach teachers and others in authority positions;
- how to be assertive but not aggressive;
- how to understand one's own needs and explain them to someone else;
- how to set realistic goals and then follow through to make them happen.

You as the parent can play an important part in helping your child develop skills needed for finding and keeping a job. For example, you can:

- Suggest that your pre-high schooler complete the Workbook page at the end of this chapter, "Checklist:

Planning for the Future";
- Communicate confidence in your young adult's abilities — emphasize the positive;
- Encourage and support your young adult in becoming independent;
- Make sure your student understands his or her rights under the law;
- Remember that self-advocacy goals can be part of the IEP for students as they advance through the grades;
- Use the suggestions in Appendix E to help your student get ready for work;
- Stay involved in your teenager's life!

TRANSITION PLANNING WHILE IN SCHOOL

The Individuals with Disabilities Education Act (IDEA) requires that students in special education have a *transition plan* as part of their IEP, starting at age 14 (or sooner, if appropriate).[1] The transition plan outlines what transition services are necessary to help the student move from school to the next step in life. According to the law, transition services are "a coordinated set of activities that...promotes movement from school to post-school activities, including post-secondary education, vocational training, integrated employment..., continuing and adult education, adult services, independent living, or community participation." These services are to be based on the needs of the individual student.

The transition plan is a VERY important part of the IEP, so students with learning disabilities who are at least 14 years old, and their parents, should play an active role in developing realistic goals and getting the services that are needed. It is at this point that responsibility for goal-setting and advocacy should begin to shift to the child or young adult. Success in the future partly

depends upon a student with a learning disability understanding his goals and being able to advocate for himself. The self-advocacy goals should be part of his IEP.

By age 14, the transition services outlined in the IEP should address which high school courses are necessary in order for the student to achieve his or her goals. For example, if college is the goal, most colleges require a certain number of English, math, science, social studies, and foreign language credits. Planning when to fit in all of these courses is vital before high school even begins.

If either vocational training or employment is the goal after high school, then the student needs to plan which courses will offer best preparation, and where and when these courses can be taken.

At age 16, the transition plan may include working with other agencies such as vocational rehabilitation, community support agencies, colleges, or apprenticeship programs.

This list of needed transition services and activities may include:
- instruction of some type, such as in daily living skills;
- related services, such as counseling, occupational therapy, etc.;
- community experiences;
- development of post-school objectives, such as employment or further schooling.

Again, the services are based on the needs of the individual student. The school acts as the coordinator of all these services. If any outside services are included in the IEP transition plan, representatives of those groups should be at the IEP meeting.

LAWS PROTECTING STUDENTS AFTER HIGH SCHOOL

Americans with Disabilities Act (ADA)

Once a student graduates from high school, IDEA no longer applies. After high school, a student with a physical or mental impairment that substantially limits one or more life activities (e.g., learning) is protected from discrimination by the ADA[2] and Section 504.

ADA prohibits discrimination solely on the basis of disability. This applies to:

- Employment
- Access to publicly funded services
- Access to accommodations — IF the person is otherwise qualified for the program, job, or service.

ADA provides for reasonable accommodations in educational activities or settings for anyone eligible. These accommodations can include (but are not limited to):

- Modification of tests (e.g., extended time, dictation versus writing, etc.)
- Redesigning of equipment
- Assigning of aides
- Provision of written communication in alternate formats (e.g., auditory tapes)
- Reassignment of services to accessible locations
- Altering of existing facilities.

Section 504 of the Rehabilitation Act

(1) Rules that benefit the student

Section 504 contains some rules that can benefit the student with learning disabilities. Colleges and universities may NOT...

- Limit the number of students with disabilities admitted;
- Make pre-admission inquiries as to whether or not an applicant has a disability;
- Use admission tests or criteria that inadequately measure the academic level of applicants with disabilities because special provisions were not made for taking the test;
- Exclude a student with a disability from any course of study solely on the basis of his/her disability;
- Counsel students with disabilities towards a more restrictive career than students without disabilities, unless such counsel is based on strict licensing or certification requirements in a profession;
- Measure student achievement using modes that adversely discriminate against students with disabilities;
- Institute prohibitive rules (such as not letting students use tape recorders) that may adversely affect the performance of students with disabilities.[3]

While a student with LD must not get in the habit of using his learning disability as an excuse, it *is* important for him or her to be aware of the rights provided under the law and to be able to advocate for those rights.

(2) Documentation needed

In order to qualify for these Section 504 protections and special services at post-secondary institutions, your son or daughter will need documentation of his or her disability. Usually, an IEP alone is insufficient. Contact the appropriate person at the post-secondary institution to find out in detail what is necessary. In general, colleges must have:

- Comprehensive information about assessments that have been done;
- A diagnostic report (performed by a

qualified examiner either from the school or in private practice), including:

> ➤ an interview
> ➤ assessment of ability, academic achievement, and how the person processes information
> ➤ a diagnosis

- Documentation of any accommodations and recommendations made by the people doing the assessment. (Your notebook file will come in handy for this! See Chapter 4, Part C.)

COLLEGE FOR STUDENTS WITH LEARNING DISABILITIES

More students with learning disabilities are heading to college than ever before. Because of this influx and the pressure from the Americans with Disabilities Act (ADA) and Section 504 of the Rehabilitation Act of 1973 to avoid discrimination against these students, many colleges and universities have been adding services for students with learning disabilities. The key to finding the right college is helping your young adult determine what he or she wants, and then finding the college that seems to offer the best fit.

Getting Ready for College
Entering college is a time of big change in the lives of all students, those with a learning disability and those without. It is also a big change for their parents.

Parents can no longer check on where the young adult is, what he's doing, and whether he's studying as he must if he's to pass his courses.

For the student, college is a time for growing up — taking care of one's own laundry, finances, and class assignments. College requires fewer hours in the classroom, but much more studying on one's own. And there are fewer opportunities to interact with the instructor.

There are several things a parent can encourage a high school student with learning disabilities to do to help make the transition process easier. These include:

- Making sure all of the prerequisite courses for entry to the chosen college are taken in high school;

- Taking a college course at the local community college or university while still in high school or during the summer;

- Finding his or her *own* reasons to attend college — not because parents said so, or because everyone else is doing it;

- Analyzing his goals, as well as what motivates him;

- Doing a self-assessment of her strengths and weaknesses (for example, realizing that she is not strong enough in math to be considering engineering a good choice of study);

- Asking for long-term projects from teachers in order to get some practice at structuring time in order to meet a deadline;
- Examining and coming to grips with how he is different from others in terms

of the amount of time needed to study, study habits, and the type of instruction that works for him (lecture, lab, etc.).

If you encourage your young adult to try these things now, while you are still nearby, you are being of help in the transition process.

Standardized Admissions Tests (SATs)

Part of the college admissions requirement is the standardized testing procedure — the Scholastic Aptitude Test (SAT) or another achievement test. There is much emphasis placed on doing well on these tests. Students with learning disabilities who have been allowed accommodations for classroom testing while in high school can also qualify for modifications to the SAT. This may include extended time, a scribe, a reader, etc. Schools will provide information about their own testing procedures, but in all cases one must fill out the standard SAT registration form AND an eligibility/request-for-modifications form. This will be needed in order to get supporting documentation from the school, so your son or daughter should ask the high school advisor or guidance counselor how to go about registering for the SAT.

What Are the College Options?

Two-year junior or community colleges offer associate degrees in many fields. These colleges often have flexible requirements and special services for students with learning disabilities. The classes are usually smaller than those in larger universities and tuition is frequently less expensive.

Four-year colleges and universities offer a variety of degree programs in settings that are characteristically larger than community colleges. At most universities, there is a center which provides special services to

support students with disabilities. Typically, the student must take the initiative to request the special services.

What Makes a College Student Successful?

Many students with learning disabilities who make a successful transition from high school to college have several of the following characteristics:[4]

- They are able to describe their special talents and abilities.

- They know the nature of their disability and the accommodations they need.

- They can talk with adults about their own strengths and weaknesses.

- They take the initiative to advocate for their own needs, without waiting for someone else to do it for them.

- They have learned which study habits make them successful and then they adhere to those habits.

- They know when to ask for help from someone else on campus, either for academics or other needs, and they seek out the right person.

- They accept that studying and graduating may take longer for them than for their classmates who don't have LD.

- They understand that they will face frustrations, but they view these as a challenge, not a defeat.

- They communicate frequently with the people who support them (friends, parents, advisors, service providers, etc.).

- They spend time evaluating themselves

and looking for ways to do better.

Parents can help their young adults develop these skills during high school so the students can have the skills firmly in place before they are needed in post-secondary situations.

What to Look for in a College

There are literally thousands of colleges and universities and they are apt to have attractive brochures and exciting programs. It is difficult to wade through all of the information to find the right fit. The best way to find that fit is to ask many, many questions about the school and its programs.

The areas to investigate and some questions to ask are included in the form, "Questions to Ask Before Applying to a College," in this chapter's Workbook pages. Take a few minutes to look through them and determine with your young adult which things you both feel are most important. It might help your fact-finding to copy a set of the questions for each school you plan to contact.

Your young adult must decide what is most important to him or her about a college. A good place to start is with admissions, academic programs, and support services. Again, helping your young adult to analyze his goals, strengths, and needs will be VITAL in finding the right place.

Services That May Be Available

Colleges offer a variety of services for students with disabilities. You and your young adult should investigate what each college that you both are interested in may offer. For example:

Compensatory services:
- Courses that students may not have had in high school that are open only to students with disabilities
- Help with note-taking in lecture classes
- Assistance in reading assigned materials

Remediation services:
- Tutoring programs
- Support services such as extra labs or extra help with labs

Psychoeducational services:
- Help with study skills
- Counseling
- Academic advising

Each college's list of services will be unique, so it is important for your student to determine his needs, and then try to match those needs with the help provided by a particular school.

Be sure to find out:
- Whether the services are available, and if so, how frequently and for what period of time;
- What is required for a student to qualify for these services;
- Whether any student support groups are available;
- Whether career counseling is available;
- The cost of the services needed;
- The qualifications of the instructors providing the help;
- The name and qualifications of the director/coordinator of the services.

How Else Can Parents Help?

There are some additional ways you can assist your student to make a successful transition to college:[5]

1. Assisting in the selection of appropriate campus housing, if your son or daughter plans to live away from home. A small residence hall, preferably with an older student or other individual as an advisor,

may be more conducive to studying and maintaining a stable environment than a large dormitory or apartment.

2. Preparing a duplicate copy of the most current testing data and any other pertinent files you have kept for your young adult to take to college. This information will be important in qualifying for services.

3 Assisting in compiling necessary aids, in addition to the usual college paraphernalia. These should include a calendar and address book, dictionary, calculator, tape recorder, and computer accessories (depending on what may also be available at the college).

4. Encouraging your son or daughter to attend any summer orientation program the college may offer. This should provide an opportunity for your student to...

- ask questions;
- meet with the assigned advisor to plan the up-coming class schedule;
- ask how instructors of different sections teach a particular course:
  - all lectures?
  - assigned reading only?
  - much parallel reading?
  - weekly tests, or
  - only a final exam?
  - multiple choice tests only?
  - discussion questions only?
  - mixtures of types of tests?
- get acquainted with individual instructors;
- review course outlines;
- check in the bookstore to determine the amount of reading required for specific courses.

5. Letting your son or daughter know that college is a big adjustment for all students. Encourage your student to ask for help when it's needed. There should be persons assigned by the college to provide support to students who have been previously identified as having LD.

6. Letting your daughter or son know *you* are always available for moral support!

VOCATIONAL EDUCATION AND JOBS

While college may be an option for many students with learning disabilities (see previous section), others may choose to pursue vocational training, hoping to secure a job following high school. *Vocational Centers* provide training for specific occupations. They combine bookwork with hands-on experiences and usually provide flexible course times (some during the day and some in the evening). Planning is again important and a good plan depends upon a thorough evaluation of the student's aptitudes and abilities.

Vocational Assessment
A vocational assessment may be conducted by the high school and/or the Vocational Rehabilitation Agency. (See Appendix B-3 for information about a web site with a state-by-state listing.) Once the evaluation has been completed, vocational and guidance counselors should meet with the student and his teachers (and you, the parent, if appropriate) to explore the test results in light of your student's career interests.

Your son's or daughter's IEP transition plan should be written to include goals and objectives in job training in the student's chosen career. These goals may then be accomplished through participation in the school's Vocational-Technical Center, special "on-the-job' placement and training which is supervised by school personnel, or any other programs available in your school system.

Parents should know that a federal law

called the Carl D. Perkins Vocational Education Act (P.L. 98-154), as well as Section 504 of the Rehabilitation Act of 1973, guarantee that students with learning disabilities shall have access to all regular vocational education programs available in the public schools. (See Chapter 4, Part D.) (For example, if a student has a reading disability which results in difficulty in reading the training manual in an auto mechanics class, this does not mean that he cannot/should not take this class. Rather, accommodations must be made to allow the student to acquire the information in the manual by some means other than reading.)

It should also be noted that the IEP transition plan should emphasize job-seeking and interpersonal skills, as well as specific job training. Students with LD must learn how to locate available positions, complete job applications, participate in an interview, etc. Likewise, the importance of interpersonal skills — being on time, knowing how to speak and relate to a supervisor or co-workers, etc. — are also increasingly recognized as critical to the success of a young person's adjustment.

Training and Employment Resources
As noted earlier, federal, state, and community resources, many of them free of charge, are available to individuals with LD seeking training and employment.

The *HEATH Resource Center* (Higher Education and Adult Training for People with Handicaps) might be one starting point. The Center provides a wealth of information, at no charge, about training and post-secondary opportunities for young people. It is listed along with other resources in Appendix B-1.

The *Vocational Rehabilitation Agency*, with

offices in every state (see Appendix C), has programs which benefit students with learning disabilities. Clients must be at least 15 years old; there is no maximum age limit.

Training is provided in over 50 job areas, as well as in work adjustment, job seeking, and independent living. Vocational evaluation is comprehensive and can include:
- Counseling and guidance
- Standardized testing
- Psychological testing
- Work sample evaluations
- Vocational exploration
- Job analysis.

Fees for these services operate on a sliding scale, based on one's ability to pay.

A major new resource, funded by the U.S. Department of Labor, is a network of *One Stop Career Centers*. These centers are being opened in localities across the United States, as mandated by the Workforce Investment Act of 1998. For information about this program in your state, look on the website www.usworkforce.org, and go to WIA STATE PLANS to find the contact person/agency for the *One Stop Career Centers* in your state.

Opportunities through the local public schools are offered, even for those beyond school age or those who have left school. Many students continue to need basic skills instruction. Those who elect to enter *Adult*

Basic Education (ABE) Programs may prove to be more receptive or ready than they were the first time they were in school because they are more mature. They also may benefit from the more practical emphasis placed on academics, and from working with more mature classmates.

In addition to ABE programs, special services or programs for the young adult with LD may be available through the local *Vocational-Technical Center* in your school system. Contact the Adult Education and Vocational Education departments in your school district.

There are many variations among communities in the services available to students out of high school. Check in the phone book under Adult Services, Adult Education, etc., for additional resources. Or refer to Appendix F, "College, Vocational, and Transitional Resources."

Jobs, Paid and Volunteer

Registering with a *temporary employment service* can prove to be an entering point to the job market. The temporary employee often does not need the level of skill a full-time employee must exhibit. This may lessen the pressure while the young person learns about the world of work from the "inside."

A *volunteer position* is sometimes the answer for one not sure of his or her ability to retain a paid job. Here, almost any effort is appreciated and some skills can be learned while confidence is being built. Sometimes volunteer positions can evolve into paid employment.

If none of these avenues seems appropriate, it might be wise to check with the *Social Security Administration* (under *U.S. Government* in the phone book), the *SSI*

Benefits division. They will advise you if any funds are available for the support of your child. A factor to be considered is that the process of determining need for financial assistance for a person with a disability is quite rigorous.

The GED Test

The **GED** test provides an alternate route to high school graduation. Detailed information is available in Appendix G concerning testing accommodations which can be made for people who have learning disabilities or ADHD.

SOCIAL ASPECTS AND SUCCESS

It has been stressed in previous sections of this book that a learning disability can have a life-long impact on an individual, in non-academic as well as academic aspects of living. It can affect areas of self-esteem, interpersonal relationships, and daily living skills needed for independence.[6]

There are no fool-proof techniques for assuring that a young person with a learning disability will grow into a self-assured adult. Everyone has a unique way of handling feelings and disappointments. (However, the suggestions in Chapter 3 for improving self-esteem are recommended for earnest study.)

Some young adults with LD will weather the transitions and storms they face by themselves, or with the help of a school counselor. Others may need more formalized help from a mental health professional. But often the guidance of a parent, teacher, a friend, or a peer support group will point the way to a successful future. Your community may have organized a support group for adults with LD where a young person can discuss his or her problems and get suggestions from others who have had similar experiences.

Social Awareness

Positive personality traits — perseverance, ambition, optimism, willingness to try hard, eagerness to continue even after failure, and willingness to ask for and receive help — ease our way through life, whether or not we have a learning disability.

But a young adult with a learning disability can have these traits and still be unsuccessful because of lack of social awareness. These young people may be less able to interpret the emotions and attitudes of others. Their problems can range from general difficulties in making and keeping friends to specific difficulties associated with social functions.

Many reported problems of people with learning disabilities of any age are related to language and communication, including the comprehension of vocabulary. This may lead to difficulty in following conversations. A person with LD may monopolize conversations so he won't have to process spoken language at a rapid rate, or engage in the give-and-take of ideas.[7] Or she may frequently interrupt the speaker. Others may stand too close to the person speaking, which may be interpreted as an "in your face" attitude.

Another problem may be one of time and energy: When the person tries to juggle his uneven combination of abilities and disabilities, he can become short of time and highly

frustrated — with himself as well as with those around him. The energy he expends in dealing with these everyday situations can leave him exhausted — and feeling unable to find uncluttered time for exploring possibilities for social interaction.

Such situations can make young adults with LD feel insecure with groups. However, one must not lose sight of the fact that there are also many individuals with LD problems who are quite skilled socially — so much so that they later become superb salesmen, politicians, owners or managers of business enterprises, and leaders in the community. Examples are:[8]

- Richard Avedon   Photographer
- Thomas Edison   Inventor
- Bruce Jenner   Olympic athlete
- James Earl Jones   Actor
- Greg Louganis   Olympic athlete
- George Patton   Army general
- Nelson Rockefeller   Vice-president of the U.S.
- Charles Schwab   Owner of investment firm
- Henry Winkler   Actor ("The Fonz")

Giftedness and Perseverance

Many people with LD are unusually gifted in the arts, math and science, global reasoning, and inventiveness.

With the extra effort required for the person with LD to meet each day, it is not surprising that, in many cases, this population achieves success in life at a later age than their peers. The perseverance they have had to exercise throughout life seems to enhance the resilience and tenacity they have needed for success — sometimes a success even greater than that found by others who do not have learning disabilities and who have similar intellectual gifts. For more information on giftedness combined with LD, see Chapter 8.

SUMMARY

It may be very difficult to begin to let go of the control of many aspects of your son's or daughter's life, even though you want your young adult to be independent and self-sufficient.

There are many ways to help in this transition, including encouraging your son or daughter to develop self-advocacy skills, to set realistic goals, and to find the right post-secondary match (college, vocational training, volunteer or paid job, etc.).

The law is clear that this planning should be a vital part of the IEP process, beginning by age 14 and continuing at least through high school. In addition, most young adults with learning disabilities who are in post-secondary settings are protected by law from discrimination due to their disability. Many services are available to help make a successful transition.

Even though social skills may be difficult for the young adult with LD to develop, they are worth the effort since they will have an impact on future success. Equally important, though, are qualities of perseverance, resilience, tenacity, and optimism — qualities often found in people with learning disabilities.

 **CHECKLIST: PLANNING FOR THE FUTURE**

For The Student to Complete

If you are in high school, or even if you haven't entered high school, it is not too early to begin thinking about YOUR FUTURE! Grab a pencil and consider the questions below:

Where am I headed right after high school?   **What lifestyle do I picture for myself?**
_____Employment   _____Having my own apartment
_____Vocational training   _____Sharing an apartment with friends
_____College   _____Receiving support from my parents:
                                                     _____financial
                                                     _____emotional
                                                     _____housing

****

Where would I like to be in five to ten years?
_____Working for a living...*or*..._____In grad. school...*or*...other:_____
_____Working indoors: _____by myself...*or*... _____with customers/clients
_____Working out-of-doors: _____alone..........*or*... _____working with customers/clients
_____Working: _____for a boss...*or*... _____for myself
_____Working: _____ by myself...*or*... _____directly with people
_____In a job with lots of responsibility
_____In a job that provides lots of support, direction and supervision

****

What kinds of experiences do I need in order to reach my goals?_____

_____

_____

_____

What courses should I take now in order to reach my goals?_____

_____

_____

_____(Continued)

CHECKLIST: PLANNING FOR THE FUTURE (cont'd.)

What kind of help (modifications) will I need...

...in classes:_____

_____

_____

_____

_____

...on the job that I picture for myself:
_____

_____

_____

_____

_____

_____

Completed by _____
                          (Initials)

Date_____

Questions to Ask Before Applying to a College

College catalogs are written for general audiences and may not indicate clearly all special support systems that are available. Furthermore, they may not communicate fully how flexible their attitudes and policies are, especially toward a student with a learning disability.

If an appointment with an admissions counselor is not possible, a phone call or letter which asks specific questions may still be of great help. Following are some suggested questions. (You may want to make several copies of this form before you start to record the college's responses, just in case you'll want to contact more than one college.)

Contact
Person_____College_____Date of
Contact_____

1. College/University Requirements

What, if any, entrance examinations must the student with LD take?_____

_____

_____

Can any of these exams be waived?_____

_____

_____

Is the untimed Scholastic Aptitude Test acceptable?_____

_____

Is a minimum score required on any of these tests?_____

_____

_____

What, if any, minimum academic standing must the student have achieved in high school?_____

_____

Are there specific course requirements (such as foreign language study) for admission?_____

_____

_____

_____

If so, can any of these requirements be waived? Or can other courses be substituted (e.g., substitute sign language or a computer language for a foreign language)?

_____

_____

_____

(continued)

Questions to Ask (cont'd)

Is admission limited to certain fields of study?

_____

_____

_____

What are the specific requirements for program completion?

_____

_____

Can any of these requirements be waived?

_____

_____

_____

Can a student take a reduced course load?

_____

_____

_____

Must the student complete the program in a specified length of time?_____

_____

_____

2. Special Services and Accommodations

Can the student tape-record classes?

_____

_____

Are oral examinations possible?

_____

_____

_____

What kinds of tutorial services are available?

_____

_____

What is the length of each tutorial session?

_____

_____

How frequently are the sessions held?

_____

_____

Has training for tutors included a variety of teaching techniques that are appropriate for students with LD?_____

_____

_____

Or, by contrast, are tutors trained to work with disabled students in general (not specifically with those with LD)?

_____

_____

Are tutors trained to work with students only in the courses the students are taking?

_____

_____

_____

(continued)

Questions to Ask (cont'd)

Is there a program that addresses remediation of basic skills, such as reading, spelling, etc.?_____

_____

_____

Is a support group available specifically for students with LD?_____

_____

What kinds of special counseling are available (e.g., career counseling)?

_____

_____

Is there a learning center, resource room, or learning lab on campus?_____

_____

_____

Would these special services involve any extra expense?_____

_____

_____

3. Experiences of Students with LD

Has the college accepted students with LD in the past?_____

_____

_____

Have these students been successful?

_____

_____

_____

_____

4. Name and qualifications of the director/coordinator of the services

_____

_____

_____

_____

_____

_____

Chapter 6 — ADULTS WITH LEARNING DISABILITIES

The term "learning disabilities" (LD) covers disorders in reading, writing, and/or mathematics, as one would expect. But there can also be problems in listening, thinking, speaking, and social interaction. A quick glance at this list makes clear why adults with LD sometimes have problems in fulfilling their roles as workers, citizens, and even as family members. Such problems understandably can affect their self-esteem.

CHARACTERISTICS OF ADULTS WITH LD

If you've scanned Chapter 1 of this book, and particularly the section, "The Hidden Disability," you're already aware that some people are skeptical that the condition called learning disabilities even exists. It's usually not obvious in a person's outward appearance, so people with LD may become labeled as "lazy," "careless," or "unmotivated," and the underlying condition may go undetected.

This unfortunate situation also arises because individuals with LD can demonstrate unusual intellectual strengths in some areas, while, at the same time, their disabilities may prevent them from excelling in other life situations — at least at the same level as their intellectual peers.

Areas that can be affected include employment, education, social interaction, community participation, a strong role as a family member, independent living, and emotional health.[1]

One has to use caution in deciding that he or she has learning disabilities after simply looking down a list of characteristics and finding that several of the behaviors "fit."

Most adults will find they have exhibited *some* of the characteristics on a list. So if you find yourself looking at the list below and checking off several items, this does not necessarily mean that you have a learning disability. But if you check off most of the items, and if you are experiencing these difficulties to a degree that it is causing you problems in employment, education, or daily living, take heed: you would perhaps benefit from having an assessment by a *qualified professional who is experienced in working with adults with learning disabilities.* After all, it is best to learn what you're dealing with and then develop your own "game plan" — that is, know what accommodations you'll need in order to be successful in life.

Identified characteristics are as follows:[2]
- May perform similar tasks differently from day to day;
- May have trouble organizing small or large daily tasks;
- May be able to learn information presented in one way, but not another;
- May have a short attention span, be impulsive, and/or be easily distracted;
- May have difficulty telling or understanding jokes;
- May have difficulty with social skills, may misinterpret social cues;
- May find it difficult to memorize information;
- May have difficulty following a schedule, being on time, or meeting deadlines;
- May be poorly coordinated;
- May have difficulty following oral directions, especially multiple directions;

- May get lost easily, either driving and/or in large buildings;
- May confuse right and left, up and down;
- May have trouble reading maps;
- May have trouble dialing phone numbers and reading addresses;
- May often misread or miscopy;
- May have difficulty reading a newspaper, following small print, and/or following columns;
- May confuse similar letters or numbers, reverse them, or confuse their order;
- May reverse numbers in checkbook and have difficulty balancing a checkbook;
- May have difficulty with math, math language, and math concepts;
- May reverse or omit letters, words, or phrases when writing;
- May have difficulty completing job applications correctly;
- May be able to explain things orally, but not in writing;
- May have had difficulty with parts or all of the process of learning to read;
- May have noticeable difficulty with oral reading, and poor oral language skills;
- May have to read materials more than one time, slowly and methodically, in order to understand them;
- May have a pronounced dislike of reading and writing;
- May read well but not write well, or write well but not read well;
- May experience continuous problems with spelling, frequently spelling the same word differently in one document;
- May have persistent problems with sentence structure, writing mechanics, and organizing written

work;
- May avoid writing letters and notes — even e-mail;
- May misinterpret language, have poor comprehension of what is said;
- May hear sounds, words, or sentences imperfectly or incorrectly.
- May be unable to tell you what has just been said;

The list above reveals that the term learning disabilities encompasses "skills that adults must use every day…. These disabilities ... may interfere with the ability to store, process, or produce information. In addition, learning disabilities may co-occur and be complicated by problems in attention and social skills." You may find helpful the Workbook page, "Could I Have a Learning Disability?," which is at the end of this chapter.[3]

THE WORK PLACE

ADA and Section 504
Adults with learning disabilities are usually protected from discrimination in their jobs by two federal laws: the Americans with Disabilities Act (ADA) and Section 504 of the Rehabilitation Act of 1973. (These laws are discussed in some detail in Chapters 4 and 5.)

In order to qualify for this protection, a person must be able to perform the essential functions of a particular job with or without reasonable accommodations. This means a person must have the same education and/or experience as anyone else who would be in that position. Reasonable accommodations to be made by the *employer* include such things as:

- making the job site accessible (this would apply particularly to physically handicapped people);
- restructuring the job (breaking down large tasks into smaller, more manageable ones);
- modifying the work schedule;
- acquiring equipment or modifying the equipment on hand;
- providing readers and interpreters;
- modifying examinations, training materials, policies, etc.;
- providing spoken memos as well as written memos.

On the other hand the *employee* (e.g., the adult with the learning disability) must be prepared to make accommodations in order to produce a satisfactory final product. These accommodations may include:

- scheduling working time for most efficient use of time;
- deciding on the equipment needed (in addition to the standard equipment provided);
- finding someone to proof the work completed, if that is necessary.

The employee cannot always expect the employer to accept changes in the final product outcome. For example, if the employer wants a written report, the employee can't automatically expect the employer to accept an oral report.

To Disclose or Not
"If you wish to request help from your employer, decide whether or not you wish to disclose your [learning] disability. Disclosure is becoming easier as the stigma lessens, but discrimination is not yet cleansed from our country.... Explain what you want [in] positive terms."[4] It is well to

realize that, while disclosure is a source of empowerment for people with disabilities, it also has risks.

"Shall I Take the Job?"
In order to make a decision about taking a job, you need to consider the following:

- Would I be able to do the job without accommodations?
- Would I be able to do the job well enough to progress and be successful?
- Would I benefit some way from doing the job without accommodations?
- How much of a struggle would the job be without accommodations?
- How would doing the job without accommodations affect my quality of life? (Would I have to spend a great deal more time at the work-place? Would I have to rely on co-workers for more than the average degree of help? Would the extra work leave me irritable and frustrated?)
- Is it a job that accentuates my talents and strengths?[5]

Appendix H has "Tips for Workplace Success for the Adult Learner." They are useful for the adult with LD before taking a job, while applying for a job, and after taking a job.

RELATIONSHIPS

Some adults with LD have difficulties in their personal contacts with others. They may misread social cues, have difficulty taking turns in conversations, and sometimes feel somewhat isolated.

On the other hand, there are other adults with LD who have excellent social skills. These abilities can help to carry them into successful careers and solid, long-lasting, loving relationships, despite their other LD problems.

The following are some tips that may prove useful for adults with LD and their partners, spouses, or roommates:

Suggestions for Adults with LD:
- Have a good understanding of the way in which learning disabilities affect your ability to process information, communicate, etc.
- Explain to your partner how learning disabilities might interfere with some aspects of everyday life.
- Request accommodations in a direct manner without feeling guilty or giving excuses.
- Avoid "crying wolf" (exaggerating the problem: you need to maintain credibility with others).
- Accept that some tasks may take longer.
- Be as self-reliant as possible by finding alternatives to overburdening your partner.

Suggestions for the Partner of an Adult with LD:

- Try to recognize, specifically, how the learning disability impacts your partner's ability to pay attention, comprehend, conceptualize, visualize, communicate, be organized, follow conversations, interpret body language, etc.

- Be aware that what appears to you to be a simple and logical way to carry out a task may not be the most logical way for the person with learning disabilities. Usually it is not helpful to try to persuade your partner to "just do it this way." Conversely, you should accept that what seems like a roundabout method may, in fact, be the easiest way for your partner to complete the task.
- Acknowledge that an adult with LD may bring to the present life situation many scars from past experiences.
- Remember that the thought processes of a person with LD may manifest themselves in a fashion which may seem confusing to others.
- Refrain from demanding that your partner "try harder" to correct a disability. This would be like expecting a deaf person to hear by trying harder.
- Be sensitive to the fact that "symptoms" of the learning disabilities may be more apparent at the end of the day or when your partner is fatigued.

SELF-ESTEEM

"The image we have of ourselves as children often affects how we feel about ourselves as adults. Children who feel overweight often turn into adults who are obsessed with their weight even though they are thin. Similarly, children who feel like failures may turn into adults obsessed with failing" even if they are successful.

"There are many ingredients that contribute to success in life that tests do not measure and that traditional teaching most likely does not reward. These include subtle ingredients that have to do with drive and determination, the setting of reachable goals, ingenuity, resourcefulness, and interpersonal skills.

"What we find with adults with learning disabilities is that often they have a wealth of untapped potential. To photograph with an unconventional eye, to build a beautiful boat, to compose a sonata, to organize a party, or to ease the last days of someone who is terminally ill — these are the skills that humanize our civilization and make life worth living. People with learning disabilities can realize that they are not stupid, or lazy, or bad, or incompetent, but, rather, that they are intelligent people with a mass of potential. They can begin to prize their uniqueness and feel better about themselves.

"To build self-esteem, a person has to know his or her strengths and interests, at the same time knowing what he or she has the most trouble with and what strategies help. As actor/director/producer Henry Winkler told children at the Lab School of Washington, 'The feeling of feeling stupid when you are not is terrible. Your person, your personality, your inner song is a lot more important than the speed at which you get things done.' When people like themselves, everything seems possible. They can dare to risk a little failure.

"Elizabeth Daniels Squire, author, says, 'It certainly is more inspiring to think of yourself as a person with a problem you can get around by working a little harder, trying alternatives, and not giving up, than trying to think of yourself as an awkward klutz who is jinxed and has bad luck...' People with learning disabilities must not view themselves as victims of fate. They must see themselves as agents of change and think of their learning disabilities not as problems but as opportunities to problem-solve.

"Accomplishing what one wants to do can be done even if it is not done the way everyone else does it. Learning disabilities are simply one of the facts of life — part of the way in which some people operate. Being learning disabled doesn't have to keep a person from chasing dreams. It just means that he or she chases them differently. No matter what we do, we are in charge of ourselves as we chase our dreams. The responsibility for learning and growing rests with us."[6]

A little advice to an adult with LD:

- Recognize your strengths and weaknesses;
- Know (and be able to explain) what accommodations you need;
- Invent your own strategies;
- Be able to ask for help when you need it;
- Believe in yourself![7]

SUCCESS

A few years ago, three college professors, Henry B. Reiff, Paul J. Gerber, and Rick Ginsberg, interviewed 71 adults with learning disabilities who were leading successful lives, to try to find out if there were any specific characteristics that had led to their successes. The participants came from 24 states and Canada.[8]

The researchers found that the characteristic that stood out as most important was the determination of those interviewed to gain control of their lives. They had decided to pursue this goal in several ways:

- They desired to succeed.
- They were goal-oriented.
- They were able to view their ordeals resulting from their learning disability as a more positive or productive experience.
- They were persistent.
- They learned ways of coping.
- They found a good fit between their abilities and their choice of environment (course choice, career, etc.).
- They displayed a strong passion for their work.
- They had a support system (e.g., spouse, family members or close friends, teachers, tutors, or secretaries).

A support system proved to be highly important. The researchers observed that "the pattern we deciphered was consistent: Support and guidance are invaluable aids, and one must be willing to seek, appreciate, and accept what others can offer."[9]

Writing about this same study but in another publication, the authors mention "the road not taken" by the adults they'd interviewed:

"*Many interviews indicated that, in one way or another, learning how to deal with learning disabilities provided the foundation for success. Indeed, many of the subjects felt that they were more determined, resilient, goal-oriented, and creative because of their learning disabilities. In a sense, they may have realized their full potential; they simply journeyed a different route to get to that destination.*"[10] (Italics added.)

SUMMARY

Even though adults with learning disabilities may have had great difficulty during some periods of their lives (especially with academics), they often have learned subtle but essential skills that give them unusual strengths, such as drive, determination, and ingenuity. Many find success in life by developing certain traits such as viewing their struggles positively, being persistent, learning ways of coping, building a support system, finding a good fit between their abilities and passions and their choices in life. Being LD doesn't have to keep a person from chasing dreams, even if they may have to be chased in new and creative ways.

Could I Have a Learning Disability?

I *may* have a learning disability, since I seem to have a good many of the characteristics listed earlier in this chapter.

For example, I SOMETIMES…

_____ read ok but I don't write well, <u>OR</u> write ok but I don't read well;

_____ can learn information presented in one way, but not another (for example, spoken but not written, or the other way around);

_____ have a short attention span, am impulsive and/or can be distracted easily;

_____ have difficulty telling or understanding jokes;

_____ find it difficult to memorize;

_____ have trouble following a schedule, being on time, or meeting deadlines;

_____ get lost easily, either in large buildings or while I'm driving;

_____ have trouble reading maps;

_____ misread or miscopy frequently;

_____ confuse similar letters or numbers (I often reverse them or confuse their order);

_____ have trouble reading a newspaper or following small print;

_____ am able to explain things orally much better than I can in writing;

_____ reverse or omit letters, words, or phrases when I'm writing;

_____ have trouble completing job applications correctly;

_____ have a lot of trouble with sentence structure, the mechanics of writing, and organizing written work;

_____ spell the same word several different ways in one document;

_____ have trouble dialing phone numbers and reading addresses;

_____ reverse numbers in my checkbook, and have trouble balancing my checkbook;

_____ have trouble following directions, especially if several are given to me at one time;

_____ feel I'm not well coordinated, and find I'm better at swimming, horseback riding and sailing than I am at baseball/softball and basketball;

_____ have a hard time repeating what someone has just said.

*　　　*　　　*

I realize the above is just a checklist, not a diagnostic test. But perhaps it gives me some guidance, as follows:

_____ I've checked many of the blanks in the list above. So I might benefit from having some testing done by a qualified professional who is experienced in working with adults who have learning disabilities.

_____ I've checked only a few of the blanks in the list above. It's possible I might not have a learning disability.

Chapter 7 — ASSISTIVE TECHNOLOGY

Advances in technology are coming at a swift pace these days, and that can be beneficial for students and adults with learning disabilities. Technologies such as speech readers and word processing programs have helped individuals with learning disabilities cross barriers to further learning or employment that otherwise would have been insurmountable. Assistive technology, however, is often overlooked or not well understood by parents, teachers, and employers.[1]

WHAT IS ASSISTIVE TECHNOLOGY?

Assistive technology is "any item, piece of equipment, or product system…that is used to increase, maintain, or improve functional capabilities of individuals with disabilities"[2] (IDEA Federal Regulations, Subpart A, Sec.300.5). IDEA requires that the IEP team consider the need for assistive technology in planning a student's program. (See Chapter 4 for detailed information on IDEA.)

In addition, the Americans with Disabilities Act (ADA) requires that employers make reasonable accommodations for employees with disabilities which include "acquisition or modification of equipment or devices" [Sec. 101(9)(b)].

Assistive technology devices can be either "high-tech," computer-based devices such as word processors or screen readers, or "low-tech" devices such as tape recorders or special pencils.

An assistive technology device allows someone with a learning disability to complete a task that he or she is capable of completing, except for a difficulty due to the disability. For example, a store manager is required to write memos to all employees. A store manager who has problems with spelling and writing may need to use a computer with special software to do the task. He understands the business, knows what he needs to tell employees, but has trouble with spelling and writing — that is where the assistive

technology provides the help. (This is discussed further in the next section.)

In addition to assistive technology *devices*, IDEA regulations define assistive technology *services* as "any services that directly assist a child with a disability in the selection, acquisition, or use of an assistive technology device" (Subpart A, Sec. 300.6). These services include such things as evaluation of a student's need for assistive technology, assistance and training in using the device, and training and technical assistance for teachers in incorporating the device into their lesson plans.

IDEA guarantees that assistive technology devices and services are made available to a child with a disability if they are required as part of the special education, related services, or supplementary aids and services, and are defined in the child's IEP.

Therefore, as you prepare for IEP meetings, think about how assistive technology may be able to help your child. Then go to the meetings prepared with specific suggestions.

HOW CAN ASSISTIVE TECHNOLOGY DEVICES HELP A CHILD OR ADULT WITH LEARNING DISABILITIES?

How does one know if and when assistive technology is needed? The best way to know is by examining...

1. the strengths and weaknesses of the individual,
2. the demands of the task he or she must complete,
3. the types of devices available, and
4. the ability of the individual to use these devices.

Examples of these steps follow:

Step 1: Determine the strengths and weaknesses of the student or adult.
Examples:

- John gets frustrated when he writes because he is constantly erasing his mistakes in grammar and punctuation and cannot get the content down.
- Maria has outstanding listening skills but difficulty reading at the same level on her own.
- Jorge understands the concept of multiplication but he cannot memorize his facts.

Step 2: Identify the demands of the task.
Examples:

- In John's English class, he must write a five-paragraph essay each week. He is graded on mechanics and content.
- In Maria's literature class, students are required to read three books per quarter and present an oral summary to the class.
- In Jorge's algebra class, multiplication facts are used daily in the completion of assignments.

Step 3: Identify the types of devices available.
Examples:

- John — word processor, spell checker, grammar checker, "talking" word processors
- Maria — talking word processor, books on tape, books on CD-ROM or the Internet
- Jorge — calculator, fact board, "talking" calculator

Step 4: Determine the student's ability to use the device.
Examples:

- John does not know how to type quickly. He will need to learn keyboarding skills first.
- Maria usually reads at an after-school program or on the couch in her home because she shares her bedroom. She needs a portable device.
- Jorge knows how to use a calculator but is embarrassed by his inability to memorize the facts. He does not want to use anything that other students do not have.

In all of these examples, the students have the ability to complete the tasks but not in traditional ways. With the help that assistive technology can provide, these students can achieve in ways similar to those used by students without disabilities.

WHAT KINDS OF TECHNOLOGIES ARE OUT THERE?

Written language

- Word processors allow students with LD to get their thoughts down and correct them later. This makes for cleaner, neater documents.

- Spell checkers allow students to check spelling for problems. Homonyms are still a problem and proofreading is still an essential skill. Some come with word processors; others are pocket-size and battery-operated; still others have speech synthesizers so the user can see and hear the word.
- Grammar checkers scan the document for punctuation, grammar, word usage, structure, spelling, style, or capitalization errors. Again, proofreading is still an essential skill.
- Outlining/brainstorming programs are found in many word processors. They enable students to write all of their ideas down in a list, then categorize and organize them afterward. There is also a graphic organizer that allows students to create visual webs or charts of their ideas.
- Abbreviation expanders are included in many word processing programs. They allow students to develop an abbreviation list for frequently used words or phrases so they do not have to type them each time they want to use them.
- Word prediction software supports both spelling and syntax by offering a list of words once a writer starts typing.
- Speech recognition programs allow students to write by speaking into the computer instead of using the keyboard. The programs require a sound board (on Windows machines) and a noise-canceling microphone; they also require training by reading an included text, which may be difficult for people with LD.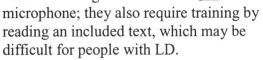
- Speech synthesis/screen reading programs read text from the computer screen in an adjustable voice. The text can be typed in,

scanned, or downloaded from the Web.

Reading

- Speech synthesis programs go beyond word processors and can read any text that is on a computer screen, including Web sites, information banks, etc.
- OCR/speech synthesis systems (Optical Character Recognition). These systems transfer information from paper pages to electronic files that can then be read out loud by the computer. Material is put through a scanner to input it to the computer; then the computer reads it.
- Variable speech-control tape recorders can be used in a variety of situations, such as listening to books on tape, or recording a lecture and listening to it later. Often students with LD need to listen to the playback at a slower speed in order to better process the information. Variable speech-control recorders allow you to control the playback speed.

Organization/Memory

- Personal Digital Assistants can be software included on a desktop computer, or can be hand-held devices used to schedule assignments, remind students about upcoming obligations, keep phone numbers, etc.

Listening aids

- Personal FM Listening systems require the speaker to wear a microphone/transmitter or have one for the group. It then transmits to a receiver with a headset that the student wears. This allows the student to hear the speaker directly and may filter out distracting noise.
- Tape recorders allow students to hear the information again at their own speed, and to make sure that their notes reflect all of the important material.

- <u>Digital Recorders</u> are like tape recorders with no tape, and allow easy recording of information and easier playback than tape.

Math
- <u>Calculators</u> are especially valuable for the student with LD who understands the concepts but whose memory difficulties get in the way of mastering basic facts.
- <u>Talking calculators</u> perform the same functions as calculators. However, they say each number and function out loud so that students can verify their input.

These are a few examples of the devices that are available. For more information, see the resources at the end of this section.

CAUTIONS AND OTHER COMMENTS

Skills Needed by Students

It is vital that your child or young adult have the skills to use technology efficiently and effectively. If he or she does not, a device designed to help could instead lead to increased frustration. For example, if your child has difficulty with the writing process so the IEP team thinks a computer with a word processor would be a good idea, then make sure your child has the keyboarding skills to use the word processor efficiently. There are a number of keyboarding programs available that would greatly enhance your child's use of a computer. Or if your child uses a tape recorder in class, make sure he or she knows how to check the batteries, keep up with the tapes, and switch tapes when one is full. Make sure that your child's IEP includes training in all of these skills.

Information Needed by Teachers

When talking with the school, make sure that all teachers are aware of the circumstances under which your child needs to use the device and when he does not. If your child has to go to another room to use a computer or

other device, help the teacher to find alternate ways that are efficient but that do not isolate your child from classroom activities. Talk to the teacher about ways that the device can be integrated into classroom activities. And make sure that the IEP team considers whether the device can be used in testing situations. Put all of this information in your child's IEP.

Technical Devices at College

If your child is going to college, make sure that you check out whether the devices are available through the university or whether you must provide them. Encourage your young adult to talk with professors or others about the use of tape recorders and other devices during class and testing situations. It is important for everyone to understand what is necessary for your child's success.

Technical Devices on the Job

For adults, assistive technology may be vital to performing a job function. If that is the case, make sure that the employer understands the individual's needs and can either provide for them or allow the use of personal equipment. In many cases, colleagues will be using similar devices (word processors, spelling checkers, personal data managers, etc.).

ON-LINE RESOURCES FOR MORE INFORMATION

ABLEDATA
NARIC and ABLEDATA
8401 Colesville Road
Silver Spring, MD 20910
1-800-227-0216
1-800-227-0216, x22 (TTY)
Web: www.abledata.com

Americans with Disabilities Act Disability and Business Technical Assistance Centers (DBTACs)
(The DBTACs provide information, referral, TA, and training on the ADA.)
6858 Old Dominion Drive, Suite 250
McLean, VA 22101 1-800-949-4232
Email: adata@adata.org

Assistive Technology Industry Association (ATIA)
www.atia.org/index.htm
A not-for-profit membership organization of organizations manufacturing or selling technology-based assistive devices for people with disabilities, or providing services associated with or required by people with disabilities. Among its primary goals is the establishment and continuation of an assistive device technology conference on an annual basis.

Center for Advanced Technology in Education (CATE)
www.cate.uoregon.edu
A research and development group in the University of Oregon College of Education investigating innovative applications of technology for middle school, secondary, and post-secondary students, their teachers and their schools.

Center for Applied Special Technology (CAST)
www.cast.org
Non-profit organization whose mission is to expand opportunities for people with disabilities through innovative multimedia computer technology.

Center for Electronic Studying
www.ces.uoregon.edu
Center investigating ways computer technology can be used to enhance students' efforts to study and learn content-area material. Funded by the U.S. Department of

Education, the Center has launched three projects blending portable computer technology with instruction on computer-based study strategies.

Closing the Gap
www.closingthegap.com
Internationally recognized source for information on the use of microcomputer related technology by and for exceptional individuals. Publishes newsletter, resource directory, and holds annual international conference each fall in Minneapolis, Minn.

Equal Access to Software and Information (EASI)
www.rit.edu/~easi
EASI's mission is to serve as a resource to the education community by providing information and guidance in the area of access-to-information technologies by individuals with disabilities.

Learning Disabilities Resources
www.ldresources.com
Technology expert (and adult dyslexic) Richard Wanderman's up-to-the-minute review of software and hardware for people with learning disabilities. He also publishes (irregularly) The LD Reader, a free e-mail newsletter with information about myriad aspects of learning disabilities. Send your order e-mail to Richard@ldresources.com from the address you want it sent to. Put "Subscribe LD Reader" in the subject area.

Literacy Instruction Through Technology (LITT)
www.edweb.sdsu.edu/SPED/ProjectLitt/LITT
A research project focusing on the use of technology to improve the reading skills of students with learning disabilities. Project LITT, located at San Diego State University, is funded by the U. S. Department of Education.

National Center to Improve Practice (NCIP)
www.edc.org/FSC/NCIP
Promotes the effective use of technology to enhance educational outcomes for students with sensory, cognitive, physical, and social/emotional disabilities. Funded by the U.S. Department of Education.

RESNA Technical Assistance Project
www.resna.org
Information and consultation to assistive technology programs in states and territories, funded under The Technology-Related Assistance For Individuals With Disabilities Act Amendments of 1994 (P.L. 103-218).

Speak to Write
www.edc.org/spk2wrt
Federally-funded project studying the use of speech recognition technology by secondary students with disabilities. Includes e-mail discussion forum *(listserv)* of the educational issues associated with using speech recognition technology to support students with disabilities in home and school settings.

The Internet: An Inclusive Magnet for Teaching All Students.
www.wid.org/tech/handbook/
World Institute on Disability has produced a handbook to help K-12 teachers promote access to the Internet for students with disabilities, students with a variety of learning styles, and those who do not speak English as their first language. The 21-page handbook provides practical tips, general access guidelines, resource listings, and success stories!

RESOURCES FOR MORE INFORMATION

Assistive Technology Pointers for Parents
by Penny Reed and Gayl Bowser
January 2000

Designed to be used as a workbook, this new publication focuses on specific questions that parents can use to help move the decision-making process forward appropriately and effectively as they work with their child's education team. Available from the **Coalition for Assistive Technology in Oregon (CATO)** for $12.00, which includes shipping and handling. Send orders to: CATO, PO Box 431, Winchester, Oregon, 97495. For additional information call **541/440-4791** (voice/TDD) or fax **541/957-4808.**

Learning Through Listening Video Series
(4 tapes):
Explore how taped textbooks can help dyslexic students improve their educational success. An excellent resource for parents, educators and school administrators.
- Volume 1: Learning About Learning Disabilities
- Volume 2: On the Right Track: K-7
- Volume 3: On the Right Track: Teens and Adults
- Volume 4: Setting up Your AIM Program

For more information, call 1-800-221-4792, Recording for the Blind & Dyslexic.

Only the Best 1999-2000
The annual guide to the highest-rated educational software and multimedia. By compiling information on the highest-rated materials in one convenient guide, educators are able to sift through the intimidating mass of programs now available and select those that are truly worthy of an A grade.
ISBN: 9990567204 Available through most booksellers.

Special Education Technology Practice
This magazine is published five times annually. For more information, call the Editorial offices: 414/962-0120.

Note

Most public libraries have computers available for the public to use in looking for on-line resources. Be sure to also check out <u>www.ldonline</u> for a broad range of information on learning disabilities.

SUMMARY

Technology has provided opportunities for many students and adults with learning disabilities to overcome the barriers their difficulties present at school, on the job, and in daily living. New devices come on the market every day, and your child may learn about them and use them more quickly than you! Assistive technology devices should be accepted in virtually every classroom, and made available to students, disabled or not.

Chapter 8 — GIFTED, WITH LEARNING DISABILITIES

Learning disabilities combined in the same person with giftedness can produce a puzzling human being. For example, this individual may be exceptionally creative, with high-level interests to which he is totally committed, but, at the same time, may be failing in English composition. When ADD (and especially ADD with hyperactivity) is added to this mix, the affected students can present challenges not only to their teachers but to their parents as well. It is important to keep in mind that these gifted individuals are valuable resources to society if they receive the kind of teaching as well as the support and guidance they need.

TRAITS OF GIFTED CHILDREN WITH LD

"How could he be *gifted* when he got two F's this semester?" "Hey, that kid can tell you the names of every bug he's ever met, and he knows the characteristics of over a hundred species of insects. How could he be learning disabled? If you ask me, he's just lazy – and careless to boot."[1]

It's not unusual for parents and teachers to hear such comments about certain students. After all, they, too, have been puzzled about how to plan for and how to teach these "conundrum kids." "Conundrum kids" is what Priscilla Vail calls them. She's a learning specialist in Bedford, N.Y., and author of *Smart Kids with School Problems*.[2]

She says these are young people in whom extraordinary talent or interest coincide with what our print-oriented verbal culture calls learning disabilities (or any of several other terms, including dyslexia). They <u>can</u> learn, they <u>do</u> learn, but not the same things or in the same way as their classmates.[3]

In Bobbie H. Jones' experience with these students, she has found that "the dyslexic student frequently does not read, spell, listen, or get his thoughts on paper at the level his intelligence predicts. His organizational skills are frequently poor. Our gifted dyslexic may not be able to read well in spite of enthusiasm for pulsars and knowledge about space. He may be a poor speller with problems in written expression, despite his creative imagination. He may write slowly and illegibly and routinely fail to finish tests, even when he has a broader knowledge of the subject than most. The spread between his capacity and his skills is great, and this is confusing to most teachers."[4]

To make the picture even more puzzling, it would not be unusual to find that he has high-level interests at home. These children may use plastic bricks to build fantastic structures, or undertake a campaign to save the whales. Clear indicators of their giftedness are their creative abilities, intellectual strength, and the passion they bring to their hobbies.[5]

At school, they may be frequently off-task; they may day-dream, complain of not feeling well; and may use their creativity to avoid tasks.

Priscilla Vail includes the following traits to describe conundrum children:[6]

- Rapid grasp of concepts;
- Awareness of patterns;
- Energy, curiosity, and concentration;
- Exceptional memory;

- Empathy, vulnerability, heightened perception;
- Divergent thinking.[7]

EXAMPLES OF LD/GIFTEDNESS

A superbly coordinated athlete or sculptor may have illegible handwriting and bizarre spelling. A student who can think through and solve complex mathematical problems may stumble over arithmetic problems he has to put down on paper. A blossoming young scientist who gets straight A's in his lab work may have a desk and a school locker in complete disarray – and he may be unable to keep track of his backpack.[8]

Vail tells about Martina, who won first place in her high school Science Fair, and yet had difficulty with reading comprehension. Her Science teacher was astonished to hear about her low scores on standardized reading tests, and her English teacher was surprised to hear about her Science project winning a first place ribbon.[9]

INCIDENCE

Two pediatricians at Rutgers Medical School in New Jersey have a theory about why we don't hear much about such children. They say that many teachers can't imagine that both superior and inferior abilities can possibly exist in one student. This lack of understanding by teachers clouds the picture when we try to find out the number of such children in the general population; however, we can get some idea if we estimate that about 10 percent of gifted children have a reading problem (i.e., two or more years behind grade level on reading tests), and approximately 30 percent of gifted children will show a "significant discrepancy

between mental age and achievement scores in reading."[10]

ADD WITH LD/GIFTEDNESS

Sometimes the condition of learning disabilities combined with giftedness is further complicated when these conditions are accompanied by Attention Deficit Disorder (ADD). The students' problems are "enormously more extensive, more dramatic, and more difficult for parents and teachers to deal with than those of a dyslexic student [who is not gifted and does not have ADD]," according to Bobbie H. Jones. She continues, "We know that children who have an attention deficit disorder are less compliant, more attention-seeking and require more supervision.... They may be more negative and interact with others less positively.

"When the child has an attention deficit disorder with hyperactivity, family negotiation and problem solving are often impaired by parental fatigue and an ongoing sense of failure, as well as by the separation that often affects couples as they attempt to cope with the demanding, lovable, but difficult child....

"The gifted dyslexic can be domineering and manipulative in response to his own frustration and helplessness. To help manage this, parents can redefine their own control of the family by closing ranks and returning to a team stance, a unit force, using both mother and father. Within limits and boundaries clearly set, the child can then be allowed appropriate freedom of choice. Clarity of the family structure lessens anxiety, and, interestingly, helps the child interact with peers more comfortably.

"Allowing the child to appreciate his own difference provides parents with an opportunity to teach him about the importance of the uniqueness of every individual. As a gifted dyslexic, he is different in at least two ways from other children (and perhaps in a third way, if attention deficit disorder is present). A great disadvantage is that two of these differences, being dyslexic and being gifted, are invisible.... If a bright dyslexic child's deficits were physically expressed, if he were unable to walk or hear or speak, then those around him would rally to diagnose and help him, not to blame and reproach him."[11]

THE SCHOOL'S RESPONSE TO LD/GIFTEDNESS

Priscilla Vail has six suggestions for teaching gifted students who are also dyslexic, in order to teach their minds while releasing their creativity:

1. "Just as unsupported weaknesses ache, unexercised talents itch. Therefore parents and educators must budget time, money and emotional resources for the exercise of talent as well as for the remediation of weakness.

2. "Benevolent tyranny has its place. As Harriet Sheridan taught us in her role as dean at Carleton College and at Brown, organization in time and space is convenient in lower school, helpful in middle school, supportive in high school and VITAL in college and graduate school. Thus, we do students a life-long service by teaching and reinforcing spatial and temporal organization from the beginning.

3. "Language development is the key to intellectual and social/emotional growth. If we hope students will be able to understand what they read and hear, we need to stimulate and nurture their receptive language capacities through exposure, and encourage their expressive capacities through opportunity and response. We must talk with young learners, read aloud to them, and listen to tapes together. Then we must elicit their responses to narrative, engage them in conversation about current events, and encourage connections among their various bits and pieces of general information.

4. "Privacy matters. Students of all ages are afraid to do what they do badly in front of the audiences they would most like to impress: their parents. Kids have many teachers but only one mother or one father. Therefore, adults need to 'find a pro you trust and then trust the pro.'

5. "Ownership of a problem belongs to the student. Why? If a parent, tutor, or teacher owns the 'problem,' the ultimate solution or victory also belongs to that adult. Victory should belong to the student: adult ownership is, actually, a type of theft.

6. "Many impressive, serious educational conferences focus on goals and test scores but make little mention of humor. Yet, what's the point if you don't save time for the joke? The legendary Katrina DeHirsch left halfway through a solemn child-study symposium that attempted to codify the childhood experiences of successful adults: how many trips to the zoo by age 5 or how many library cards by age 10. The plan was to feed these facts into a computer that would, in retrospect, produce a recipe for precursors for perfect adulthood. Mrs. DeHirsch deduced that one common factor, which resisted formulaic analysis, existed among those adults who were living productive, juicy, joyful, yeasty lives. Each one of the successful adults said, 'my parents [or a parent, or someone who cared for me], got a kick out of me.' To 'get a kick out of' implies trust, faith, and enjoyment. We don't laugh with people we don't think are intact. Thus to get a kick out of is to say 'You are OK.' 'Conundrum kids' need this message."[12]

SUMMARY

These students who are both LD and gifted are enigmas — and fascinating challenges. They can flounder as they try to deal with the opposing forces of their gifts and their learning disabilities, and may be particularly vulnerable when they have the added complication of Attention Deficit Disorder. But they are a resource that society can't afford to waste. It is imperative that they have support from their families and schools, in order to "negate the anger, fear, self-doubt, frustration, pressure, and blame they often feel," as Vail has observed.[13] We must respond to their possibilities and provide them with the help they deserve. They are a gift to us all.[14]

APPENDICES

APPENDIX A

DEFINITIONS OF LEARNING DISABILITIES

In the Individuals with Disabilities Education Act (IDEA) of 1997, the federal government defines a learning disability as follows:

A. *IN GENERAL--The term "specific learning disability" means a disorder in one or more of the basic psychological processes involved in understanding or in using language, spoken or written, that may manifest itself in an imperfect ability to listen, think, speak, read, write, spell, or to do mathematical calculations.*
B. *DISORDERS INCLUDED--Such term includes conditions such as perceptual disabilities, brain injury, minimal brain dysfunction, dyslexia, and developmental aphasia.*
C. *DISORDERS NOT INCLUDED--Such term does not include a learning problem that is primarily the result of visual, hearing, or motor disabilities, of mental retardation, of emotional disturbance, or of environmental, cultural, or economic disadvantage [IDEA – 20 U.S.C. 1401(26)].*

Some states and schools have tried to clarify the federal definition and criteria by adding their own specific criteria. For example, while many state definitions include the concept of a learning disability as a discrepancy between achievement and potential, some go a step further in qualifying how large that discrepancy must be, as manifested by various test scores. It is interesting to note the lack of consensus, with each state using a slightly different "yardstick."

It is important for parents to be very clear about the criteria that will be used to determine if their child has a learning disability. Contact both your state Department of Education (see Appendix C) and your local school to request a copy of the definition and criteria that will be used in evaluating your child.

Other organizations concerned with learning disabilities have developed their own definitions. One of those is the National Joint Committee on Learning Disabilities, which defined learning disabilities in 1990 as follows:

"Learning disabilities is a general term that refers to a heterogeneous group of disorders manifested by significant difficulties in the acquisition and use of listening, speaking, reading, writing, reasoning, or mathematical skills.

"These disorders are intrinsic to the individual, presumed to be due to central nervous system dysfunction, and may occur across the life span. Problems in self-regulatory behaviors, social perception, and social interaction may exist with learning disabilities but do not, by themselves, constitute a learning disability.

"Although learning disabilities may occur concomitantly with other disabilities (for example, sensory impairment, mental retardation, serious emotional disturbance), or with extrinsic influences (such as cultural differences, insufficient or inappropriate instruction), they are not the result of those conditions or influences."

To find out more about definitions, look for LD-In Depth on the LDOnline Web page (www.ldonline.org) or contact any of the national organizations listed in Appendix B.

APPENDIX B

EXPLANATION OF RESOURCE PAGES

This Appendix offers lists of resources for further information on topics related to learning disabilities. It is divided into the following sections:

Appendix B-1 is "NCLD's Resource List," reprinted from *Their World 2000*, National Center for Learning Disabilities, 381 Park Avenue South, Suite 1401, New York, N.Y. 10016-8806. It is used with permission of NCLD. The reader may find updates to this list of resources on the Website www.ld.org.

Appendix B-2, "Additional Resources," has been assembled by the Learning Disabilities Council. It supplements the list in Appendix B-1.

Appendix B-3 lists Websites which offer a starting point for parents wishing to locate official agencies in each state.

Further additions to those listed in Appendix B-1, pertaining to college, vocational training, and transitional programs, may be found in Appendix F. Additional technology resources are listed at the end of Chapter 7.

The resources listed in Appendices B-1, B-2, B-3, F, and Chapter 7 are included for information purposes only. No endorsement by the Learning Disabilities Council is intended or implied.

NATIONAL CENTER FOR LEARNING DISABILITIES

381 Park Avenue South, Suite 1401
New York, NY 10016
212/545-7510 Fax 212/545-9665
National Information & Referral Service: 888/575-7373
www.ncld.org or www.ld.org

NCLD'S RESOURCE LIST

INTRODUCTION:

The National Center for Learning Disabilities (NCLD) is pleased to provide our readers with an updated and expanded Resource List. Please feel free to duplicate and distribute these pages and to contact us with any suggestions for enlarging this list. Many of the organizations listed can be visited on the Internet, and most will provide useful literature and recommendations for local resources at little or no cost.

While NCLD has found these to be excellent and reliable resources, we do not endorse any specific program, product, or organization.

CONTENTS

Introduction
National Organizations on Learning Disabilities
Related Organizations
Local Advocacy and Support
Continuing Education
· College Resources
School Testing Issues
Employment and Related Issues
Legal Issues
Government Departments/Agencies
Financial Support
Summer Camps
Information Guides and Directories
Gifted/LD
ADD/ADHD
Literacy
Homeschooling
Independent Living
Technology Resources
Books on Tape
Web Sites
Bibliography
Journals
Videotapes and Audiotapes

NATIONAL ORGANIZATIONS ON LEARNING DISABILITIES

SERVING ALL AGES

National Center for Learning Disabilities (NCLD): 381 Park Avenue South, Suite 1401, New York, NY 10016. Telephone: 212/545-7510, Fax: 212/545-9665, Toll-free National Information & Referral: 888/575-7373, Web: www.ncld.org. National non-profit membership organization that offers a free Information & Referral Service, conducts educational programs, raises public awareness of learning disabilities (LD), and advocates for improved legislation and services for those with LD.

Learning Disabilities Association of America (LDA): 4156 Library Road, Pittsburgh, PA 15234. Telephone: 888/300-6710 or 412/341-1515, Fax: 412/344-0224, Web: www.ldanatl.org, Email: ldanatl@usaor.net. National non-profit membership organization, with state and local chapters, that conducts an annual conference and offers information and various publications.

The International Dyslexia Association (formerly The Orton Dyslexia Society): Chester Building, 8600 La Salle Road, Suite 382, Baltimore, MD 21286-2044. Telephone: 410/296-0232 or 800/ABCD-123, Fax: 410/321-5069, Web: interdys.org, Email: info@interdys.org. International non-profit membership organization that offers training in language programs and provides publications relating to dyslexia. Chapters are located in most states.

The Council for Exceptional Children (CEC): 1920 Association Drive, Reston, VA 20191-1589.

Telephone: 888/232-7733, Fax: 703/264-9494, Web: www.cec.sped.org, Email: service@cec.sped.org. A non-profit, membership organization that has 17 specialized divisions including the Division for Learning Disabilities (DLD), the Division for Children's Communication Development (DCCD), and The Association for the Gifted (TAG). CEC and its divisions hold conferences and publish newsletters and journals.

Council for Learning Disabilities (CLD): P.O. Box 40303, Overland Park, KS 66204. Telephone: 913/492-8755, Fax: 913/492-2546, Web: coe.winthrop.edu\cld. National membership organization dedicated to assisting professionals who work in the field of learning disabilities. The *Learning Disabilities Quarterly,* a professional publication, is available through CLD.

Learning Disabilities Association of Canada (LDAC): 323 Chapel Street, Suite 200, Ottawa, Ontario, K1N 7Z2 Canada. Telephone: 613/238-5721, Fax: 613/235-5391, Web: educ.queensu.ca/~lda, Email: ldactaac@fox.nstn.ca. Non-profit membership organization with provincial and territorial offices that conducts programs and provides information for children and adults with LD. Resources include books and pamphlets that may also be useful to U.S. residents.

National Institute of Child Health and Human Development (NICHD): National Institutes of Health (NIH), Building 31, Room 2A32, 31 Center Drive MSC 2425, Bethesda, MD 20892-2425. Telephone: 301/496-5133, Fax: 301/496-7101, Web: www.nichd.nih.gov. Provides reviews of literature and information related to NICHD research.

National Information Center for Children and Youth with Disabilities (NICHCY): P.O. Box 1492, Washington, DC 20013-1492. Telephone: 800/695-0285 or 202/884-8200, Fax:

202/884-8441, Web: www.nichcy.org, Email: nichcy@aed.org. Information clearinghouse that provides free information on disabilities and disability-related issues.

National Center for Law and Learning Disabilities (NCLLD): P.O. Box 368, Cabin John, MD 20818. Telephone: 301/469-8308. Non-profit organization that provides education, advocacy, analysis of legal issues, policy recommendations, and resource materials.

Schwab Foundation for Learning: 1650 South Amphlett Boulevard, Suite 300, San Mateo, CA 94402-2516. Telephone: 800/230-0988 or 650/655-2410, Fax: 650/655-2411, Web: www.schwablearning.org, Email: infodesk@schwablearning.org. Membership organization that provides information and referral to national and local resources as well as research and guidance for parents, teachers, clinicians, and others who work with children who have learning differences.

ADULT RESOURCES

HEATH Resource Center (National Clearinghouse on Postsecondary Education for Individuals with Disabilities): One Dupont Circle, NW, Suite 800, Washington, DC 20036. Telephone: 800/544-3284 or 202/939-9320, Fax: 202/833-4760, Web: www.heath-resource-center.org, Email: heath@ace.nche.edu. National clearinghouse that provides information on postsecondary education and related issues for a nominal cost.

National Association for Adults with Special Learning Needs (NAASLN): 1444 I Street, NW, Su[...] e: 20[...] **NO LONGER IN OPERATION** it organization comprised of professionals, advocates, and consumers, whose purpose is to educate adults with special learning needs. Publishes a newsletter and holds annual conferences.

NCLD'S RESOURCE LIST

RELATED ORGANIZATIONS

American Speech-Language-Hearing Association (ASHA): 10801 Rockville Pike, Rockville, MD 20852. Telephone: 800/638-8255 or 301/897-5700, Fax: 301/571-0457, Web: www.asha.org, Email: irc@asha.org. Membership organization comprised of speech pathologists and audiologists that provides information and referrals to the public on speech, language, communication, and hearing disorders.

Association of Educational Therapists (AET): 1804 West Burbank Boulevard, Burbank, CA 91506. Telephone: 818/843-1183, Fax: 818/843-7423, Email: aetla@aol.com. National professional organization that maintains standards for professional educational therapists. Offers publications and audio tapes.

ERIC Clearinghouse on Disabilities and Gifted Education (ERIC/CEC): The Council for Exceptional Children, 1920 Association Drive, Reston, VA 20191-1589. Telephone: 800/328-0272, Web: www.cec.sped.org/ericec.htm, Email: ericec@cec.sped.org. A national information system on education with a large database of educational materials. Publishes and disseminates information, serves as a resource center for the general public, and promotes the dissemination of research (see also The Council for Exceptional Children).

National Association for the Education of Young Children (NAEYC): 1509 16th Street, NW, Washington, DC 20036-1426. Telephone: 800/424-2460 or 202/232-8777, Fax: 202/328-1846, Web: www.naeyc.org/naeyc, Email: chaudry@naeyc.org. National membership organization that focuses on children from birth to age eight. Sponsors an annual conference, publishes a bimonthly journal, and has a catalog of books, brochures, videos, and posters.

National Association of Private Schools for Exceptional Children (NAPSEC): 1522 K Street, NW, Suite 1032, Washington, DC 20005. Telephone: 202/408-3338, Fax: 202/408-3340, Web: www.napsec.com, Email: napsec@aol.com. Provides referral service for persons interested in private special education placements. Offers publications and sponsors annual conferences.

National Parent Network on Disabilities (NPND): 1200 G Street, NW, Suite 800, Washington, DC 20005. Telephone: 202/434-8686, Fax: 202/434-8707, Web: www.npnd.org, Email: npnd@cs.com. Membership organization open to all agencies, organizations, parent centers, parent groups, professionals, and individuals concerned with the quality of life for people with disabilities.

National Association for Bilingual Education (NABE): 1220 L Street, NW, Suite 605, Washington, DC 20005-4018. Telephone: 202/898-1829, Fax: 202/789-2866, Web: www.nabe.org, Email: NABE@nabe.org. Non-profit advocacy membership organization that provides literature, including a newsletter and quarterly research journal.

National Association of State Directors of Special Education, Inc. (NASDSE): 1800 Diagonal Road, Suite 320, Alexandria, VA 22314. Telephone: 703/519-3800, Fax: 703/519-3808, Web: www.nasdse.org, Email: nasdse@nasdse.org. Not-for-profit corporation that promotes and supports educational programs for students with disabilities and holds annual meetings.

National Center to Improve the Tools of Educators (NCITE): 805 Lincoln Street, Eugene, OR 97401. Telephone and Fax: 541/683-7543. Web: Darkwing.Uoregon.EDU. Organization that is funded by the U.S. Department of Education. Dedicated to the improvement of instructional methods and materials. Publishes articles on educational practices.

NCLD'S RESOURCE LIST

National Association of School Psychologists (NASP): 4340 East West Highway, Suite 402, Bethesda, MD 20814. Telephone: 301/657-0270, Fax: 301/657-0275, Web: www.naspWeb.org, Email: nasp8455@aol.com. International not-for-profit membership association of school psychologists. Provides a nationally-recognized certification system, promotes children's rights, produces videos, and sponsors conferences. Publishes books, a newspaper, and the quarterly *School Psychology Review.*

LOCAL ADVOCACY AND SUPPORT

Parent Training and Information Project (PTI): PACER Center, 4826 Chicago Avenue South, Minneapolis, MN 55417-1098. Telephone: 888/248-0822 or 612/827-2966, Fax: 612/827-3065, Web: www.pacer.org, Email: pacer@pacer.org. Federally funded program that provides local resources and advocacy training for disability and special education issues.

Parent to Parent: National Parent-to-Parent Support and Information System, P.O. Box 907, Blue Ridge, GA 30513. Telephone: 800/651-1151 or 706/374-3822, Fax: 706/374-3826, Web: www.nppsis.org, Email: eppis@ellijay.com. Networking program that matches parents with other parents based on the disabilities of their children.

Sibling Support Project: P.O. Box 5371, CL-09, Seattle, WA 98105-0371. Telephone: 206/368-4911, Fax: 206/368-4816, Web: www.chmc.org/departmt/sibsupp, Email: dmeyer@chmc.org. Organization for families that publishes a newsletter and holds support group meetings. Provides regional and statewide training for sibling support groups and makes referrals internationally to sibling support groups.

CONTINUING EDUCATION

Association on Higher Education and Disability (AHEAD): P.O. Box 21192, Columbus, OH 43221-0192. Telephone: 614/488-4972, Fax: 614/488-1174, Web: www.ahead.org. International organization that provides training programs, workshops, conferences, and publications.

Higher Education Consortium for Special Education (HECSE): Department of Special Education, Room 100, Whitehead Hall, Johns Hopkins University, Baltimore, MD 21218. Telephone: 410/516-8275, Fax: 410/516-8424, Web: edscsjhuvms.hcs.jhu.edu. Non-profit membership organization for colleges and universities that promotes the improvement of special education training programs.

General Educational Development Testing Service (GEDTS): One Dupont Circle, Suite 250, Washington, DC 20036. Telephone: 202/939-9490, Fax: 202/775-8578, Web: www.acenet.edu, Email: Web@ace.nche.edu. Administers the GED exam and publishes information on disability-related accommodations.

GED Hotline: P.O. Box 81826, Lincoln, NE 68501. Telephone: 800/626-9433. 24-hour service that provides information on local GED classes and testing services. An accommodations guide for people with learning disabilities is available.

Vocational Rehabilitation Agencies: U.S. Department of Education, Office of Special Education and Rehabilitative Services (OSERS), Switzer Building, 330 C Street, SW, Washington, DC 20202. Telephone: 202/205-5465, Fax: 202/205-9252, Web: www.ed.gov/office/osers. These agencies can provide job training, counseling, financial assistance, and employment placement to individuals who meet eligibility criteria.

American Association for Vocational Instructional Materials (AAVIM): 220 Smithonia Road, Winterville, GA 30683. Telephone: 800/228-4689 or 706/742-5355, Fax: 706/742-7005, Web: aavim.com, Email: seabaugh@msn.com. Provides information on educational materials including the *Performance Based Teacher Education* catalog.

Learning Resources Network (LERN): 1550 Hayes Drive, Manhattan, KS 66502. Telephone: 800/678-5376 or 785/539-5376, Fax: 785/539-7766, Web: www.lern.org, Email: hq@lern.com. Provides information on adult continuing education.

COLLEGE ISSUES

Dispelling the Myths: College Students and Learning Disabilities (by Katherine Garnett and Sandra LaPorta, 1990). Available from NCLD. 888/575-7373.

Guidelines for Learning Disabled College Students (AHEAD, 1997). Available from AHEAD. 614/488-4972.

Guidelines for Documentation of a Learning Disability i ~~NO LONGER APPLICABLE~~ Available from AHEAD. 614/488-4972.

Assisting College Students with Learning Disabilities: A Tutor's Manual (by Pamela Adelman and Debbie Olufs, 1996). Available from AHEAD. 614/488-4972.

K&W Guide to Colleges for the Learning Disabled (by Marybeth Kravets and Imy Wax, 4th edition, 1997). Princeton Review, New York, NY.

Colleges with Programs for Students with Learning Disabilities or Attention Deficit Disorder (edited by Charles T. Mangrum, II and Stephen S. Strichart, 5th edition, 1997). Peterson's, Princeton, NJ.

Counseling Secondary Students with Learning Disabilities: A Ready-To-Use Guide to Help Students Prepare for College & Work (by Marybeth Kravets and Mike Koehler, 1998). Center for Applied Research in Education, West Nyack, NY.

Survival Guide for College Students with ADD or LD (by K. Nadeau, 1994). New York, NY: Magination Press.

The College Student with a Learning Disability: A Handbook (by Susan Vogel, 6th edition, 1997). Available from LDA. 412/341-1515.

SCHOOL TESTING ISSUES

Students with documented learning disabilities may request information on testing accommodations. For more information contact:

ACT Universal Testing Special Testing: P.O. Box 4028, Iowa City, IA 52243-4028. Telephone: 319/337-1332, Fax: 319/337-1285, Web: www.act.org. Provides college admissions testing nationally.

Educational Testing Service (ETS): Rosedale Road, Princeton, NJ 08541. Telephone: 609/921-9000, Fax: 609/734-5410, Web: www.ets.org. Tests administered include: SAT, GRE, GMAT.

Law School Admission Council (LSAC): P.O. Box 2000-T, Newtown, PA 18940-0998. Telephone: 215/968-1001, Fax: 215/968-1277, Web: www.LSAC.org, Email: LSACinfo@LSAC.org. Tests administered include: LSAT.

General Educational Development Testing Service (GEDTS): One Dupont Circle, Suite 250, Washington, DC 20036. Telephone: 202/939-9490, Fax: 202/775-8578, Web: acenet.edu, Email: Web@ace.nche.edu. Administers the GED exam and publishes information on disability-related accommodations.

Educational Records Bureau (ERB):
220 East 42nd Street, New York, NY 10017.
Telephone: 800/989-3721, Fax: 212/370-4096,
Web: www.erbtest.org, Email: info@erbtest.com.
Tests administered include: Independent School
Entrance Examination (ISEE).

EMPLOYMENT AND RELATED ISSUES

RESOURCES

Job Accommodation Network (JAN):
West Virginia University, P.O. Box 6080,
Morgantown, WV 26506-6080. Telephone:
800/232-9675 or 304/293-7186, Fax:
304/293-5407, Web: janWeb.icdi.wvu.edu,
Email: jan@jan.icdi.wvu.edu. International information network and consulting resource that
answers questions about workplace accommodations, the Americans with Disabilities Act, and
the Rehabilitation Act of 1973. Offers individualized information packets to employers, rehabilitation professionals, and persons with disabilities.

Mainstream, Inc.: 6930 Carroll Avenue,
Suite 240, Tacoma Park, MD 20912. Telephone:
301/891-8777, Fax: 301/891-8778,
Web: www.mainstreaminc.org, Email:
info@mainstreaminc.org. Non-profit organization
that works with employers, service providers, and
individuals with disabilities to increase opportunities for persons with disabilities. Provides technical assistance on compliance with the Americans
with Disabilities Act.

**Equal Employment Opportunity Commission
(EEOC):** 1801 L Street, NW, Washington, DC
20507. Telephone: 800/669-4000 or
202/275-7377, Fax: 202/663-6834, Web:
www.eeoc.gov. Key federal agency for the implementation of Title I (employment) of the
Americans with Disabilities Act.

PUBLICATIONS

Latham, P.S. & Latham, P.H. (1994). *Succeeding in
the Workplace: Attention Deficit Disorder and Learning
Disabilities in the Workplace.* Washington, DC: JKL
Communications.

LDA of Canada. (1993). *Learning Disabilities and
the Workplace.* Ottawa, Ontario: LDA of Canada.
Call LDAC at 613/238-5721.

Witt, M.A. (1992). *Job Strategies for People with
Disabilities.* Princeton, NJ: Peterson's Guides.

LEGAL ISSUES

RESOURCES

**American Bar Association Center on Children
and the Law:** 740 15th Street, NW, Washington,
DC 20005-1009. Telephone: 202/662-1720,
Fax: 202/662-1755, Web: www.abanet.org/child,
Email: ctrchildlaw@abanet.org. Provides information on legal issues and referrals to local services.

**National Association of Protection and
Advocacy Systems:** 900 2nd Street, NE, Suite
211, Washington, DC 20002. Telephone:
202/408-9514, Fax: 202/408-9520, Web:
www.protectionandadvocacy.com, Email:
NAPAS@EARTHLINK.NET. Provides
literature on legal issues and referrals to federally-mandated programs that advocate for the rights
of people with disabilities.

ADA Information Hotline: Telephone:
800/949-4232, Web: www.disabilityact.com.
Provides technical assistance and information
regarding the Americans with Disabilities Act.

ADA Information Line: U.S. Department of
Justice, P.O. Box 66738, Washington, DC 20035-6738. Telephone: 202/514-0301 or
800/514-0301, Web: www.usdoj.gov/crt/ada/ada-hom1.htm. Answers questions about Title II

(public services) and Title III (public accommodations) of the Americans with Disabilities Act. Provides materials and technical assistance on the provisions of the ADA.

Disability Rights Education and Defense Fund, Inc. (DREDF): 2212 Sixth Street, Berkeley, CA 94710. Telephone: 800/466-4232 or 510/644-2555, Fax: 510/841-8645, Web: www.dredf.org, Email: dredf@dredf.org. A national law and policy center that provides services, including technical assistance, information and referrals on disability rights laws, legal advocacy, and legal representation.

PUBLICATIONS

Gordon, M. & Kaiser, S. (1998). *Accommodations in Higher Education under the Americans with Disabilities Act (ADA): A No-Nonsense Guide for Clinicians, Educators, Lawyers, and Administrators.* New York, NY: Guildford Press.

Latham, P.S. & Latham P.H. (1993). *Learning Disabilities and the Law.* Washington, DC: JKL Communications.

Turnbull, H. R., III, & Turnbull, A. (1997). *Free Appropriate Public Education: The Law and Children with Disabilities.* 5th edition. Denver, CO: Love Publishing Company.

GOVERNMENT DEPARTMENTS/ AGENCIES

Office of Special Education and Rehabilitative Services (OSERS): U.S. Department of Education, Switzer Building, 330 C Street, SW, Suite 3006, Washington, DC 20202-2500. Telephone: 202/205-5465, Fax: 202/205-9252, Web: www.ed.gov/offices/osers. Contact OSERS for information about special education programs, vocational rehabilitation programs, and information about national and international research regarding disabilities and rehabilitation.

State Departments of Education: State Departments of Education can provide information about Individuals with Disabilities Education Act (IDEA) implementation requirements and regulations. Contact directory assistance in your state capital or NCLD for further information.

Office for Civil Rights (OCR) of the U.S. Department of Education: 600 Independence Avenue, SW, Washington, DC 20202. Telephone: 800/421-3481 or 202/205-5413, Fax: 202/205-9862, Web: www.ed.gov, Email: ocr@ed.gov. Contact OCR for information about how to file a formal civil rights complaint.

FINANCIAL SUPPORT

Social Security Administration (SSA): 6401 Security Boulevard, Baltimore, MD 21235. Telephone: 800/772-1213, Web: www.ssa.gov. Provides financial assistance to those with disabilities who meet eligibility requirements.

Federal Student Aid Information Center: P.O. Box 84, Washington, DC 20044. Telephone: 800/433-3243, Web: www.fafsa.ed.gov. Answers questions and produces several publications about financial aid.

Family Resource Center on Disabilities: 20 East Jackson Boulevard, Suite 300, Chicago, IL 60604. Telephone: 312/939-3513, Fax: 312/939-7297. Publishes the brochure *Tax Guide for Parents* that outlines many of the income tax deductions available to parents.

The Foundation Center: 79 Fifth Avenue, New York, NY 10003. Telephone: 800/424-9836 or 212/620-4230, Fax: 212/807-3677, Web: fdncenter.org. Provides referrals to local centers for information regarding scholarships and grants.

NCLD'S RESOURCE LIST

SUMMER CAMPS

The Advisory Service on Private Schools and Camps: 501 East Boston Post Road, Mamaroneck, NY 10543. Telephone: 914/381-8096, Web: www.westnet.com/advisoryservice, Email: asops@westnet.com. A referral service for sleep-away camps and private boarding schools.

Learning Disabilities Association of America: 4156 Library Road, Pittsburgh, PA 15234. Telephone: 888/300-6710 or 412/341-1515, Fax: 412/344-0224, Web: www.ldanatl.org, Email: ldanatl@usaor.net. Publishes the *Summer Camp Directory*.

American Camping Association: 5000 State Road, 67 North, Martinsville, IN 46151. Telephone: 800/428-2267 or 765/342-8456, Fax: 765/342-2065, Web: www.aca-camps.org. Publishes directory of special summer camps entitled Guide to Accredited Camps.

National Camp Association: 610 Fifth Avenue, P.O. Box 5371, New York, NY 10185. Telephone: 212/645-0653 or 800/966-CAMP, Fax: 914/354-5501, Web: www.summercamp.org, Email: info@summercamp.org. Provides personalized guidance and referrals to sleep-away camps.

INFORMATION GUIDES AND DIRECTORIES

Exceptional Parent: Psy-Ed Corporation, 555 Kinderkamack Road, Oradell, NJ 07649. Telephone: 800/562-1973 or 800/247-8080, Web: www.familyeducation.com. This organization produces a comprehensive, yearly resource guide that lists many sources of help (both private and government) for professionals and families.

The Complete Learning Disabilities Directory: Grey House Publishing, Inc., Pocket Knife Square, Lakeville, CT 06039. Telephone:

800/562-2139 or 860/435-0868, Fax: 860/435-0867, Web: www.greyhouse.com.

Peterson's Private Secondary Schools: Peterson's, P.O. Box 2123, Princeton, NJ 08543-2123. Telephone: 800/338-3282 or 609/243-9111, Fax: 609/452-0966, Web: petersons.com, Email: custsvc@petersons.com.

NCLD Regional Resource Listing
Contact NCLD for a listing of private schools, colleges, clinics, programs, summer camps, and other national and local resources. Toll-free National Information & Referral: 888/575-7373. Web: www.ncld.org.

GIFTED/LD

RESOURCES

The Council for Exceptional Children (CEC): 1920 Association Drive, Reston, VA 20191-5989. Telephone: 888-232-7733, Fax: 703/264-9494, Web: www.cec.sped.org. A non-profit, membership organization that has 17 specialized divisions including The Association for the Gifted (TAG).

ERIC Clearinghouse on Disabilities and Gifted Education (ERIC/EC): The Council for Exceptional Children, 1920 Association Drive, Reston, VA 20191-5989. Telephone: 800/328-0272, Web: www.cec.sped.org/ericec.htm, Email: ericec@cec.sped.org. Electronic Answering System: askeric@ericir.syr.edu. A national information system on education with a large database of education materials. Publishes and disseminates information, serves as a resource center for the general public, and promotes the dissemination of research.

National Association for Gifted Children (NAGC): 1707 L Street, NW, Suite 550, Washington, DC 20036. Telephone: 202/785-4268, Web: www.nagc.org, Email:

nagc@nagc.org. Membership advocacy group that offers information to educators, administrators, and parents. Publishes a quarterly parents' magazine.

Hollingworth Center for Highly Gifted Children: 827 Central Avenue, Suite 282, Dover, NH 03820-2506. Telephone: 207/655-3767. National membership organization that provides information and referrals. Publishes a quarterly newsletter and sponsors conferences.

Institute for the Academic Advancement of Youth (IAAY): Johns Hopkins University, 3400 North Charles Street, Baltimore, MD 21218. Telephone: 410/516-0337 or 0278, Fax: 410/516-0108 or 0325, Web: www.jhu.edu/~gifted, Email: durdenwg@jhunix.hcf.jhu.edu. A comprehensive, university-based initiative for gifted students throughout the world. Offers education programs in mathematics, the sciences, and the humanities tailored to the students' abilities.

Talent Identification Program (TIP): Duke University, 1121 West Main Street, Suite 100, Durham, NC 27701. Telephone: 919/683-1400, Fax: 919/683-1742, Web: www.tip.duke.edu. Identifies gifted students and provides model programs and services to ensure that students develop and realize their full potential.

Center for Talent Development (CTD): Northwestern University, 617 Dartmouth Place, Evanston, IL 60208. Telephone: 847/491-3782, Fax: 847/467-4283, Web: www.ctd.nwu.edu, Email: t-mikolyzk@nwu.edu. Offers programs that identify, promote, and develop abilities of gifted children. Programs include talent searches and summer academic programs.

Rocky Mountain Talent Search: University of Denver, 2135 East Wesley, Denver, CO 80208. Telephone: 303/871-2983, Fax: 303/871-3422, Web: www.du.edu/education/ces/rmts.html,

Email: rradclif@du.edu. Provides information and programs for gifted students.

PUBLICATIONS

Baum, S.M., Owen, S.V., & Dixon, J. (1991). *To Be Gifted & Learning Disabled*. Mansfield Center, CT: Creative Learning Press.

Center for Talented Youth. (1994). *The Gifted Learning Disabled Student*. Baltimore, MD: CTY Publications and Resources, The Johns Hopkins University.

ADD/ADHD

RESOURCES

Children and Adults with Attention Deficit/Hyperactivity Disorder (CHADD): 8181 Professional Place, Suite 201, Landover, MD 20785. Telephone: 800/233-4050 or 301/306-7070. Fax: 301/306-7090. Web: www.chadd.org, Email: national@chadd.org. National non-profit membership organization that provides information, sponsors conferences, holds meetings, and has support groups.

The Attention Deficit Information Network, Inc. (AD-IN): 475 Hillside Avenue, Needham, MA 02194. Telephone: 781/455-9895, Fax: 781/444-5466, Web: www.addinfonetwork.com, Email: adin@gis.net. Non-profit volunteer organization with a network of affiliated support groups that provides information and support to families, children, adults, and professionals. Sponsors an annual conference.

The National Attention Deficit Disorder Association (ADDA): P.O. Box 1303, Northbrook, IL 60065-1303. Web: www.add.org, Email: mail@add.org. National membership organization that focuses on adults and families. Provides referrals to local support groups, holds national conferences and symposiums, and offers materials on ADD and related issues.

ADDult Support Network: 20620 Ivy Place, Toledo, OH 43613. Volunteer organization that provides referrals to local support groups.

PUBLICATIONS

Alexander-Roberts, C. (1995). *ADHD and Teens: A Parent's Guide to Making It Through the Teen Years.* Dallas, TX: Taylor Publishing Company.

Barem, M. (1994). *Hyperactivity and Attention Disorders in Children.* San Ramon, CA: HIN, Inc.

Barkley, R.A. (1995). *Taking Charge of ADHD: The Complete Authoritative Guide for Parents.* New York, NY: Guildford Press.

CH.A.D.D. (1992). *CH.A.D.D. Educator's Manual.* Plantation, FL: CH.A.D.D.

Dendy, C.A.Z. (1995). *Teenagers with ADD: A Parents' Guide.* Bethesda, MD: Woodbine House.

Hallowell, E.M. & Ratey, J. (1996). *Answers to Distraction.* New York, NY: Bantam Books.

Hallowell, E.M. & Ratey, J. (1995). *Driven to Distraction.* New York, NY: Simon & Schuster.

Nadeau, K.G. (ed). (1995). *A Comprehensive Guide to Attention Deficit Disorder in Adults: Research, Diagnosis, Treatment.* New York, NY: Brunner Mazel Inc.

Parker, H. (1992). *The ADD Hyperactivity Workbook for Schools.* San Luis Obispo, CA: Impact Publications, Inc.

Parker, H. (1988). *The ADD Hyperactivity Workbook for Parents, Teachers and Kids.* San Luis Obispo, CA: Impact Publications, Inc.

Quinn, P.O. (1995). *Adolescents and ADD: Gaining the Advantage.* New York, NY: Magination Press.

Quinn, P.O. & Stern, J.M. (1993). *The "Putting on the Brakes" Activity Book for Young People with ADHD.* New York, NY: Magination Press.

Quinn, P.O. & Stern, J.M. (1992). *Putting On the Brakes: Young People's Guide to Understanding Attention Deficit Hyperactivity Disorder.* New York, NY: Magination Press.

Rief, S.F. (1998), *The ADD/ADHD Checklist: An Easy Reference for Parents and Teachers.* Saddle River, NJ: Prentice Hall.

Rief, S.F. (1993). *How to Reach and Teach ADD/ADHD Children.* West Nyack, NY: The Center for Applied Research in Education.

LITERACY

Literacy Volunteers of America (LVA): 635 James Street, Syracuse, NY 13203. Telephone: 315/472-0001, Fax: 315/472-0002, Web: www.literacyvolunteers.org, Email: lvanat@aol.com. National non-profit organization that provides literacy opportunities for adults.

National Center for Family Literacy (NCFL): Waterfront Plaza, 325 West Main Street, Suite 300, Louisville, KY 40202-4251. Telephone: 502/584-1133, Toll-free Literacy Infoline: 877/326-5481. Fax: 502/584-0172. Web: www.famlit.org, Email: ncfl@famlit.org. Non-profit educational organization whose mission is to advance and support family literacy services for families across the United States. Programs include dissemination of information about family literacy, advocacy, research, and training.

National Institute for Literacy (NIFL): 1775 I Street, NW, Suite 730, Washington, DC 20006. Telephone: 800/228-8813 or 202/233-2025,

THEIR WORLD 2000

NCLD'S RESOURCE LIST

Fax: 202/233-2050, Web: www.nifl.gov. Federal agency that provides leadership through advocacy, information sharing, and collaboration.

National Clearinghouse for ESL Literacy Education (NCLE): 4646 40th Street, NW, Washington, DC 20001. Telephone: 202/429-9292, Fax: 202/362-3740 Web: cal.org/ncle, Email: ncle@cal.org. Provides literacy education for adults and out-of-school youth who are learning English as a second language.

International Reading Association (IRA): 800 Barksdale Road, P.O. Box 8139, Newark, DE 19714-8139. Telephone: 800/336-7323 or 302/731-1600, Fax: 302/731-1057, Web: www.reading.org, Email: pubinfo@reading.org. Non-profit membership organization that publishes journals and a newsletter for teachers, researchers, and professionals. A catalog of books, videos, and other materials is available.

HOMESCHOOLING

Homeschool Legal Defense Association: P.O. Box 3000, Purcellville, VA 20134. Telephone: 540/338-5600, Fax: 540/338-2733, Web: www.hslda.org. Membership organization that offers legal assistance on homeschooling issues.

National Homeschool Association (NHA): P.O. Box 290, Hartland, MI 48353-0290. Telephone: 513/772-9580, Web: www.n-h-a.org. Non-profit membership organization that offers lists of support groups, magazines, books, and organizations.

INDEPENDENT LIVING

Independent Living Research Utilization Program (ILRU): 2323 South Shepherd, Suite 1000, Houston, TX 77019. Telephone: 713/520-0232, Fax: 713/520-5785, Web: www.ilru.org, Email: ilru@ilru.org. National

resource center that produces materials, develops and conducts training programs, and publishes a quarterly newsletter.

National Council on Independent Living (NCIL): 1916 Wilson Boulevard, Suite 209, Arlington, VA 22201. Telephone: 703/525-3406, Fax: 703/525-3409, Email: ncil@tsbbs02.tnet.com. Cross-disability grassroots national advocacy organization that provides referrals to independent living facilities around the nation.

TECHNOLOGY RESOURCES

Alliance for Technology Access: 2175 East Francisco Boulevard, Suite L, San Rafael, CA 94901. Telephone: 800/455-7970 or 415/455-4575. Fax: 415/455-0654. Web: www.atacess.org, Email: atainfo@ataccess.org. National network of 40 community-based resource centers that offer information and assistance about technology for people with disabilities. Contact the headquarters for local listings.

Rehabilitation Engineering and Assistive Technology Society of North America: 1700 North Moore Street, Suite 1540, Arlington, VA 22209-1903. Telephone: 703/524-6686. Web: www.resna.org, Email: natloffice@resna.org. Maintains a listing of State Assistive Technology Programs which are funded under the Technology-Related Assistance for Individuals Act of 1988 and its amendments.

BOOKS ON TAPE

Recording for the Blind & Dyslexic (RFB&D): 20 Roszel Road, Princeton, NJ 08540. Telephone: 800/221-4792 or 609/452-0606, Fax: 609/520-7990, Web: www.rfbd.org. International non-profit organization that loans recorded and computerized books at all academic levels to people who cannot read standard print.

NCLD'S RESOURCE LIST

National Library Service for the Blind and Physically Handicapped: Library of Congress, 1291 Taylor Street, NW, Washington, DC 20542. Telephone: 800/424-8567 or 202/707-5100, Fax: 202/707-0712, Web: www.loc.gov\nls, Email: nls@loc.gov. Provides books on tape to children and adults with learning disabilities. Contact your local library for further information.

WEB SITES

Listed below are Web sites that have information applicable to the field of LD. In addition to the information that can be found on these sites, they offer links to many other sites.

LD OnLine: This comprehensive Web site offers information on all aspects of LD, an events calendar, bulletin boards, chats with experts, publications, and videos as well as artwork and writing by children with LD. This site is provided by WETA Public Television in association with the Coordinated Campaign for Learning Disabilities. **www.ldonline.org**

U.S. Department of Education: This official Web site of the U.S. Department of Education lists many educational programs, policies, and news updates. **www.ed.gov**

National Center for Education Statistics: This program's site, run though the U.S. Department of Education, offers publications, statistics, and surveys on education-related issues. **http://nces.ed.gov**

National Academy of Sciences: This Web site has information relating to the work of the programs within the National Academy of Sciences, which includes research in education. **www.nas.edu**

National Institutes of Health: This site features the work of the various Institutes at the National Institutes of Health and includes information on LD and related issues. **www.nih.gov**

National Library of Medicine's MEDLINE*plus*: This site offers access to a free database on medical and education-related topics. **www.nlm.nih.gov/medlineplus**

The National Reading Panel: This Web site offers literature about reading and links to related groups. **www.nationalreadingpanel.org**

Library of Congress: This site offers book and topical index searches and it also links to the Web sites of many local government offices. **http://lcweb.loc.gov**

THOMAS: This site, which is a service of The Library of Congress, allows for searches of current and pending legislation. **http://thomas.loc.gov**

BIBLIOGRAPHY

BOOKS ABOUT LEARNING DISABILITIES AND RELATED TOPICS

Adams, M.J. (1994). *Beginning to Read: Thinking and Learning About Print.* Bradford Books.

Adams, M.J., Foorman, B.R., Lundberg, I., et al. (1997). *Phonemic Awareness in Young Children: A Classroom Curriculum.* Baltimore, MD: Paul H. Brookes Publishing Co.

Algozzine, B. & Ysseldyke, J. (1997). *Strategies and Tactics for Effective Instruction: Time Savers for Educators.* Longmont, CO: Sopris West.

Algozzine, B. & Ysseldyke, J. (eds.) (1995). *Tactics for Improving Parenting Skills.* Longmont, CO: Sopris West.

NCLD'S RESOURCE LIST

Bain, A.M., Lyons, B.L., & Moats, C.L. (1991). *Written Language Disorders: Theory into Practice.* Austin, TX: PRO-ED.

Blevins, W. (1997). *Phonemic Awareness Activities for Early Reading Success.* New York, NY: Scholastic Inc.

Blevins, W. (1998). *Phonics from A to Z: A Practical Guide.* New York, NY: Scholastic Inc.

Bloom, J. (1991). *Help Me To Help My Child.* Waltham, MA: Little Brown and Company.

Bos, C.S. & Vaughn, S. (1997). *Strategies for Teaching Students with Learning and Behavior Problems.* Needham Heights, MA: Allyn & Bacon.

Brooks, R. (1991). *The Self-Esteem Teacher.* Circle Pines, MN: American Guidance Service.

Brown, F.R., Aylward, E.H., & Keogh, B.K. (1992). *Diagnosis and Management of Learning Disabilities: An Interdisciplinary/Lifestyle Approach.* San Diego, CA: Singular Publishing Group, Inc.

Carnine, D.W., Silbert, J., & Kameenui, E.J. (1997). *Direct Instruction Reading* (3rd edition). Upper Saddle River, NJ: Prentice-Hall, Inc.

Clark, R., Hawkins, D., & Vachon, B. (1999). *The School-Savvy Parent: 365 Insider Tips to Help You Help Your Child.* Minneapolis, MN: Free Spirit Publishing Inc.

Clarke, L. (1996). *SOS: Help for Parents.* KY: Parent Press.

Cramer, S.C. & Ellis, W. (eds.) (1996). *Learning Disabilities: Lifelong Issues.* Baltimore, MD: Paul H. Brookes Publishing Co.

Dane, E. (1990). *Painful Passages: Working with Children with Learning Disabilities.* Silver Spring, MD: NASW Press.

Deshler, D., Ellis, E., & Lenz, K. (eds.) (1996). *Teaching Adolescents with Learning Disabilities: Strategies and Methods.* Denver, CO: Love Publishing Company.

Dunn, K.B. & Dunn, A.B. (1993). *A Family Story About Learning Disabilities.* Rockville, MD: Woodbine House.

Gadbow, N.F. & DuBois, D.A. (1998). *Adult Learners with Special Needs: Strategies and Resources for Postsecondary Education and Workplace Training.* Kreiger Publishing Co.

Gerber, P. & Brown, D. (eds.) (1997). *Learning Disabilities and Employment.* Austin, TX: PRO-ED.

Gerber, P. & Reiff, H.B. (eds.) (1994). *Learning Disabilities in Adulthood: Persisting Problems and Evolving Issues.* Austin, TX: PRO-ED.

Gerber, P., Reiff, H.B., & Ginsberg, R. (1997). *Exceeding Expectations: Successful Adults With Learning Disabilities.* Austin, TX: PRO-ED.

Gregg, N., Hoy, C., & Gay, A.F. (eds.) (1996). *Adults with Learning Disabilities: Theoretical and Practical Perspectives.* New York, NY: Guilford Press.

Hall, J.K., Grimes, A.E., & Salas, B. (1999). *Evaluating and Improving Written Expression.* (3rd edition). Austin, TX: PRO-ED.

Hallahan, D.P., Kauffman J.M., & Lloyd, J.W. (1998). *Introduction to Learning Disabilities.* Needham Heights, MA: Allyn & Bacon.

Hallowell. E. (1997). *When You Worry About the Child You Love.* New York, NY: Simon & Schuster.

Harris, K.R. & Graham, S. (1996). *Making the Writing Process Work: Strategies for Composition and Self-Regulation.* Cambridge, MA: Brookline Books.

NCLD'S RESOURCE LIST

Harris, K.R., Graham, S., Deshler, D., & Pressley, M. (1997). *Teaching Every Child Every Day: Learning in Diverse Schools and Classrooms.* Cambridge, MA: Brookline Books.

Johnson, P.F. (1997). *125 Ways to Be a Better Writer.* East Moline, IL: LinguiSystems, Inc.

Kozloff, M.A. (1994). *Improving Educational Outcomes for Children with Disabilities: Principles for Assessment, Program Planning, and Evaluation.* Baltimore, MD: Paul H. Brookes Publishing Co.

Kranowitz, C.S. (1998). *The Out-of-Sync Child: Recognizing and Coping With Sensory Integration Dysfunction.* New York, NY: Perigree.

Lauren, J. (1997). *Succeeding with LD: 20 True Stories About Real People with LD.* Minneapolis, MN: Free Spirit Publishing.

Lerner, J. (1997). *Learning Disabilities: Theories, Diagnosis, and Teaching Strategies.* (7th edition). Boston, MA: Houghton Mifflin.

Levine, M. (1994). *Educational Care: A System for Understanding and Helping Children with Learning Problems at Home and in School.* Cambridge, MA: Educators Publishing Service, Inc.

Levine, M. (1991). *Keeping A Head in School.* Cambridge, MA: Educators Publishing Service, Inc.

Lyon, G.R. (1996). *Neuroimaging: A Window to the Neurological Foundations of Learning and Behavior in Children.* Baltimore, MD: Paul H. Brookes Publishing Co.

Lyon, G.R. (ed.) (1994). *Frames of Reference for the Assessment of Learning Disabilities: New Views on Measurement Issues.* Baltimore, MD: Paul H. Brookes Publishing Co.

Lyon, G.R. (ed.) (1993). *Better Understanding Learning Disabilities: New Views from Research and Their Implications for Education and Public Policies.* Baltimore, MD: Paul H. Brookes Publishing Co.

Lyon, G.R. & Krasnegor, N.A. (1996). *Attention, Memory, and Executive Function.* Baltimore, MD: Paul H. Brookes Publishing Co.

Mastropieri, M. & Scruggs, T. (1992). *Teaching Test Taking Skills: Helping Students Show What They Know.* Cambridge, MA: Brookline Books.

Mastropieri, M. & Scruggs, T. (1991). *Teaching Students Ways to Remember: Strategies for Learning Mnemonically.* Cambridge, MA: Brookline Books.

McGuinness, D. (1999). *Why Our Children Can't Read and What We Can Do About It: A Scientific Revolution in Reading.* New York, NY: Simon & Schuster.

Murphy, S.T. (1996). *On Being LD: Perspectives and Strategies of Young Adults.* New York, NY: Teachers College Press.

National Commission on Teaching & America's Future (1996). *What Matters Most: Teaching for America's Future.* New York, NY: National Commission on Teaching & America's Future.

Nosek, K. (1995). *The Dyslexic Scholar: Helping Your Child Succeed in the School System.* Dallas, TX: Taylor Publishing.

Novick, B.Z. & Arnold, M.M. (1991). *Why is My Child Having Trouble at School? A Parent's Guide to Learning Disabilities.* New York, NY: Villard Books.

Olivier, C. & Bowler, R. (1996). *Learning to Learn.* New York, NY: Fireside.

Osman, B.B. (1997). *Learning Disabilities and ADHD: A Family Guide to Living and Learning Together.* New York, NY: John Wiley & Sons, Inc.

Osman, B.B. (1996). *No One to Play With.* Novato, CA: Academic Therapy Press.

Rief, S.F. & Heimburge, J.A. (1996). *How to Reach & Teach All Students in the Inclusive Classrooms: Ready-To-Use Strategies, Lessons and Activities.* West Nyack, NY: Center for Applied Research in Education.

Rourke, B. (1989). *Non Verbal Learning Disabilities: The Syndrome and The Model.* New York, NY: Guilford Press.

Sedita, J. (1989). *The Landmark Study Skills Guide.* Prides Crossing, MA: Landmark School (also available in Spanish).

Silver, L.B. (1998). *The Misunderstood Child: Understanding and Coping With Your Child's Learning Disabilities.* (3rd edition). New York, NY: Times Books.

Smith, C. & Strick, L. (1999). *Learning Disabilities A to Z: A Parent's Complete Guide to Learning Disabilities from Preschool to Adulthood.* New York, NY: Simon & Schuster.

Smith, S.L. (1996). *No Easy Answers: The Learning Disabled Child at Home and at School.* New York, NY: Bantam.

Smith, S.L. (1994). *Different is Not Bad, Different is the World: A Book About Learning Disabilities.* Longmont, CO: Sopris West.

Smith, T.E.C., Dowdy, C.A., et al. (1997). *Children and Adults with Learning Disabilities.* Needham Heights, MA: Allyn & Bacon.

Spear-Swerling, L. & Sternberg, R. (1996). *Off Track: When Poor Readers Become Learning Disabled.* Westview Press.

Stevens, S.H. (1996). *Classroom Success for the Learning Disabled.* Winston-Salem, NC: John F. Blair.

Tuttle, C. & Tuttle, G.A. (1995). *Challenging Voices: Writings By, For, and About People with Learning Disabilities.* Los Angeles, CA: Lowell House.

Vail, P. (1992). *Learning Styles: Food for Thought and 130 Practical Tips.* Rosemont, NJ: Modern Learning Press - Programs for Education.

Vogel, S.A. & Reder, S. (1998). *Learning Disabilities, Literacy, and Adult Education.* Baltimore, MD: Paul H. Brookes Publishing Co.

West, T.G. (1997). *In the Mind's Eye.* Buffalo, NY: Prometheus Books.

Wong, B. (1996). *The ABC's of Learning Disabilities.* New York, NY: Academic Press Inc.

BOOKS FOR AND ABOUT CHILDREN WITH LEARNING DISABILITIES

Aiello, B. (1993). *Secrets Aren't Always for Keeps.* Twenty-First Century Books.

Banks, J.T. (1995). *Egg-Drop Blues.* Boston, MA: Houghton Mifflin Company.

Bentancourt, J. (1994). *My Name is Brian.* New York, NY: Scholastic Inc.

Bezzant, P. (1994). *Angie.* Fawcett Book Group.

Blue, R. (1979). *Me and Einstein Breaking Through the Reading Barrier.* New York, NY: Human Sciences Press.

Carris, J. (1990). *Aunt Morbelia and the Screaming Skulls.* Demco Media.

Gehret, J. (1996). *The Don't-Give-Up Kid and Learning Differences.* Fairport, NY: Verbal Images Press.

NCLD'S RESOURCE LIST

Griffith, J. (1997). *How Dyslexic Benny Became a Star: A Story of Hope for Dyslexic Children and Their Parents.* Yorktown Press.

Hughes, S. (1990). *Ryan: A Mother's Story of her Hyperactive/Tourette Syndrome Child.* Duarte, CA: Hope Press.

Janover, C. (1988). *Josh: A Boy with Dyslexia.* USA: Waterfront Books.

Kline, S. (1986). *Herbie Jones.* New York, NY: Puffin Books.

Levine, M. (1993). *All Kinds of Minds: A Young Student's Book About Learning Abilities and Learning Disorders.* Cambridge, MA: Educators Publishing Service, Inc.

McNamara, B. & McNamara, F. (1995). *Keys to Parenting a Child with Learning Disabilities.* Long Island, NY: Barron Educational Series, Inc.

Moss, D.M. (1989). *Shelly the Hyperactive Turtle.* Rockville, MD: Woodbine House, Inc.

Philbrick, W.R. (1993). *Freak the Mighty.* New York, NY: Scholastic Inc.

Polacco, P. (1998). *Thank You, Mr. Falker.* New York, NY: Putnam Publishing Group.

Roby, C. (1994). *When Learning is Tough: Kids Talk About Their Learning Disabilities.* Morton Grove, IL: Alberter Whitman and Company.

Stern, J. & Ben-Ami, U. (1996). *Many Ways to Learn: Young People's Guide to Learning Disabilities.* New York, NY: Magination Press.

JOURNALS AND PERIODICALS

Journal of Learning Disabilities
Remedial and Special Education
Journal of Special Education
Pro-Ed
8700 Shoal Creek Boulevard
Austin, TX 78757-6897
Telephone: 800/897-3202 or 512/451-3246
Fax: 800/397-7633
Web: http://www.proedinc.com

The DLD Times Newsletter
Exceptional Children
Teaching Exceptional Children
The Council for Exceptional Children
1920 Association Drive
Reston, VA 20191-5989
Telephone: 888/232-7733.
Fax: 703/264-9494.
Web: www.cec.sped.org

Annals of Dyslexia
Perspectives
The International Dyslexia Association
(formerly The Orton Dyslexia Society)
Chester Building, Suite 382
8600 LaSalle Road
Baltimore, MD 21286-2044
Telephone: 410/296-0232
Fax: 410/321-5069
Web: http://www.interdys.org
Email: info@interdys.org

LDA Newsbriefs
Learning Disabilities: A Multi-Disciplinary Journal
Learning Disabilities Association of America
4156 Library Road
Pittsburgh, PA 15234
Telephone: 412/341-1515 or 888/300-6710
Fax: 412/344-0224
Web: www.ldanatl.org
Email: ldanatl@usaor.net

THEIR WORLD 2000

NCLD'S RESOURCE LIST

Learning Disabilities: Research and Practice
Lawrence Erlbaum Associates
10 Industrial Avenue
Mahwah, NJ 07430
Telephone: 800/926-6579 or 201/236-9500
Fax: 201/236-0072
Web: http://www.erlbaum.com
Email: orders@erlbaum.com

Learning Disabilities Quarterly
Council for Learning Disabilities
P.O. Box 40303
Overland Park, KS 66204
Telephone: 913/492-8755
Fax: 913/492-2546
Web: coe.winthrop.edu\cld\

VIDEO TAPES AND AUDIO TAPES

Every Child is Learning: A 45-minute video with accompanying manual to help parents, teachers, and early-care providers recognize early warning signs for language and learning disabilities. Produced by NCLD. $89.90, including postage and handling. Contact: NCLD, 381 Park Avenue South, Suite 1401, New York, NY 10016. Telephone: 888/575-7373.

Bridges to Reading: A comprehensive kit of first-step strategies to help identify, understand, and address reading problems. Kit includes eight booklets, two audio tapes, and resources. Produced by Schwab Foundation for Learning. Contact: Schwab Foundation for Learning at 1650 South Amphlett Boulevard, Suite 300, San Mateo, CA 94402-2516. Telephone: 800/230-0988.

Learning Disabilities/Learning Abilities: A comprehensive video series consisting of six tapes that draws on current research from the National Institutes of Child Health to understand and improve the teaching of students with learning disabilities. Contact: Vineyard Video Productions, P.O. Box 370, West Tisbury, MA 02575-0370.

Telephone: 800/664-6119.

How Difficult Can This Be? F.A.T. CITY: A 70-minute video by Rick Lavoie that explores the difficulties faced by children with learning disabilities. $49.95 + $5.00 shipping and handling. Contact: CACLD, 25 Van Zant Street, Suite 15-5, East Norwalk, CT 06855-1729. Telephone: 203/838-5010.

I'm Not Stupid: A 53-minute video that depicts the constant battles the child with learning disabilities has in school. $22.00 (handling not included). Contact: Learning Disabilities Association of America, 4156 Library Road, Pittsburgh, PA 15234. Telephone: 412/341-1515.

Last One Picked...First One Picked On: (Parent and teacher versions) A video by Rick Lavoie that addresses the social problems of children with learning disabilities. Offers practical solutions for teachers and parents. $49.95 + $6.00 shipping and handling. Contact: PBS Video, 1320 Braddock Place, Alexandria, VA 22314-1698. Telephone: 800/344-3337.

L.D. Stories/L.D. Stories II/On the Edge: A 13-minute animated video produced by Lab School students about what it is like to have learning disabilities. Contact: The Lab School of Washington, 4759 Reservoir Road, NW, Washington, D.C. 20007. Telephone: 202/965-6600.

Lab School Audiotape Series: Collection of audiotapes featuring 12 of the most popular programs from The Lab School Lecture Series for parents and professionals. Topics include: social problems of children with LD, controversies about ADD and treatment, and confidence in parenting. For a complete listing and more information, contact: The Lab School of Washington. Telephone: 202/965-6600.

NCLD'S RESOURCE LIST

Reaching Minds: An audio cassette subscription series hosted by Mel Levine, M.D., that is geared to helping parents help their children with learning differences. For further information, call 800/720-AKOM.

NATIONAL CENTER FOR LEARNING DISABILITIES

381 Park Avenue South, Suite 1401
New York, New York 10016
Toll-free National Information & Referral:
888/575-7373
Telephone: 212/545-7510
Fax: 212/545-9665
Web: www.ncld.org

ADDITIONAL RESOURCES AVAILABLE
FROM NCLD'S NATIONAL INFORMATION &
REFERRAL SERVICE

Information on these and other topics is available free of charge:
Early Warning Signs of Learning Disabilities
Learning Disabilities Awareness Checklist
Learning Disabilities: General Information
Adults with Learning Disabilities
College Issues (including a
    Financial Aid Information packet)
Inclusion
Juvenile Delinquency and Learning Disabilities
The Evaluation Process
Choosing the Right School
Legal Rights of Children and Youth
    Who Have Learning Disabilities
Dyscalculia (Difficulty With Mathematics)
Dysgraphia (Difficulty With Written Expression)
Dyspraxia (Difficulty with Motor Planning)
Dyslexia (Difficulty with Language)
Visual and Auditory Processing Disorders
Giftedness and Learning Disabilities
Attention-Deficit/Hyperactivity Disorder
Social Skills and Self-Esteem
Technology and Computer Software
NCLD's Tips (several one-page tips for parents

and teachers of children with LD as well as adults with LD)

Regional Resource Listing (request resources for up to three states): private schools, colleges, clinics, programs, summer camps, and other sources of help from our resource database.

APPENDIX B-2

ADDITIONAL RESOURCES

The following list of resources, assembled by the Learning Disabilities Council, are additions to those in Appendix B-1, "NCLD's Resource List."

CONTENTS

ADD/ADHD
Employment and Related Issues
Gifted/LD
Independent Living
Legal Issues
Literacy
Related Organizations

ADD/ADHD

ADD-Parents
A forum for parents of children with Attention Deficit Disorder. New subscriptions must be approved by the list owner. The list owner is Deborah J. Ruppert (phoenix@clearspring.com).

> To subscribe, send mail to:
> listserver@ourfriends.com
> In the body of your message, type:
> subscribe addparents

ADD-Adults
A forum for discussing the more personal aspects of living as or with an adult with Attention Deficit Disorder and for professionals who work with ADDults. **This is a high volume list, averaging between 75 and 150 messages every day.** The list owners are Jim McLean-Lipinsk (jmclip@world.std.com) and Beth Dodge (dodge@pcnet.com).

> To subscribe:
> 1. Send e-mail message to address: listserv@maelstrom.stjohns.edu
> 2. Leave subject blank

3. In the body of your e-mail note write the following (start in column 1)
subscribe ADDult firstname lastname
ADDULT@MAELSTROM.STJOHNS.EDU

Employment and Related Issues

Council for Exceptional Children, Division on Career Development and Transition
1110 North Glebe Road, Suite 300
Arlington, VA 22201-5704
703-620-3660
1-888-CEC-SPED
FAX: 703-264-9494#
TTY: (text only)703-264-9446
Web: www.cec.sped.org/

ERIC Clearinghouse on Adult, Career, & Vocational Education at the Center for Employment, Education & Training at Ohio State University
College of Education
The Ohio State University
1900 Kenny Road
Columbus OH 43210-1090
614-292-7069
1-800-848-4815 ext 2-7069
FAX: 614-292-1260
TTY/TDD: 614-688-8734
E-mail: ericacve@postbox.acs.ohio_state.edu
Web: www.ericacve.org

National Rehabilitation Information Center (NARIC)
8455 Colesville Road, Suite 935
Silver Spring, MD 20910-3319.
301-588-9284
1-800-346-2742
TTY: 301-495-5626

E-mail: naric@capaccess.org
Web: www.naric.com

President's Committee on Employment of People with Disabilities
1331 F Street NW, Suite 300
Washington, DC 20004
202-376-6200
FAX: 202-376-6219
TTY: 202-376-6205
E-mail: info@pcepd.gov
Web: www.pcepd.gov
Web: www.50.pcepd.gov/pcepd

Gifted/LD

Parents of Gifted/LD Children, Inc.
2420 Eccleston Street
Silver Spring, MD 20902
301-986-1422
FAX: 301-565-7809
FAX: 301-929-9304
E-mail: Jilmeyers@aol.com
Web:
www.geocities.com/athens/1105/gtld.html

Independent Living

Research and Training Center on Independent Living
University of Kansas
4089 Dole Building
Lawrence, KS 66045-2930
913-864-4095 (Voice/TTY)
FAX: 785-865-5063
E-mail: rtcil@kuhub.cc.ukans.edu
Web: www.lsi.ukans.edu/rtcil/rtcil.htm

Legal Issues

Center for Children's Advocacy, Inc.
University of Connecticut School of Law
63 Elizabeth Street
Hartford, CT 06105
860-510-5327
Web: www.kidscounsel.org

Children's Defense Fund Action Council
25 E Street, NW
Washington, DC 20001
202-662-3576
(legal rights information)

E-mail:
cdfactioncouncil@childrensdefense.org

Council of Parent Attorneys and Advocates (COPAA)
1321 Pennsylvania Ave., SE
Washington, DC 20003-3027
Voice - (202) 544-2210
P.O. Box 81-7327
Hollywood, FL 33081-0327
954-966-4489
FAX: 954-966-8561
Web: www.copaa.net

FAPE – Family & Advocates Partnership for Education
A project which aims to inform and educate families and advocates about IDEA, the Individuals with Disabilities Education Act of 1997. For legal and advocacy topics addressed at this site see:
www.fape.org/main.html

IDEA – The Individuals with Disabilities Education Act is available at:
www.ed.gov/offices/OSERS/IDEA/index.html

National Center for Law and Learning Disabilities (NCLLD)
Up-to-date information about effective advocacy for children with disabilities.
P.O. Box 368
Cabin John, MD 20818
301-469-8308
FAX: 301-469-9466
Web: www.his.com/~plath3/nclld.html

Wright's Law
Peter W.D. Wright
P.O. Box 1008
Deltaville, VA 23043
804-776-7008
E-mail: pwright@wrightslaw.com
Web: www.Wrightslaw.com

(See also "The Nation's Disability Rights Network" in Appendix B-3.)

Literacy

National Institute for Literacy
1775 I Street, NW Suite 730
Washington, DC 20006-2401
202-233-2025

FAX: 202-233-2050
E-mail: listproc@literacy.nifl.gov
Web: http://novel.nifl.gov/

E-mail: webmaster@seriweb.com
Web: www.seriweb.com

Related Organizations

ASPEN of America
An organization for Asperger's Syndrome
and Nonverbal Learning Disabilities.
P.O. Box 2577
Jacksonville, FL 32203-2577
904-745-6741
Web: www.asperger.org

Developmental Delay Resources (DDR)
6701 Fairfax Road
Chevy Chase, MD 20815
Developmental Delay Resources
4401 East West Highway, Suite 207
Bethesda, MD 20814
301-652-2263
E-mail: devdelay@mindspring.com
Web: www.devdelay.org

Federation of Families for Children's Mental Health
1101 King Street, Suite 420
Alexandria, VA 22314
703-684-7710
Web: www.ffcmh.org

Learning Disabilities Council
PO Box 8451
Richmond, VA 23226
804-748-5012

National Council on Educational Outcomes (NCEO)
University of Minnesota
350 Elliott Hall
75 East River Road
Minneapolis, MN 55455
612-626-1530
FAX: 612-624-0879
Web: www.coled.umn.edu/nceo

Special Education at About.com
Valuable resources for information on
disabilities and special education topics.
Web: www.specialed.guide@about.com/

Special Education Resources on the Internet (SERI)
List of internet resources on disabilities and
special education topics.

APPENDIX B-3

AGENCIES BY STATE

The following Websites offer a starting point for parents wishing to locate official agencies in each state. Most public libraries offer internet access, and a reference librarian is usually available to help you view Websites.

1. State Education Agencies – Provide information, resources, and technical assistance on educational matters to schools and residents. For a state-by-state listing, see:
www.ed.gov/Programs/bastmp/SEA.htm

2. State Directors of Special Education – Ensure appropriate services and opportunities for children and youth with disabilities. For a state-by-state listing, see:
www.ed.gov/Programs/bastmp/SDSE.htm

3. State Vocational Rehabilitation Agency – Coordinates and provides counseling, evaluation, and job placement services for people with disabilities. For a state-by-state listing, see:
www.ed.gov/Programs/bastmp/SVRA.htm

4. State Parent Training and Information Centers (Disabilities) – Provide training and information to parents of infants, toddlers, children, and youth with disabilities, and to people who work with these parents. The goal is to enable the adults to participate more fully and effectively with professionals in meeting the educational needs of children with disabilities. For a state-by-state listing, see:
www.ed.gov/Programs/bastmp/SPTIC.htm

5. The Nation's Disability Rights Network (Protection and Advocacy Office) – Lists Websites of agencies in each state in the U.S. that provide protection and advocacy information and legal assistance to persons with disabilities. For a state-by-state listing, see:
www.protectionandadvocacy.com/demofile.htm

APPENDIX C

WHAT IF YOUR CHILD REQUIRES DISCIPLINARY ACTION BY THE SCHOOL?

Unfortunate as it may be, some students with LD find themselves faced with the possibility of suspension or expulsion as a result of some type of unacceptable behavior. The federal law, Individuals with Disabilities Education Act (IDEA), has provided safeguards which go into effect if disciplinary measures seem necessary.

There are Disciplinary Due Process procedures that apply to ALL students — those in regular education as well as special education. However, there are additional procedures under IDEA that apply only to students with IEPs.

The first step for you as a parent if you are faced with this situation is to find out what your school district's Discipline Due Process procedures are — those that apply to ALL students. With this information in hand, you should then obtain a copy of the additional disciplinary procedures that apply to children in your school district who have IEPs.

As you digest this information, you will be confronted with acronyms such as "FBA" and "BIP" and "IAES." Don't despair! These are all defined in this book's Glossary. They have to do with such topics as assessment of behavior (FBA), or a plan for dealing with the behavior (BIP), or a temporary alternative setting for the student whose behavior involves weapons, drugs, or a controlled substance (IAES).

There are several resources to help you through this maze. Start with your child's special education teacher. If needed, next see the school principal. If your district has an LD Coordinator, that person can be an additional contact, followed, if you still have uncertainties, by your district's Special Education Director. In case you're still floundering, call your *state's* Director of Special Education (you may want to follow up with an appointment with this person).

In Appendix B-3, you can find out how to locate your state's Parent Training and Information Center, as well as your Protection and Advocacy Office. They are both valuable resources.

APPENDIX D

HOW IS AN LD CLASSROOM DIFFERENT FROM A REGULAR EDUCATION CLASSROOM?

HOW IS ACCOMMODATION DIFFERENT FROM REMEDIATION?

The LD Classroom

At some point you may find yourself asking one of the following questions:

- How is the LD classroom different from the regular classroom in which my LD child has been so frustrated?

- What does the LD teacher do that is so different from what the regular classroom teacher does?

If you were to observe an LD class, you would discover that the instruction used by the LD teacher is neither magical nor mysterious, though the approaches should be different from the ones used in the classroom where your child was not successful. The strategies comprise teaching techniques which are more appropriate for the learning styles of the students in the class, applied in a consistent manner in a small class setting. Your child's former regular education teacher may not have been familiar with these needed techniques.

Not all LD classrooms or programs are alike, but you should note the following features that many LD programs have in common:

Low teacher-pupil ratio: Instruction is usually provided in small groups and sometimes on a one-to-one basis.

Individualized instruction: The instruction the students receive is based upon their IEP goals, not what is next in the textbook. The teacher matches the instruction and materials to the students' needs.

Use of task analysis: The teacher analyzes concepts and skills and breaks them down into small, incremental steps to teach to students.

Acknowledgment of learning style: The teacher recognizes that students learn differently (some by doing, some by example, etc.) and tries to match the instructional style to the students' particular learning styles.

Success philosophy: By presenting instruction on each student's level and in small steps, the teacher tries to insure that every student is successful at each step of the process. "Success breeds success."

High degree of structure and organization: The teacher's expectations of the students are clearly stated so that students know what is required, what will happen next, etc. The classroom environment may also be highly structured with routines, checklists and furniture arranged to designate certain activities and areas of study.

Availability of a variety of instructional materials and approaches: The teacher of students with LD will use many approaches and materials to get information to students, instead of being limited to what is available in many regular classrooms.

Multisensory approach to learning: This approach incorporates as many senses as possible into the instructional program. For example, a student may study spelling words by looking at the word, while simultaneously saying the letters and tracing them in a sand tray.

Instruction in coping strategies (Accommodation): Students are taught ways to "work around" their specific learning disabilities; for example, they may learn strategies for improving memory, focusing attention, completing an assignment, etc.

Mastery learning (Remediation): Teachers present and students practice concepts and skills until they over-learn or master them. The goal is for the student to practice a skill until it becomes automatic.

Close monitoring of student progress: A "test-teach-test" approach may be used to determine what skills a student lacks or whether he has mastered them during instruction. This means students are given immediate feedback about their performance so they "know where they are." This is an on-going process.

Use of motivational system: Points and contract systems may be used to motivate and reward students for their work and effort.

Direct instruction in social skills: Some LD students need direct help in relating to other people effectively.

Accommodation vs. Remediation

While it is difficult and even unwise to make generalizations about educational programming for all students with LD, professionals usually agree that, in order to be successful in both the long and short terms, educational programs for the learning disabled must include a balance of both *accommodation* and *remediation*.

- **Accommodation** is the modification and adaptation of materials (textbooks, workbooks, worksheets, etc.), assignments, class requirements, etc., so that the student with LD is able to work around or bypass his specific disabilities and still participate in and benefit from classroom activities.

Examples of accommodations include:

— Securing books on tape (see Appendix B-1) or individually tape-recording textbook material so a student with a reading disability may listen to the material;

— Permitting a student who has difficulty expressing his thoughts in writing to make oral, instead of written, presentations (such as book reports);

— Allotting additional time for the completion of tests and other written work;

— Providing information already written or printed, instead of asking students with LD to copy the material from the board or textbook;

— Allowing hand-held calculators for students who are unable to memorize the multiplication tables, even though they have tried diligently to do so;

— Permitting students with LD who are easily distracted by visual or auditory stimulation to do seat work at a desk that is removed from the other desks. (This arrangement should not be viewed by the student or his classmates as punishment.)

- **Remediation** is the improvement in specific skills through individualized instruction. For example, students with difficulties in the area of reading might receive specific instruction in those reading skills that have not yet been mastered.

- **Balancing these approaches:** It is important to develop a balance in these two approaches. For the student who has just begun to receive LD assistance or for the student with a severe learning disability, accommodations in the regular classroom are especially critical.

While the student may be working with the LD teacher to remediate basic deficits, it does take time to build these skills. In the meantime, then, it is important to minimize the student's frustration and lack of success in the regular classroom by making modifications and accommodations, so that the youngster is not penalized for the learning disability.

Likewise, it is not sufficient to just modify the student's classroom environment in order to accommodate the existing disabilities. This sometimes occurs at the secondary level where LD teachers often go to great lengths to encourage regular classroom teachers to allow students to take tests orally, give oral reports, have shorter assignments, etc. This may be necessary for the student's immediate, short-term success; however, it must be supplemented by remediation of the basic skills (reading, spelling, composition, etc.) which necessitated the accommodations in the first place. Only then is long-term success possible, going beyond just making a passing grade in a particular class.

Graduation, with a successful, fulfilling life beyond school, is the goal. The LD instruction may provide the last chance the student has to learn basic skills. Once the student has graduated, the opportunities to gain these skills are very limited.

It is important to note here that, despite remediation in school, many individuals with LD will need accommodations as adults, whether in the context of their job, day-to-day living, or social relations. Learning disabilities are never really "cured." However, it is appropriate to expect that, *when they have had the advantage of receiving proper help in school,* young adults with LD will assume increasing responsibility for devising their own accommodations and solutions in surmounting daily obstacles.

APPENDIX E

GET YOUR CHILD READY FOR WORK

Someday your learning disabled child will have to find a job if he is to become self-supporting. Hopefully, this work will challenge him and contribute to the economy. It's hard for parents to focus on their child's future work when simply to get him an education is such a struggle. Yet, school years usually make up less than a third of his life. He will "make it or break it" according to his ability to work. And many people are successful in the "real world" who have failed in school.

This article will discuss how you can help your child become a valuable employee.

Teach Your Child to Become a Successful Worker

Teach your child to feel good about work. As your child achieves in school, at play, and at home, praise him. Let him brag. When he produces something or finishes a task, encourage him to take a moment and feel pride. Inner pride in a job well-done should become its own reward.

Make him a productive part of the household. Don't relegate him to traditional children's chores of washing dishes and taking out the garbage. Give him more challenging tasks such as cooking simple meals, folding laundry, shopping, or helping with simple repairs. Of course, be sure the jobs are not too difficult for him.

Show pride in your own job. Your children should understand that you are earning the money the family needs for survival. Let them know what you do. If possible let them visit you. One cashier always has her husband bring the children shopping and is sure to ring up their groceries. A lawyer took his son to his office one weekend and showed his diplomas and awards. A political activist regularly takes his children to speeches. If a visit is impossible, consider bringing home samples of what you do. Work should be a frequent topic of conversation in your house. Discuss your job at dinner and ask your children to talk about their daily achievements.

Teach them that all work is important. No job is below them or above them, provided they find it challenging and can do it well.

Point out other people working. Arrange for your family to tour a factory. Also, let them be aware of the lawyers, doctors, teachers, and other professionals the family contacts.

When you are inconvenienced by sloppy work, let your child know. For example, one father had to take his new car into the shop to be repaired. The transmission was built in a shoddy way. "I don't even know the person who made it," he told his daughter, "but someone put a screw in wrong, and now we can't use the car for a week." These relationships are not obvious to your child, because most of our goods are produced by strangers.

As you show your child the world of work, explain how what he learns in school will help him someday. For example, when you eat in a restaurant, show him how the waitress had to add up the checks. Point out the cash registers, which require elementary math to operate. Point to people on the bus who are reading papers from their briefcases. Tell him that doctors, lawyers, policemen, and other professional workers have to go to school for a long time.

Here are some areas where learning disabled children need particular help:

- *Social Skills* are part of the handicap of learning disabilities for many children. Help your child interpret social situations and get along with others. *Help for the Lonely Child* by Ernest and Rita Seigel offers many suggestions.

- *Time* is important in the world of work. Many learning disabled children don't feel the passage of time in a normal way. Help her to overcome this part of her handicap. Talk about the time of day in your conversations. Give her ten minutes' warning before going somewhere and then give five minutes' warning. Ask her to tell you when half an hour is up so you know when to turn off the roast beef. As she grows older, have her take more responsibility for finishing tasks and getting to places on time. When she graduates from high school, she should be able to awaken independently with an alarm clock. Getting to work on time is essential for almost every job.

- *Transportation.* Ability to get from home to work is important in most jobs. Encourage your child to use public transportation if it's available.

Teach him to drive, but keep in mind that it takes many learning disabled people extra time and effort to learn. If there is no public transportation and your child cannot drive, consider moving to a location where your child can be independent.

- *Encouragement of Abilities.* The most important and most neglected areas for learning disabled children is their abilities. Help your child find his strengths. What is he really good at? What does he enjoy doing?

When you and your child find an interesting talent, support your child in developing it. Encourage her to feel inner pride about that talent. It's worth the same time and effort to encourage the strengths as it is to remediate the handicaps. For instance, a learning disabled teenager was interested in science and electronics. The parent went to a local technical school and recruited a student to help their son develop a "robot" that he showed at the science fair. The match-up was successful, and the boy won an honorable mention.

Choosing a Career

During adolescence, your child should be developing his strengths even more. He might be athletic, academic, attractive, good with his hands, or socially adept. Whatever the strengths, effort and encouragement can help them to grow.

His career choice will be based on his strengths, and you should encourage him to think about future jobs. Can he fix items so they work? Can he wash small delicate items without breaking them? Coordination and mechanical ability are useful in many careers from car mechanic to dentist. Has he always been expert at knowing which parent to approach first to get what he wants? Can he charm grades out of his teachers? These skills are also important for many jobs from salesperson to diplomat.

It's not easy to determine which career uses your child's strengths. Many books about job hunting have practical exercises to help your child make that match. Private job placement firms can administer tests and advise adolescents. Vocational rehabilitation counselors can also help. Vocational skills tests can serve as a valuable guide, but they are not accurate for everyone. Some school systems offer career education, systematically exposing the students to the world of work.

If your child's school doesn't have such a course, perhaps you could recommend establishing one.

After the teenager thinks of a potentially interesting job, he should learn more about it and try to talk to people doing that job. If possible, he should visit the actual office, factory, or worksite. Volunteering, internships, apprenticeships, and part time jobs will enable him to experience the work and find out if he can do it well and enjoy it.

Careful career exploration is especially important to learning disabled youth since they must be careful to avoid their areas of disability. For example, Carla, who is talkative and friendly, thought she might want to be a telephone operator. She volunteered at a small community agency to try it and found that she could not sit in one place for the full work day. Her hyperactivity interfered with the job. James wanted to enter the field of television production. He became an intern at a neighborhood cable TV station and found that the mechanical aspects of production were difficult for him. Now he is thinking about scriptwriting.

Your child should know about his disabilities. It will help him avoid his weak areas. Without clear information on his disabilities, he may still think of himself as stupid, lazy, crazy, or personally weak. These explanations lead to a low self-image and paralyze the desire to improve. Tell your child what you know. If you feel uncomfortable about this, ask a professional to talk to him. Let him know what the handicap is and how it affects him. Teach him the scientific words. Be sure he knows about what he has to overcome. Improvement should be ascribed to his efforts, not to "outgrowing it," upbringing, or treatment. Most learning disabled people feel relieved when they find out about their disabilities, although some initially deny them.

They deserve to be proud of what they have overcome, a pride that will make them feel good about themselves. A strong and realistic self-image is one of the most important qualities in success. It will be vital during the time your child is looking for work.

Looking for Work

Looking for work is difficult for everyone. Chances are strong that your child will face this challenge while living at your home. How can you make your home a supportive place for job hunting? Here are some ideas:

1. *Insist your child actively look for work.* Do not let him spend extensive time watching TV, reading, shopping, or entertaining friends. If necessary, tell him that looking for work is his full-time job which he must do in order to earn your financial support. Help him by not overloading him with chores during working hours on the weekdays when employers are in. Help him overcome his failures, but do not accept lack of effort.

2. *Help him to organize himself.* Some learning disabled people do not know how to look for work. There are many books about job hunting, each with a slightly different approach. Together, you might decide on a plan of action. Or help might be needed with the fine points of planning and scheduling. You could remind him of necessary follow-up telephone calls or letters.

3. *Be a good listener.* Ask him how the day went. Listen carefully to his adventures. Let him express his feelings of frustration, anger, and nervousness. Emphasize his actions and behavior, rather than the results. If he is actively seeking work, he deserves your respect and praise, even if he does not succeed in finding work. For example, praise your child if he does a good job of describing his qualifications at an interview even if he is not selected for the opening.

4. *Help with reading and writing.* You may have to read classified ads for her and check addresses of her letters. Some job banks have computer printouts on a screen, which are especially difficult for dyslexic people to read. It may be helpful if the parent types or handwrites job applications since childish handwriting and misspellings tend to disturb employers.

5. *Help with transportation if necessary.*

6. *Grooming is important.* Learning disabled people with visual perceptual problems often are unaware of tears and stains on their clothing, sloppy hair, or dirt on their hands. It helps if someone looks them over before an interview.

7. *Use your social network to help your child find work.* Talk to your friends, co-workers, and other parents of learning disabled children. Tell them about your child. Stress your child's positive qualities and

describe her as a capable worker. Don't spend a lot of time describing her learning disability. Ask her to follow up any leads that you discover.

8. *Be aware of community resources.* Know the applicable civil rights laws. Consider government programs such as vocational rehabilitation and job service. If you know of other parents whose children are job hunting, you may want to form a support group for yourselves and/or your children.

With your help, your child will be able to locate a satisfying job. However, this is only half the battle. Your child will have to work hard in order to keep that work. Be sure your child gets a complete job description and check for problem areas. If your child might have difficulty with any task because of his disability, he may want to consider trading that task with a co-worker in return for another task that he can do.

Equipment such as calculators and tape records can solve problems. A learning disabled person should not accept a job that includes many tasks in his area of disability.

Social skills are important to job success. Help your child to understand the point of view of co-workers and to adjust to the many hidden rules of the organization.

Many learning disabled adults are successful. Learning disabled people work in every conceivable job—salesperson, optometrist, pilot, doctor, psychologist, computer programmer, janitor, and waiter.

Remember to pay as much attention to your child's abilities as to his disabilities. Teach him to feel pride in his achievements. Help him select an interesting career that does not emphasize his area of disability. And support him as he hunts for a job. With your help and your clear belief that your child *can* succeed, he can "make it."

Dale S. Brown is author of the above, which originally appeared in full in **Newsbriefs** *(September-October, 1988). Ms. Brown has also published* **Learning a Living, a Guide to Planning Your Career** *and* **Finding a Job: For People with Learning Disabilities, Attention Deficit Disorder, and Dyslexia**. *The above abridgment of "Get Your Child Ready for Work" is printed with permission of the author and* **Newsbriefs**, *Learning Disabilities Association of America.*

APPENDIX F

COLLEGE, VOCATIONAL, AND TRANSITIONAL RESOURCES

Note: The following resources are additions to those in Appendix B-1 — "NCLD's Resource List." No endorsement by the Learning Disabilities Council is intended or implied.

- **Directories and Guides for College**

CollegeView
CollegeView is a free online college search service with profiles of 3,500+ colleges and universities, virtual tours, electronic applications, financial aid info, career planning tools, and more.
www.collegeview.com

Peterson's Colleges with Programs for Students with Learning Disabilities
(4th Edition, 1994)
Peterson's Guides
Princeton, NJ
A state-by-state guide. Available from NCLD.
212/545-7510.

SchoolSearch Guide to Colleges with Programs or Services for Students with Learning Disabilities
(by Midge Lipkin, 1992)
SchoolSearch Press
Belmont, MA.
A state-by-state guide.

Unlocking Potential: College and Other Choices for Learning Disabled People: A Step-by-Step Guide
(by Barbara Scheiber, 1992)
Woodbine House
Bethesda, MD. A guide to post-secondary options.

- **Financial Support**

Fastweb
A free scholarship Internet search for financial aid for postsecondary education.
www.fastweb.com

The Financial Aid Information Page
A free, comprehensive, independent and objective guide to student financial aid.
www.finaid.org

Project EASI...Easy Access for Students and Institutions
A guide to financial aid resources for education beyond high school.
www.easi.ed.gov

- **Post-Secondary Information Resources**

National Association for College Admissions Counseling
An educational association of secondary school counselors, college and university admissions officers and counselors, and related individuals.
1631 Prince St
Alexandria, VA 22314-2818
1-800-822-6285
www.nacac.com/index.html

National School-to-Work Learning and Information Center
400 Virginia Avenue SW, Suite 150,
Washington, DC 20024
1-800-251-7236
FAX: 202-488-7395
E-mail: stw-lc@ed.gov
www.stw.ed.gov/index.htm

National Transition Alliance for Youth with Disabilities
The NTA is working to create a brighter future for all youth transitioning from school to employment, post-secondary experiences and independent living.
Transition Research Institute
University of Illinois

113 Children's Research Center
51 Gerty Dr.
Champaign, Illinois 61820
217-333-2325
www.dssc.org/nta/html

- **School Testing Issues**

College students with documented learning
disabilities can apply for test accommodations as
appropriate. For more information contact AHEAD.
The information which follows replaces that found on
the NCLD Resources List under "College Issues."
AHEAD provides training and insight pertaining to
Section 504 of the Rehabilitation Act. AHEAD is a
resource for college faculty re: accommodations.

Association on Higher Education and
Disabilities (AHEAD)
University of Mass., Boston
100 Morissey Blvd.
Boston, MA 02125-3393
617-287-3880
FAX: 617-287-3881
www.ahead.org

- **Transitional Post-Secondary
  Programs**

Beacon College
105 East Main Street
Leesburg, Fl 34748
352-787-7660
FAX: 352-787-0721

Chapel Haven
1040 Whalley Avenue
Westville, CT 06515
203-397-1714 ext. 113

Landmark College
River Rd. South
Putney, VT 05346
802-387-6718

Life Development Institute
18001 N. 79th Ave., E71
Glendale, AZ 85308
623-773-2774
FAX: 623-773-2788
E-mail: LDIinARIZ@aol.com

Pace University Coordinator for Disabled
Students
New York City Campus
41 Park Row, 4th Floor
New York, NY 10038
212-346-1200
www.pace.edu/statemen.html

The Berkshire Ctr.
P.O. Box 160, 18 Park St.
Lee, MA 01238
413-243-2576
FAX: 413-243-3351

The Grow Program:
Getting Ready for the Outside World
Riverview School
551 Route 6A
East Sandwich, MA 02537
508-888-0489
FAX: 508-888-1315
www.riverviewschool.com

Threshold
Lesley College
29 Everett Street
Cambridge, MA 02138-2790
617-349-8181
www.lesley.edu/threshold

APPENDIX G

THE GED TEST

GED stands for *General Educational Development,* and that's what is tested when one takes the GED tests. They are offered to people who have not completed high school, giving them an opportunity to earn a high school diploma. GED diplomas are accepted by more than 90 percent of employers, colleges, and universities.

The tests are administered at approximately 3,400 sites in the United States and its territories, as well as in eleven Canadian provinces and territories, and internationally through Sylvan Learning Centers.

Accommodations Allowed

The good news for adults with documented disabilities is that every testing site allows the very same accommodations. Learning disabilities and ADHD (see Chapter 1) are included in the disabilities covered. The accommodations allowed for disabilities in general are:

- extended time
- frequent, supervised breaks
- private room in which to take the test
- use of a calculator
- use of an audio cassette edition of the test
- use of a Braille edition
- scribe (person who writes or records answers)
- other accommodations if approved individually by the GED Testing Service (GEDTS).

All candidates, even those whose learning disability has <u>not</u> been documented, are entitled to additional, reasonable accommodations, such as:

- a large-print version of the test
- colored overlays
- a non-ruled straight edge
- magnifying strips
- graph paper
- other strategies that do not compromise the reliability or validity of the GED tests.

Form Needed

After your learning disability has been documented, you will need to fill out Form L-15. It is available at your nearest Official GED Testing Center, which you can locate by contacting GED Testing Service (1-800-626-9433 or (202) 939-9490, or www.gedtest.org).

The L-15 form requires a candidate (or parent/guardian, if the candidate is under 18) to sign a statement authorizing release of information. This allows the Testing Center to obtain psychological or medical information about an individual, but only if the information is necessary to support the request for accommodations.

Completion of the Forms

Because this L-15 form asks GED candidates for information that is critical to the approval of the request, it must be filled out completely if the process is to move quickly. Accommodations cannot be granted without the completion of Form L-15. A letter from the GED Testing Center which accompanies the form provides an introduction and some sample cases of requests for accommodations.

IMPORTANT: Your completed L-15 form should be in the hands of the Chief Examiner of your GED Testing Center <u>at least one month before your testing date.</u>

Approval of Request for Accommodations

The GED State Administrator reviews the completed L-15 form and usually approves the request quickly. If the Administrator is unable to approve the request, the Form L-15 may either be returned to the candidate for further information, or sent to the GEDTS in Washington, DC., for expert review. The request may then be approved, or additional information may be requested, or the request may not be approved. The GED candidate may appeal a denial of approval.

Documentation for ADHD must be provided by a professional who is licensed to make that diagnosis. This person must provide a letter clearly stating that the candidate meets the most recent DSM criteria for ADHD. The letter must also state how the requested accommodations meet the candidate's needs.

The following has been used in the preparation of this appendix: "Taking the GED Tests: Accommodating Accommodations," by Neil Sturomski. It appeared in the January/February 2001 **LDA Newsbriefs***, published by the Learning Disabilities Association of America.*

APPENDIX H

TIPS FOR WORKPLACE SUCCESS

✓ Know your learning style and how that style matches up with different jobs.

✓ Apply for job positions for which you have the knowledge, skills, and abilities to perform at the level required by the employer.

✓ Know your strengths and be able to describe them; present yourself as a capable individual who can competently perform the job.

✓ Pursue informational interviews and on-site visits in order to get a feel for different workplace environments and job tasks.

✓ Request and review job descriptions before applying for positions.

✓ Disclose learning disabilities to the personnel/human resources staff person after the job has been offered; do so in person (never over the phone) after you have accepted the job. Then make arrangements to speak with the job-site supervisor if and when necessary.

✓ At the time of disclosure, describe the strategies you have developed that assist you in performing job requirements and state workplace accommodations that can help you.

✓ Ask the supervisor for written job performance expectations — what you will be required to learn and apply within the job setting.

✓ Ask for specific time lines for performance evaluations; be sure you understand when and how your performance will be evaluated.

✓ Know when and how to request appropriate accommodations.

✓ If accommodations are provided, establish an evaluation process through which you and your supervisor can review the effectiveness of the accommodations and the possibility of adjustments.

✓ Do not use your learning disability as an excuse for not doing your best.

*The above, written by Nancie Payne, is reprinted from **Linkages** (Vol.2, No.1, Spring 1995). National Adult Literacy & Learning Disabilities Center. Washington, D.C.: Academy for Educational Development. The National Institute for Literacy served as the funding agency.*

PERSONAL STORIES

The following pages include several personal stories describing actual people with learning disabilities and their own experiences.

As described in Chapter 1, "Learning Disabilities: the Hidden Handicap," individuals with learning disabilities vary greatly as to the nature and severity of the disability.

Read individually, no one study is necessarily representative of what learning disabilities are. Read as a group, however, the stories do provide a glimpse at the diversity of learning disabilities. They also illustrate the manner in which the problems can manifest themselves, the different ages at which the learning disability can become apparent, and the range of experiences, both positive and negative, which individuals can undergo.

These stories may also serve as a starter for discussions between you and your youngster, and with other members of your family. Many parents have reported that they were able to open up a helpful exchange of ideas about learning disabilities through shared reading of stories such as the ones in this section.

THE LIFELONG IMPACT OF A LABEL

BY JANET M. BELL

Last Sunday morning the congregation began to sing the opening song. I had done it again. The congregation was singing the hymn on page 130. I was on page 310. I'm dyslexic; I'll always be dyslexic. But I didn't always know that.

In June of 1928, my mother walked me to school and enrolled me in first grade. I was so excited. I was going to learn wonderful things and have lots of fun. Wrong! In the years that followed, I found school wasn't the fun place I had dreamed about. It was filled with fear and frustration. I quickly was labeled as the "dumb" kid.

My mother and aunt spent many hours reading aloud to me as a child. I remember those times as the only positive part of my struggle with learning to read.

Every day in school, I hid behind the child in front of me so the teacher wouldn't call on me. Writing the alphabet was easy, but reading it was a problem. I couldn't seem to pronounce the words right. This played havoc with my spelling, and I worked hard to memorize words for weekly tests. School was a living nightmare.

I studied every night, but my father would get frustrated with me. He'd bang his fist on the table and say something like, "Use your head" or ask, "Where's your brain, girl?"

In spite of all this, I managed to keep my grades up and receive a high school diploma, but my belief that I was dumb overshadowed my entire adult life. I made no attempt to attend college. I chose to work in the fields of general office work, accounting, and technical writing and survived by inventing my own peculiar ways to get things done and still appear confident and knowledgeable.

When I worked as a technical writer, a co-worker told me she thought I had dyslexia. At the time, I didn't believe her and ignored her comment. But her words stayed with me.

Three years ago my curiosity prompted me to purchase a book about dyslexia. As I read the first few pages, I was in shock and tears. I thought the author had been peering into my life. My immediate and joyful reaction was, "Dear Blessed God, I am not dumb. I have dyslexia." I was ecstatic. I didn't care that my brain worked differently from others. At last I knew there was a reason for my being different — yes, different, not dumb.

I struggle every day with dyslexia in one way or another, but I no longer hide my disability. I am now focusing on dreams I once thought were impossible, such as writing a book for children about dyslexia. While children may not be able to read every word I write, it's my hope that teachers, parents, or other family members will read aloud to them.

Today a teacher or counselor can say to parents, "Your daughter has dyslexia, and we can help her." How I wish my parents could have heard these words!

The author discovered she was dyslexic at age 76. Her story is reprinted with permission of Schwab Learning © Copyright 2001 Schwab Learning ™. For more information, please visit www.schwablearning.org.

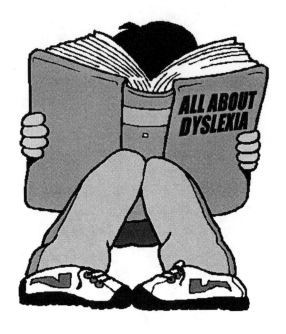

ONE MAN'S BATTLE AGAINST DYSLEXIA

BY CYNTHIA ROBINS

At the mention of that awful old joke: "Dyslexics of the world, untie!," Charles Schwab, emperor of a 3,500-person, 160-office, San Francisco-based discount brokerage fiefdom, frowns. It is not a joke he appreciates. And Schwab is a man who laughs easily.

But dyslexia is something with which Schwab lives every day of his life. He says he's tried to read "Shogun" six or seven times to no avail. And were it not for Cliff Notes and illustrated Classic Comic Books, he probably wouldn't have gotten through his English courses in high school and at Stanford.

Back in the early '40s, when Schwab was growing up in Woodland, the Yolo County seat, there wasn't a name for his learning disability. He had to wait nearly 30 years to discover that what made it so difficult for him to read, write and take notes was called dyslexia. And Schwab discovered his *own* dyslexia when he and his wife found out through a teacher that their son Michael, then 8, was dyslexic.

"Where did he get it?" Schwab asks rhetorically. "Well, you start looking back at all the symptoms, I realized he inherited it from me."

"I should have known that Charles was dyslexic when our first child was born," says his second wife, Helen Schwab, the statuesque, softly pretty woman Schwab met and married nearly 20 years ago. "When Katie was born, he sent me flowers in the hospital addressed to 'our lovely daughter Cadey.' Of course he doesn't know how to spell."

In 1988 the Schwabs founded the Parents' Educational Resources Center to provide information and counseling for other parents of learning-disabled children. "When you're a parent of this kind of child," says Helen Schwab, "you don't know where to go or who to ask. We feel that people will be served if Chuck admits that he's dyslexic. It's a way for people to learn that having a disability like this doesn't handicap you for life."

Through their foundation, the highly philanthropic Schwabs

have endowed the PERC, located at 1730 S. Amphlett Blvd. in San Mateo, with more than $300,000 per year. The center offers services for parents that include information and referral, guidance counseling, a resource library, a monthly support group and seminars on social, emotional, physical, cognitive and academic issues.

For all of its services, however, the PERC may have come too late for Chuck and Helen Schwab. "Yeah," he says, running his hand down his red paisley tie. "Obviously, what Helen and I learned is something we didn't want to have other parents go through. They could learn in a two-hour introduction what took us about three years of pain."

The Schwabs worked very hard with Michael, now 15. Helen recorded books he had to read, and he would listen to the tapes while he struggled through the texts. Michael's textbooks are obtained from Records for the Blind. "You can be a member for life for $25," Helen says. "In August, I call the school and find out about the books, and in three weeks, I have his texts."

No one recorded "Huckleberry Finn" or "Hamlet" for young Charles Schwab.

By the time he was 15, he knew he wanted to go to Stanford, and he knew he had to work very

hard to get there. He only got in, he says, "because I was highly motivated. My reading speed was probably half of what the average kid at Stanford was able to read.

"When you have this disability, you are not able to decode linearly. When you read, your eyes go slowly ...when you read that slowly, what goes is your comprehension."

Charles Schwab says that he has fairly good comprehension, but only because "I read all the Classic Comics. When you say a picture is worth a thousand words, for me, it was."

Comparatively speaking, numbers were a snap for him. Charles Schwab carries on a business in which, Forbes estimates, he has a $400 million stake.

One of the few personal tales told about him in the canon of business writing is the "chicken story," illustrative of a very motivated kid with high self-esteem. Charles Schwab was 10 or 11 when he discovered that he could make some money out of the three-dozen chickens his attorney-father was raising:

"When they got to a certain age, of course, the hens laid eggs. And you had to keep the place very clean, so at the end of the day we had an accumulation of chicken droppings — a very profitable source of material for gardeners.

And then when these babies got a little old, we turned them into fryers. It was kinda like the food chain. So we did the whole deal. It was my first fully integrated operation."

At 54, Charles Schwab is a youthfully handsome man with a flawless, unwrinkled complexion (the result, he says, of excellent genes, not plastic surgery). He is passionate about his business, his family and about golf. Now about a 10 handicapper, he played behind Al Geiberger in high school, was on the varsity golf team at Stanford and played recently in the AT&T Pro-Am at Pebble Beach with touring pro Hal Sutton.

From the 28th floor of his company's headquarters building at 101 Montgomery St., the founder, chairman of the board and chief executive officer can look out onto the northern edge of the Financial District and the Bay. The subtly decorated, art-bedecked office is a testament to Charles Schwab's prodigious abilities to keep a finger on the pulse of investing America. With his considerable profits, he has been able to educate and indulge himself as a well-known collector and connoisseur of modern American art. He has even

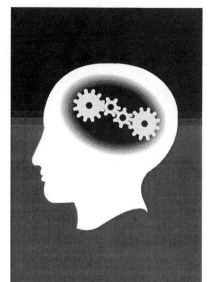

selected the art for his office, choosing pieces by Diebenkorn, Sam Francis, Al Held and sculptor Mark di Suvero.

It is the office of a low-key tycoon, a fiscal genius who is respected in the world of finance. It is obvious that Chuck Schwab, son of a Yolo County district attorney, is very successful. The result, he says, of a healthy dose of self-esteem, one of the factors that can be missing if a child is dyslexic.

"A large percentage of parents who don't understand it, who haven't made inquiry, find out that Johnny isn't reading well," he explains. "They think he's stupid, or that he's under-performing or that he's disinterested. Which is possibly not the answer at all.

"Self-esteem. That's the real problem with these kids. Some of them feel like they're really stupid. If there is anything I'd want them to know, it is that they're not stupid. They just have a learning disability. And once they understand that, then they can feel good about themselves."

*Condensed from **San Francisco Examiner** with permission. March 8, 1992.*

ONE PERSON'S PATH TO LITERACY

BY RICHARD WANDERMAN

I'm 48 years old, married, live in a nice house, have a successful career as an educational consultant, and I have a learning disability, dyslexia. My life was not always so great. I was a premature breech birth, had meningitis, polio, and every childhood illness. I was tested for everything including language problems from an early age so I was labeled "dyslexic" early. I went to a special school until 6th grade where I had plenty of extra help and remediation. Still, I had to repeat 6th grade at that school. I suffered the rest of my school days in public schools where I did poorly.

When I went to college my life improved markedly because this is where I discovered art. The art world gave me a chance to express myself without words, so I took a lot of art courses. I got good at making things with clay and I learned my first important lesson about my language disability: I could be smart and articulate with clay and still have a language disability which made it hard to be smart and articulate with words.

My next big life lesson happened a few years later. I drove Volkswagens because they were the only cars I could afford. I knew little about cars and had never even changed the oil in one. One day the engine in my VW bus seized up and I didn't have the money to have it fixed. I bought the book *How to Fix Your Volkswagen for the Complete Idiot.* I started reading, slowly. I bought a few metric tools, pulled the engine, and dragged it into the backyard where I took it apart. Two weeks later when I got the engine into the car and it started I learned that when you feel good about yourself and are willing to take risks you can transfer confidence from one domain to another. I knew nothing about engines but took the confidence I'd gotten with art into a totally new domain.

My next domain was rock climbing. Hey, I don't bungi jump; I'm not crazy. I got into climbing because it was a fun thing to do with friends. We all got into it at the same time and were all chicken from the start. However, we noticed that the more we did it the easier it was to take "exposure." So we did it more. And the more I did it the better I got. It wasn't a talent thing, it was practice. After about five years of climbing I found myself in Yosemite Valley on a big wall. What had I learned? I'd learned that if you enjoy something and do it all the time you get better at it. Practice makes better.

Later I took that idea into a very scary place. I decided to see if I could actually learn how to read and write by practicing. I read and wrote every day for two years. This may seem obvious to you but it wasn't to me; I had no idea that most people read things every day. I had avoided reading things as much as possible and avoided writing completely. Nevertheless, for two years I took my prior experiences and mapped them into learning how to read and write, and at the end of two years I'd learned a lot. Most importantly, I was literate.

Then came the dawn of personal computers. Once I used one, and then bought one, my writing and then my reading improved at a rapid clip.

Here's the point: had I been given a computer as a child in school I doubt I'd have been mature

enough to take full advantage of it and I doubt the school would have allowed me to use it in a way that would have been meaningful to me. I needed to go through the long, messy process that I went through with art, cars, climbing, and reading and writing to get to a place in my life where I knew I was smart enough to dive into an area that was totally unknown, hard, but interesting.

For me growing up was particularly painful and messy. My father used to tell me the bumps would build character and I would roll my eyes. Well, he was right. And even though I wouldn't want to go through it all again I have plenty of character because of it all. And I can read and write.

IT'S NEVER
TOO LATE

BY PAT WALTER

Jose, a 9th grader, arrived in my resource room reading at a third grade level. Over the years, he had attended eleven different schools and had been exposed to a number of different (and often not complementary) reading approaches. Jose stormed out of classrooms when he felt "disrespected" by teachers or students. He liked math, came to school every day, and was never late. I learned that he had been previously arrested on the way home from a church retreat and spent two weeks in Spofford Correctional Facility. (He claims mistaken identity and he and his mother pursued the justice system until his file was sealed.) Jose's vocabulary skills were limited and he had difficulty processing language and recalling words. I learned that he can repair machines — printers and projectors — because he could "see" what needs to be done.

His frustrations led him to avoid academic work and hide his problems. What could I possibly do to help him? Was it too late?

Our school uses an interdisciplinary, block scheduling program. Jose had three teachers each day for math/science, humanities, and Spanish. As his resource room teacher, I was able to coordinate strategies with his teachers for his success and development and tutor him during resource room time.

Jose's humanities class was studying the Mayan civilization from its golden age until the Spanish conquests. His teacher and I got picture books with controlled vocabulary from the elementary school's library, and helped him to use them as references for a paper. Unfortunately, the elementary books could not explain complex concepts such as "imperialism," but he was able to use knowledge gained from class discussions to supplement the books. I suspect that this was the first time that Jose handed in a well-prepared written assignment. He was acutely aware that his skill level was far below those of his classmates. Imagine his pride when he handed in his work!

When the class read novels like *To Kill A Mockingbird*, he listened to the books on tape. Some books we had on tape, and some we didn't. Sometimes he would get so frustrated in class that he would burst out in a rage and leave the room. This especially happened when the class was asked to work on a writing assignment. At first, Jose dictated his ideas and I typed them for him. Eventually, he began to write his own papers and I helped with editing and spelling. Thank goodness for the computer.

It took until April before Jose was ready to admit to me that he wanted to learn to read. He insisted that his problems remain private and not be shared with the other kids, so he started coming to my room before school and we worked on phonics, starting with consonant and vowel sounds, working our way through a phonics workbook. We spent a lot of time working on auditory discrimination. Then he wouldn't appear for several days. I'd then catch up with him and we'd start again.

After a year of this process, Jose began to show a thirst for reading, and he started to take simple elementary books out in front of his peers, saying, "I have reading problems." I knew that he was on his way.

Jose was stronger with basic mathematics skills. He was able to succeed with basic algebra and physics in a math/science class. I had to help him write the exhibitions, but he understood the calculations and the concepts. Jose had difficulty solving word problems and difficulties with fractions. We worked on those areas during resource room time.

He left the 9/10 grade cluster and moved to the 11/1 2 grade cluster. There he had to write portfolios for graduation. He had problems with Greek Literature, a course that I tried to discourage him from taking. He also had problems with the Toni Morrison class. The problem with a small school is that there is a limited number of courses offered. He spent a lot of time in the resource room getting help with reading and writing for his classes.

Jose started out doing very well in his math class. At midterm, the math teacher wanted his students to discover and interpret the physical significance of the "y intercept" in real world situations, such as a flooding dam. The students were asked to graph and interpret several pieces of information. Twice, Jose approached the teacher and asked for help, and each time he told Jose to "struggle with it" and "try to figure it out." Jose could not stand the tension of not knowing.

He cursed at the teacher and did next to no work for that class for the rest of the semester, saying that the teacher was unwilling to help him. By the time his advisor figured out why he had stopped working, he had failed the semester. Finally, the advisor, teacher, and Jose talked, and Jose was able to repeat the course. This time, he passed satisfactorily.

Jose may or may not be graduating in June, depending on his meeting the deadlines for the portfolio presentations and passing all of his Regents Competency Tests. He may need to spend an extra year in our school, but he will be the first person in his family to graduate from high school. He has already been accepted to a two-year college in upstate New York, but he plans to join the Marines.

I am continually amazed and energized by the resilience and courage of the students whom I teach. It took a lot of support and individualized help on the part of all of his teachers, not just one special teacher, to allow Jose to feel safe enough to stop hiding and to learn. Working with students like Jose has taught me that it is never too late to reach a kid and to turn a potentially tragic situation into a success.

*Reprinted with permission from **Their World** 1999, National Center for Learning Disabilities, 381 Park Avenue South, Suite 1401, New York, N.Y. 10016-8806.*

A BROTHER'S PERSPECTIVE

BY ALESSANDRO UZIELLI

Anyone who knows Allegra knows that she is like a bright ray of sunshine, always smiling, though quick to cry, usually from a loss or over someone else's pain. But growing up with a sister like Allegra was unique in that it forced me to learn acceptance. The hardest part about being the brother of a child (now an adult) with learning disabilities (LD) was accepting the fact that my sister was — and still is — unable to perform certain everyday activities that have become routine to me.

My mother is the Chairman of the Board at the National Center for Learning Disabilities (NCLD). Sometimes I would imagine myself as Chairman of NCSPLDWDNNHLDT, or National Center for Siblings of People with Learning Disabilities Who Do Not Necessarily Have LD Themselves. Of course, we may need to come up with a shorter acronym. Our mission would be to teach parents and teachers of children with LD how to cope with their children who do not have learning disabilities.

In reaction to the limitations faced by their children with LD, parents of LD children should be wary of expecting too much from their children who do not have LD. I always felt that because Allegra could not perform as a regular student, the weight of scholastic achievement rested on my shoulders. And when I did not pull in A's and B's I was quick to read the disappointment in my mother, not to mention my own frustration. I think I even envied Allegra at times; she had a diagnosis, but what was my reason? In hindsight I wonder if my poor grades were not an attempt to divert attention away from Allegra to myself.

It is extremely important to educate siblings of children with LD as to exactly what their brothers or sisters are experiencing. It was very hard for me to understand why Allegra could learn to become an expert figure skater but met with constant frustration with her reading, writing, or math skills. I saw my mother's heart sink and Allegra's teachers become resigned to their lack of success in helping her to learn. I did not buy that for one minute. But then again, I did not know what a lot of parents and teachers know. So while I was punished for bad grades, I saw Allegra getting comforted. While I was pushed to do better, Allegra was allowed to move on and sidestep the problems arising from her education.

I am not a parent yet, though I have a rough idea of the level of responsibility it entails. If that responsibility includes the nurturing of a child with learning disabilities, I cannot stress enough how important it is to allow your other children to share in what you are learning about LD. If I knew then what I know now, everything would have been a lot clearer.

And now I look at Allegra through different eyes. I have a better understanding of what she is going through and I am constantly learning more about Allegra's world and its boundaries. She has created her own world. She lives in a small town and has a small circle of friends. She structures her day around carefully planned routines and, most importantly, she has her independence.

On a recent trip to Europe, my mother and I could not understand why Allegra was so homesick. I soon learned that she cried because she missed her friends and her familiar surroundings. This angered me at first. How could she not appreciate the elegance and beauty of a foreign country? But Allegra's tears washed my anger away. It was that very event that made me truly understand the extent of my sister's situation.

Here she was in Vienna, a bustling European city with foreign languages and foreign currencies. To Allegra, making sure she gets the correct change is like speaking a foreign language. I suddenly realized that Christmas in Vienna was, to Allegra, like having everything familiar, everything comfortable, and everything safe pulled out from under her. It also made me understand the limitations she had to face growing up and still faces today. I only wish that I had such realizations when we were younger. I think I would have been able to better accept what Allegra was going through and better able to understand what was expected of me and what my own goals should have been.

When all is said and done, I am truly blessed. I cannot say enough about my sister. Of course, we have our little secrets, the same as any brother and sister (she does some pretty mean impersonations of family friends). But everything

that comes out of that golden girl's
mouth is straight from the heart
and smothered in love. What a
better place this whole world
would be if we were all that way.

*This article is an adaptation of a speech
that Alessandro Uzielli presented at the
1999 NCLD Benefit. It is reprinted with
permission from **Their World** 2000,
National Center for Learning
Disabilities, 381 Park Avenue South,
Suite 1401, New York, N.Y. 10016-8806.*

JONATHAN'S STORY

BY BOB AND KATHY NIED

Our son, Jonathan, the second of three boys, was born in August 1981. There was excitement in the delivery room that night, although we did not know it was about Jon. The doctors lost Jon's heartbeat. At one week old, Jon experienced a seizure and was rushed to the emergency room with a very high fever. After several days in the hospital we were told that they did not know the source of the problem; however, Jon then seemed to be OK.

Five years and several sets of ear tubes later, Jon started school. My husband and I are teachers, and we looked forward to starting his formal educational process. "Quiet and happy" was how most people saw Jon; however, from the start, there were questions about his educational progress. During our first "open house" in first grade, everything seemed to be quite normal, but by Christmas signs of difficulties appeared. There, in front of the room, was a "reading tree" with each child's name attached to a branch, except Jon's. This surprised us, for we read to him every night, and he really understood and enjoyed what we read. He just could not read by himself. Perhaps he was simply maturing a bit more slowly than the other children; that is what we hoped, that was what we were told. Our parent conference left us distraught.

At the advice of the school, Jon repeated first grade, and a new set of problems became apparent. He showed a distinct weakness on his right side, which was soon diagnosed as mild cerebral palsy. An electroencephalogram (EEG) showed that he was having several hundred absence seizures (one form of epilepsy) each day. Psychological testing at school showed him to have a high IQ, yet his achievement was well below normal. It was at this point that Jon was classified as having learning disabilities.

We cannot begin to describe how hard this second year of first grade was for us. Our perfect family, our perfect children, turned out to be far from perfect. We really did not understand what the doctors and psychologists were telling us, and the more we researched, the more confused we became. Could Jon have a normal life? No one could answer that question for us. We took one day at a time, and sometimes they were awfully long days. His grandparents did not understand Jon's problems, our friends did not know about his problems, and our personal time was being sapped trying to find out how we could help him learn.

Soon after the cerebral palsy was diagnosed, the physical education teacher in Jon's school took a special interest in Jon's physical progress. She later suggested that her husband, who was the athletic trainer for a local university, might be able to help. He was the first of many miracle workers who came to Jon's assistance. Over the summer, Jon's strength and balance were improved through a specially developed program of exercise and stretching. This had an incredibly positive impact on Jon's self-esteem.

As fate would also have it, Jon has had exceptional teachers and has had them at the most opportune times. His fourth grade teacher realized his intelligence and found ways to allow Jon to demonstrate his knowledge. She understood the need for people with disabilities to demonstrate their knowledge and feel good about themselves. She would often tell us that Jon was her "best listener." (Jon learns mostly by listening to his materials; he has all his textbooks on tape.) Fourth grade was the year that Jon received his first "A" report card. When he came home that afternoon he said, very proudly, "This is the kind of report card I've always wanted."

During this period of Jon's education, he was assigned a "learning support" teacher who knew how to access the support services available for children like Jon. She shared with us a copy of *Their World*. We finally understood that we were not alone and there were services and support for families and their children with learning disabilities.

We also became familiar with the services of the Recording for the Blind & Dyslexic (RFB&D) and became members. For the first time in his life, books on tape allowed Jon the freedom to do his own "reading." He would follow along while the tape read his book. Before this, when he would to read by himself, he tired quickly and he would get extremely frustrated and angry. "Why can't I read?" he would shout after about a half-hour of trying. It soon became apparent that writing and the transfer of information from one learning situation to another were also areas that Jon could not master. His handwriting looked perfect, but it took him hours to do a simple assignment.

Jon's sixth grade teacher was another very special person who came into our lives at just the right time. She saw Jon's wisdom and understanding, and afforded him the opportunity to demonstrate what he understood. Despite his need for assistance, Jon was teamed with the brightest students in his grade, which allowed him to contribute to their success and they to his. The friendships that developed in this class have lasted to today. This group of friends continues to support each other in high school and their loyalty to each other is truly phenomenal.

Over the years, Jon has come to understand what he needs in order to demonstrate what he knows. He often uses a speech-to-text program on the computer to write long papers, has textbooks on tape, takes tests in a very quiet environment, and is allowed extra time to complete tests and assignments. Accommodations are not easy to define, and even harder to implement.

Life was not always smooth and easy in our house, and sometimes we wonder how we survived it all. Jon's older brother found that the "new kid" not only took up more space, but he took up most of his parents' time. There was resentment for quite some time, and the relationships in our house were strained. Eventually, he began to understand that all the time we spent with Jon was not fun. It was often the hardest, most frustrating work done all day. Jon's younger brother seemed to accept the time spent with Jon as a normal part of family life, but is still confused and a bit surprised when we are amazed at Jon's accomplishments. Today, both brothers have a better understanding of how difficult it is for someone to have a learning disability. Even the grandparents have a better understanding about how much energy and time it takes to just maintain your equilibrium.

Jon is currently in eleventh grade and is in the upper 25 percent of his class. Recently, he achieved the rank of Eagle Scout, the highest rank a Boy Scout can attain. He is a varsity player on his high school's baseball and soccer teams, is well liked by his classmates, and makes us very proud every day. Jon's successes are a combination of his own hard work, his determination, and a wonderful support team which includes doctors, physical therapists, sports trainers, teachers, and caring friends.

It is not easy to live with a child with disabilities; every day is a challenge. Some of the suggestions we make to other parents of children with disabilities are:

- Always try to be aware of the changes in personality or moods of your child, as they can show you if something is or is not working. These changes do not always tell you what frustration there is. Sometimes it just comes out in conversation; always listen.
- Be involved in your child's education and participate in the Individualized Education Program (IEP) meetings.
- Remember that you have the right to change the IEP at any time, and make it work to help your child.
- Be firm in getting the accommodations that your child needs. Make sure that accommodations are followed.
- Talk with teachers and support personnel. Keep your child involved in monitoring his or her progress. With maturity, he or she will be better able to communicate with the support team about what is working and what is not.

Jon is a goal setter, and rarely does he ever miss the mark. He has learned that to expect success means to plan for success, and work hard to achieve it. He is currently planning to attend college and play college baseball and soccer. We are confident that he will achieve this goal, too.

*The authors are parents of three sons and live in Pennsylvania. Reprinted with permission from **Their World** 2000, National Center for Learning Disabilities, 381 Park Avenue South, Suite 1401, New York, N.Y. 10016-8806.*

ADDITIONAL READING

Two of the major organizations representing the interests of people with learning disabilities have provided lists of pertinent print and electronic materials, which follow here.

Orders for any of the items listed should be directed to the organizations at their addresses or Web sites.

LEARNING DISABILITIES ASSOCIATION OF AMERICA
4156 LIBRARY ROAD - PITTSBURGH, PA 15234-1349

9/01

QTY.	AUTHOR	PUBLICATION	COST PER	TTL.

ADOLESCENT-YOUNG ADULT

QTY.	AUTHOR	PUBLICATION	COST PER	TTL.
____	Cordoni, B.	Living with a Learning Disability (1990)	17.50	____
____	Crooker, J.	Campus Opportunities for Students with Learning Disabilities (1996)	7.00	____
____	duChossois, G.	Choosing the Right College: A step-by-step system to aid the student w/ LD (1992)	6.00	____
____	East, J.	YES YOU CAN! Helping Young People w/ LD Understand/Help Themselves (1993)	5.50	____
____	Greenbaum, J.	Performance Breakthroughs for Adolescents with LD or ADD (1996)	21.95	____
____	LDA	Adolescent Support Group Kit	10.00	____
____	LDA	Secondary Education & Beyond: Providing Opportunities for Students w/ LD (1996)	8.00	____
____	Lee/Jackson	FAKING IT: A Look into the Mind of a Creative Learner (1992)	17.95	____
____	Nadeau, K.	Survival Guide for College Students with ADD or LD (1994)	9.95	____
____	Satcher, et.al.	Bridges to Career Success - A Model for Training Career Counselors	10.00	____
____	Vogel, S.	*The College Student with a Learning Disability: A Handbook (2000)	8.00	____
____	Vogel, S.	*Postsecondary Decision-Making for Students with LD - Student Manual (2001)	8.50	____
____	Vogel, S.	*Postsecondary Decision-Making for Adults with LD - Teacher Manual (2001)	9.00	____
____	Vogel, S.	*Postsecondary Decision-Making for Adults w/ LD-Overhead Transparencies (2001)	5.50	____

ADULTS

QTY.	AUTHOR	PUBLICATION	COST PER	TTL.
____	Citro, T.	Successful Lifetime Management - Adults with Learning Disabilities (1999)	18.99	____
____	Jordon, D.	*Understanding & Managing LD in Adults-Professional Practices (2000)	22.50	____
____	Kelly/Ramundo	You Mean I'm Not Lazy, Stupid or Crazy?! (Adults and ADD) (1996)	16.00	____
____	LDA	They Speak for Themselves: A Survey of Adults w/ Learning Disabilities (1996)	8.00	____
____	LDA of Canada	Job Interview Tips for People with Learning Disabilities (1990)	18.00	____
____	Lewis, E.	Help Yourself:Advice for College-Bound Students with Learning Disabilities (1996)	20.00	____
____	Mooney/Cole	*Learning Outside the Lines: 2 Ivy League Students w/ LD & ADHD (2000)	13.00	____
____	Reiff, et.al.	Exceeding Expectations: Successful Adults with Learning Disabilities (1997)	27.00	____
____	Smith, C.	FOR YOU: Adults w/ Learning Disabilities (1991)	11.00	____
____	Weiss, L.	A.D.D. on the Job: Making Your A.D.D. Work for You (1996)	13.00	____

ASPERGER SYNDROME

QTY.	AUTHOR	PUBLICATION	COST PER	TTL.
____	Klin, et.al.	*Asperger Syndrome (2000)	45.00	____
____	Klin/Volkmar	Guidelines for Parents: Assessment, Diagnosis, and Intervention of Asperger (1995)	3.00	____
____	Smith/Simpson	Asperger Syndrome: A Guide for Educators and Parents (1998)	28.00	____

ASSESSMENT

QTY.	AUTHOR	PUBLICATION	COST PER	TTL.
____	Silver, L.	Psychological & Family Problems Associated w/ LD: Assess. & Intervention (1989)	1.00	____

ATTENTION DEFICIT DISORDER / HYPERACTIVITY

QTY.	AUTHOR	PUBLICATION	COST PER	TTL.
____	Alexander, C.	ADHD & Teens: A Parent's Guide to Making It Through the Tough Years (1995)	12.95	____
____	CH.A.D.D.	ADD and Adolescence: Strategies for Success (1996)	17.00	____
____	Coleman, W.S.	Attention Deficit Disorders and Hyperactivity (1993)	12.95	____
____	Crook, W., MD	Help for the Hyperactive Child-A Guide Offering Alternatives to Ritalin (1997)	16.95	____
____	Duane, D.	Reading & Attention Disorders - Neurobiological Correlates (1999)	38.00	____
____	Fowler, et.al.	ADD: An In-Depth Look From An Educational Perspective (1992)	12.50	____
____	Fowler, M.	Maybe You Know My Kid-A Parent's Guide to Identifying, Understanding & Helping (1994)	12.95	____
____	Green, G.	The A.D.D. Quest for Identity: Inside the Mind of Attention Deficit Disorder (1999)	13.95	____
____	Greenbaum,et.a	*Helping Adolescents with ADHD and Learning Disabilities (2001)	29.00	____
____	Guyer, B.	*ADHD-Achieving Success in School & in Life (2000)	30.00	____
____	Haber, J.	*ADHD: The Great Misdiagnosis (2000)	14.95	____
____	Hartman, et.al.	Think Fast! The ADD Experience (1996)	12.95	____

* = New Addition

ATTENTION DEFICIT DISORDER/HYPERACTIVITY cont...

_____	Jordon, D.	Attention Deficit Disorder - ADHD and ADD Syndrome (1992)	16.00	_____
_____	Lerner, et.al.	Attention Deficit Disorders: Assessment and Teaching (1995)	34.00	_____
_____	McEwan, E.	Attention Deficit Disorder - A Guide for Parents and Educators (1995)	11.99	_____
_____	Millichap, J.G.	Attention Deficit Hyperactivity and Learning Disorders: Questions & Answers (1998)	14.95	_____
_____	Nadeau/Dixon	Learning to Slow Down and Pay Attention (1997)	11.00	_____
_____	Nadeau, K.	Help4ADD @ High School-The Book You'll Want to Read even if Mom Bought It (199	19.95	_____
_____	Parker, R.	Making the Grade: An Adolescent's Struggle with ADD (1992)	12.00	_____
_____	Quinn/Stern	Putting on the Brakes - Young People's Guide to Understanding ADHD (1991)	9.95	_____
_____	Quinn, P.	ADD and the College Student (1994)	13.95	_____
_____	Rief, S.	How to Reach and Teach ADD/ADHD Children (1993)	28.00	_____
_____	Silver, L.	Controversial Approaches to Treating LD and ADD (Reprint)	3.00	_____
_____	Silver, L.	Dr. Larry Silver's Advice to Parents on ADHD (paperback-revised & updated)(1999)	15.00	_____
_____	Weiss, L.	Attention Deficit Disorder in Adults (1997)	13.00	_____
_____	Wodrich, D.	What Every Parent Wants to Know-Attention Deficit Hyperactivity Disorder (1994)	19.95	_____
_____	Zeigler Dendy	Teenagers with ADD: A Parent's Guide (1995)	18.95	_____
_____	Zeigler Dendy,C	*Teaching Teens with ADD/ADHD:Quick Reference Guide for Teachers/Parents (200	18.95	_____

AUDITORY

_____	Gillet, P.	AUDITORY PROCESSES (1993)	15.00	_____

CHILDREN'S BOOKS

_____	Denison, K.	I Wish I Could Fly Like A Bird! (Includes Audiotape) (1996)	17.95	_____
_____	Gehret, J.	I'm Somebody Too (Fiction Story) (1992)	13.50	_____
_____	Griffith, J.	How Dyslexic Benny Became A Star (1998)	12.95	_____
_____	Janover, C.	Josh: A Boy With Dyslexia (1988)	10.00	_____
_____	Janover, C.	How Many Days Until Tomorrow? (2000)	12.00	_____
_____	Moss, D.	Shelley, The Hyperactive Turtle (1989)	12.95	_____
_____	Munsch	Love You Forever (1996)	5.95	_____
_____	Roberts, B.	Phoebe Flower's Adventures: That's What Kids Are For (1998)	6.00	_____
_____	Roberts, B.	Phoebe Flower's Adventures: Phoebe's Lost Treasure (1999)	6.00	_____
_____	Romain, T.	Bullies Are a Pain in The Brain (1997)	9.95	_____
_____	Romain, T.	*What on Earth Do You Do When Someone Dies? (1999)	7.95	_____
_____	Romain/Verdick	*True or False? Tests Stink! (1999)	9.95	_____
_____	Romain/Verdick	*Stress Can Really Get on Your Nerves (2000)	9.95	_____

CRIMINAL JUSTICE SYSTEM

_____	LDA	Learning Disabilities and Juvenile Justice (1996)	2.00	_____
_____	Life Skills Edu.	Juvenile Delinquency: Children at Risk: Children in Need (1996)	2.50	_____
_____	NCLLD	The Criminal Justice System and Individuals with ADD and LD (1995)	2.50	_____

DIRECTORIES-SCHOOLS / COLLEGES / CAMPS

_____	LDA	List of Colleges/Universities That Accept Students with LD (1999)	4.00	_____
_____	LDA	Summer Camp Directory (1997)	4.00	_____
_____	Lipkin, M.	Guide to Private Schools with Programs or Services for Students with LD (1992)	35.00	_____
_____	Mangrum, et.al.	*Peterson's-Colleges with Programs for Students with LD or ADD (2000)	29.95	_____

DYSLEXIA

_____	Chase, et.al.	Developmental Dyslexia-Neural, Cognitive & Genetic Mechanisms (1996)	40.00	_____
_____	LDA of Canada	DYSLEXIA: An Introduction for Parents, Teachers and/or Individuals (1991)	7.50	_____
_____	Nosek, K.	Dyslexia in Adults - Taking Charge of Your Life (1997)	12.95	_____
_____	Nosek, K.	The Dyslexic Scholar - Helping Your Child Succeed in the School System (1995)	11.95	_____
_____	Shapiro, et.al.	Specific Reading Disability: A View of the Spectrum (1998)	33.50	_____
_____	Tuley, A.	Never Too Late to Read: Language Skills for the Adolescent with Dyslexia (1997)	27.50	_____

* = New Addition

EARLY CHILDHOOD

_____	Bricker, et.al.	An Activity-Based Approach to Early Intervention (1992)	29.00	_____
_____	Cook, et.al.	Adapting Early Childhood Curricula for Children in Inclusive Settings (1996)	37.00	_____
_____	Hall/Moats	Straight Talk About Reading: How Parents Can Make A Difference During the Early Years (1999)	12.95	_____
_____	LDA	When Pre-Schoolers Are Not "On-Target" In Their Development (1998)	4.00	_____
_____	LDA	When Pre-Schoolers Are Not "On-Target" In Their Development (spanish) (1998)	5.00	_____
_____	Lerner, et.al.	Preschool Children w/ Special Needs: Children At-Risk, Children w/ Disabilities (1998	52.00	_____

LANGUAGE

_____	Sorenson, S.	Working with Special Students in English/Language Arts (1991)	14.95	_____
_____	Weiss/Weiss	Basic Language Kit (1992)	16.75	_____

LEGAL

_____	Bateman, B.	Better IEPs - Third Edition	22.50	_____
_____	Bete, C.	Understanding IDEA and Section 504 - A Guide for Parents (1999)	2.50	_____
_____	Huefner, D.	*Getting Comfortable with Special Education Law (2000)	51.95	_____
_____	Latham/Latham	The Armed Forces (and ADD/LD) (1996)	3.00	_____
_____	Latham/Latham	Attention Deficit Disorder and the Law (1997)	29.00	_____
_____	Latham/Latham	Documentation and the Law (1996)	29.00	_____
_____	Latham/Latham	Higher Education Services for Students with LD and ADD - A Legal Guide (1999)	29.00	_____
_____	Latham/Latham	*Learning Disabilities and the Law (2000)	29.00	_____
_____	LDA Advocacy	Self-Advocacy Resources for Persons with Learning Disabilities (1990)	1.50	_____
_____	Siegel, L.M.	The Complete IEP Guide: How to Advocate for Your Special Ed Child (1999)	24.95	_____

LITERACY

_____	LDA	A Learning Disabilities Digest for Literacy Providers (1996)	3.00	_____
_____	Rosa Hagin Ctr.	Another Chance: The Comprehensive Learning Program for Adults w/ LD (1991)	15.00	_____

MATH

_____	Miller/Mercer	Addition Facts 0 to 9 (set of dice included) (1991)	17.00	_____
_____	Miller/Mercer	Subtraction Facts 0 to 9 (set of dice included) (1991)	17.00	_____
_____	Miller/Mercer	Multiplication Facts 0 to 81 (set of dice included) (1991)	17.00	_____
_____	Nolting, P.	Winning at Math - Your Guide to Learning Mathematice (1997)	18.95	_____

MENTAL HEALTH

_____	Dane, E.	PAINFUL PASSAGES: Working with Children with Learning Disabilities (1990)	10.00	_____

MISCELLANEOUS

_____	Boy Scouts	Scouting for Youth with Learning Disabilities (1998)	7.00	_____
_____	Johnson, et.al.	Stress and You - A Guide to Better Living (1988)	3.50	_____
_____	Kauffman, et.al.	The Illusion of Full Inclusion: A Comprehensive Critique (1995)	29.00	_____
_____	LDA	INCLUSION (1994)	3.00	_____
_____	LDA	Mark Twain Poster 13"x 20" Folded or Flat	2.00	_____
_____	LDA	Pins	3.75	_____
_____	LDA	What's Cooking With LDA? (1998)	7.00	_____
_____	Moss, P.	P. Buckley Moss - The People's Artist, An Autobiography (1989)	12.00	_____
_____	NJCLD	*Collective Perspectives on Issues Affecting LD: Position Papers/Statements (2001)	10.00	_____
_____	Smith, S.	*Power of the Arts-Creative Strategies for Teaching Exceptional Children (2001)	35.00	_____
_____	Szatmari, et.al.	A Follow-Up Study of High-Functioning Autistic Children (1989)	3.00	_____
_____	Tuttle/Tuttle	Challenging Voices (1995)	25.00	_____

PARENTS

_____	Barrett, et.al.	Playing Together, Learning Together (1996)	9.00	_____
_____	Bete, C.	What Every Parent Should Know About L.D. (1999)	2.25	_____
_____	Bishop/Olson	*Clayton's Path (2001)	13.00	_____
_____	Brooks, et.al.	*Raising Resilient Children (2001)	23.00	_____

---

* = New Addition

PARENTS cont.

_____	Citro, T.	The Experts Speak-Parenting the Child with Learning Disabilities (1998)	18.99	_____
_____	Clark, L.	S.O.S.! Help for Parents (1996)	12.00	_____
_____	Cohen, M.	The Attention Zone: A Parent's Guide to ADHD (1998)	21.95	_____
_____	Fritz, R.	Avoiding the Potholes: Having Your Child Evaluated for Learning Disabilities (1993)	3.00	_____
_____	Hays, M.	The Tuned-In, Turned-On Book About Learning Problems (1994)	12.00	_____
_____	Life Skills Edu.	Self Image (1995)	2.95	_____
_____	Life Skills Edu.	Family Stress (1997)	3.25	_____
_____	Life Skills Edu.	Understanding Peer Pressure and Helping Your Kids Cope With It (1996)	2.50	_____
_____	Ogan, G.D.	Can Anyone Help My Child? (1994)	17.95	_____
_____	Osman, B.	No One To Play With: Social Problems of LD and ADD Children (1995)	13.00	_____
_____	Pacer Center	Unlocking Doors - How to work better with my child's school & teachers (1996)	5.00	_____
_____	Rich, D.	Mega-Skills - In School and in Life: The Best Gift You Can Give Your Child (1992)	13.95	_____
_____	Rosner, J.	Helping Children Overcome L.D. (paperback) (1993)	18.95	_____
_____	Shaya/Windell	Coping With Your Attention Deficit Disorder Child (1995)	3.50	_____
_____	Silver, L.	The Misunderstood Child-Understanding and Coping with Your Child's Learning (199	15.00	_____
_____	Smith, S.	No Easy Answers - The L.D. Child at Home and at School (paperback) (1995)	13.95	_____
_____	Smith, S.	No Easy Answers (spanish)	20.95	_____
_____	Smith, S.	Succeeding Against the Odds: How the LD Can Realize Their Promise (1992)	13.95	_____
_____	Smith, et.al.	An Introduction to Learning Disability: A Practical Guide for Parents (1991)	3.00	_____
_____	Stevens, S.H.	The LD Child and the ADHD Child: Ways Parents and Professionals Can Help (1996	12.95	_____
_____	Umansky, P.	Homework Manager-All In One Assignment Book & Homework Folder (1999)	11.99	_____
_____	Wild, K.	A Mother's Book of Ideas for the LD Child (1995)	24.95	_____
_____	Wren, C.	*Hanging by a Twig-Understanding & Counseling Adults w/ Learning Disabilities (200	32.00	_____

PARENTS / TEACHERS

_____	Accardo, P.	The Invisible Disability: Understanding LD in the Context of Health & Education (199€	9.00	_____
_____	Anderson, et.al.	Negotiating the Special Education Maze:A Guide for Parents & Teachers (1997)	16.95	_____
_____	DePorter, et.al.	Quantum Teaching:Orchestrating Student Success (1990)	27.95	_____
_____	Guyer, B.	The Pretenders: Gifted People Who Have Difficulty Learning (1997)	24.50	_____
_____	Heacox, D.	Up From Under-Achievement (Teachers, students, parents working together) (1991)	16.95	_____
_____	Kranowitz, C.	The Out-of -Sync Child-Recognizing and Coping with Sensory Integration Dysfunction (1998)	14.00	_____
_____	LDA of Canada	A Guide to Understanding Learning and Behavior Problems in Children (1996)	20.00	_____
_____	Levine, M.	Educational Care:A System for Understanding & Helping Children (1994)	35.00	_____
_____	McGuinnis, D.	Why Our Children Can't Read and What We Can Do About It (1997)	25.00	_____
_____	McMurchie, S.	Understanding LD (1994)	21.95	_____
_____	Rief, S.	*Ready Start School:Nurturing & Guiding Your Child through Preschool and Kindergarten (2001)	15.00	_____
_____	Smith, S.	Different is Not Bad, Different is the World-A Book About Disabilities (1994)	9.50	_____
_____	Sternberg, et.al.	Negotiating the Disability Maze (critical knowledge for parents,professionals, etc.)(19	35.00	_____
_____	West, T.	In The Minds Eye (Visual Thinkers, Gifted People w/ LD, Computer Images) (1997)	28.00	_____

PRE-ADOLESCENT / ADOLESCENT

_____	Cummings,et.al.	The School Survival Guide for Kids w/ LD-Making Learning Easier/More Fun (1991)	13.95	_____
_____	Cummings,et.al.	The Survival Guide for Teenagers with LD (Learning Differences) (1993)	13.95	_____
_____	Cummings,et.al.	The Survival Guide for Kids with LD (Learning Differences) (1990)	10.95	_____
_____	Levine, M.	All Kinds of Minds: A Young Student's Book about Learning Disabilities & LD (1993)	23.00	_____
_____	Levine, M.	Keeping a Head in School-Student's Book about Learning Abilities & LD (1990)	23.00	_____
_____	Mannix, D.	Ready-to-Use Self-Esteem Activities for Secondary Students w/ Special Needs (199€	29.95	_____
_____	Roby, C.	When Learning is Tough: Kids Talk About Their Learning Disabilities (1994)	14.50	_____
_____	Stern/Ben-ami	Many Ways to Learn: Young People's Guide to LD (1996)	12.95	_____

RESEARCH / EDUCATIONAL

_____	Duane/Gray	The Reading Brain: The Biological Basis of Dyslexia (1991)	35.00	_____
_____	Kratoville, B.	Great Medical Milestones - Stories from Doctors (1996)	14.00	_____
_____	Lyon/Gray et.al.	Better Understanding Learning Disabilities: New Views from Research (1993)	42.00	_____
_____	Schettler, et.al.	Generation at Risk - Reproductive Health & the Environment (1999)	29.00	_____

* = New Addition

SOCIAL PERCEPTION

| | Giler, J. | *Socially ADDept-Manual for Parents of Children w/ ADHD and/or LD (2000) | 30.00 | |

SPELLING

| | Laurita, R. | Spelling as a Categorical Act | 1.50 | |

TEACHERS

	Aaron/Baker	Reading Disabilities in College & High School:Diagnosis & Management (1991)	24.00	
	Algozzine, et.al.	Simple Ways to Make Teaching Math More Fun	14.95	
	Anderson, W.	VAK Tasks for Vocabulary and Spelling (1993)	9.00	
	Anderson, W.	VAK Tasks for Vocabulary and Spelling-Teacher's Manual & Answer Key (1994)	7.00	
	Arena, J.	How to Write an IEP (1989)	12.00	
	Banas, N.	WISC-III Prescriptions-how to work creatively w/ individual learning styles (1993)	14.00	
	Beninghof, A.	SenseAble Strategies, Including Diverse Learners Through Multisensory Strategies	19.95	
	Blachman, et.al.	*Road to Code-A Phonological Awareness Program for Young Children (2000)	50.00	
	Brown/Connelly	Simplified Phonics Teaching Package:Includes:The Simplified Phonics Teaching Manual-Diagnostic Testing Materials & Six Student Booklets (1998)	25.00	
	Cross, T.	Essential Roots Word Book (1990)	10.00	
	Cross, T.	Essential Roots Workbook (1990)	10.00	
	Cross, et.al	Essential Roots Workbook - Teacher's Manual (1990)	15.50	
	Cross, et.al	Essential Root Cards (to be used with above three books) (1990)	18.00	
	DLD/CEC	The DLD Competencies for Teachers of Students with LD (1992)	5.50	
	Dornbush/Pruitt	Teaching the Tiger (1995)	35.00	
	Giles/Kovitz	Helping Learning Disabled Music Students	0.75	
	Goldstein	Teacher's Guide-Attention Deficit Hyperactivity Disorder in Children (1990)	5.50	
	Goldstein, et.al.	Overcoming Underachieving-Action Guide-Helping Your Child Succeed in School (19	16.95	
	Hagin, et.al.	Teaching Reading:Definitions of Commonly Used Terms (1996)	4.00	
	Heilman, A.	Phonics in Proper Perspective (1998)	16.00	
	Hull/Fox	Phonics for the Teacher of Reading (1998)	16.00	
	Jenson, et.al.	The Tough Kid Tool Box	16.95	
	Kirk/Minskoff	Phonic Remedial Reading Lessons (1985)	15.00	
	Kirshner, A.	Remediation of Reversals (1994)	25.00	
	Kratoville, B.	Phonograms: For The Fun Of It-Exercises and Answer Key (1999)	15.00	
	Kratoville, B. L.	Sentence Tracking: High Frequency Words (1991)	14.00	
	LDA	L.D. in the High School:A Method Booklet for Secondary Special Subject Teachers	3.00	
	Lerner, J.	Learning Disabilities: Theories, Diagnosis and Teaching Strategies (1997)	69.25	
	Light/Morrison	Beyond Retention-A Survival Guide for Regular Classroom Teachers (1990)	15.00	
	Mather/Goldstein	*Learning Disabilities and Challenging Behaviors:A Guide to Intervention and Classroom Management (2001)	44.95	
	Mercer, C.	Students with Learning Disabilities (5th Edition) (1997)	69.00	
	Moats, L.	Spelling: Development, Disability, and Instruction (1995)	23.00	
	Moats, L.	*Speech to Print - Language Essentials for Teachers (2000)	30.00	
	Moats, et.al.	LANGUAGE! Instructional Resource Guide for Teachers	45.00	
	Patton, et.al.	Exceptional Individuals in Focus (1996)	34.00	
	School/Cooper	The IEP Primer and the Individualized Program (1997)	15.00	
	Smith, C.R.	Learning Disabilities: The Interaction of Learner, Task & Setting (1998)	62.00	
	Stevens, S.	Classroom Success for the LD and ADHD Child (1997)	13.95	
	Stewart, L.	Help for the Learning Disabled Child - Symptoms and Solutions (1991)	25.00	
	Tamaren, M.	I Make A Difference (1992)	13.50	
	Tilton, L.	Inclusion - A Fresh Look (1996)	29.95	
	Watkins/Rice	Specific Language Impairments in Children (1994)	36.00	
	Winebrenner, S.	Teaching Kids with LD in the Regular Classroom (1996)	27.95	

TECHNOLOGY

	Bender/Bender	Computer-Assisted Instruction for Students at Risk for ADHD, Mild Disabilities, etc.(19	31.95	
	I B M	Computers in Head Start Classrooms (1990)	7.00	
	Lekotek	Innotek Software Resource Guide:Selecting Software for Children w/ Special Needs	26.00	
	Raskind, M.	Assistive Technology for Children with Learning Disabilities (1996)	3.00	

* = New Addition

TOXINS / LEAD

_____	Am. People's	America's Choice-Children's Health or Corporate Profit (1999)	8.00 _____
_____	Channing Bete	What Everyone Should Know About Lead Poisoning (1994)	1.50 _____
_____	Channing Bete	What Everyone Should Know About Lead in Your Water (1992)	2.00 _____

VISUAL

_____	Dawkins, et.al.	The Suddenly Successful Student-How Behavioral Optometry Helps (1990)	9.00 _____

VOCATIONAL

_____	Brown, D.	*Learning a Living:Guide to Planning Your Career-Finding a Job for People w/ LD (20	18.95 _____
_____	Latham, et.al.	Tales from the Workplace (1997)	15.00 _____
_____	LDA of Canada	Learning Disabilities and the Workplace (1993)	29.00 _____
_____	Gerber/Brown	Learning Disabilities and Employment (1997)	36.00 _____
_____	Reisman, E.S.	Guidelines for Supervising Employees with Learning Disabilities (1993)	13.00 _____
_____	Washburn, W.	Vocational Entry-Skills for Secondary & Adult Students w/ LD:Teacher's Guide(1994)	18.00 _____
_____	Washburn, W.	Vocational Entry-Skills-Student Workbook (1994)	10.00 _____

WRITING

_____	Carlisle	Models For Writing Tch Manual (1996)	15.00 _____
_____	Carlisle	Models For Writing Workbook A (1996)	16.50 _____
_____	Carlisle	Models For Writing Workbook B (1996)	16.50 _____
_____	Carlisle	Models For Writing Workbook C (1996)	16.50 _____
_____	Cavey, D.	Dysgraphia: Why Jonny Can't Write (1993)	11.00 _____

VCR TAPES   (ALL SALES FINAL)

_____ **I'm Not Stupid** - This video depicts the constant battle of the learning disabled child in school. It points out how the LD child is often misdiagnosed as slow, retarded, emotionally disturbed, or even just a lazy kid. This highly recommended documentary is for parents, teachers, administrators, students or anyone who wants to learn what it is like to live with learning disabilities. (53 Minutes, 1987)   22.00 _____

_____ **Picture of Success** - Featuring Pat Buckley Moss and Dr. Larry Silver, this inspiring video tells the story of a successful dyslexic (16 Minutes)   25.00 _____

_____ **A Leaders Guide for Youth with Learning Disabilities** - This video shows how leaders of groups can integrate individuals with learning disabilities into regular programs, similar to the Boy Scouts. This would be appropriate to show to groups such as the PTA, churches, and other agencies. (10 Minutes)   23.00 _____

_____ **Look What You've Done - Helping Learning Disabled Children Build Self-Esteem** - Whether they've failed a spelling test or dropped an easy pop fly, kids who have trouble learning hear those words far too often. Here are practical strategies for helping children develop the competence and resilience they need to succeed. (Robert Brooks, 1 Hour)   49.95 _____

_____ **When the Chips are Down - Strategies for Improving Children's Behavior** - Do you ever have days when the kids seem totally out of control? Host Richard Lavoie offers practical advice on dealing with behavior problems quickly and effectively, showing how preventive discipline can head off many problems before they start. (Rick Lavoie, 1 Hour)   49.95 _____

_____ **Last One Picked...First One Picked On - Helping Learning Disabled Children Strengthen Social Skills** - Playing with friends usually is a happy ritual for children. But kids with learning disabilities are often isolated and rejected. This program addresses social problems these children face -- and offers some practical solutions. (Rick Lavoie, 1 Hour)   49.95 _____

_____ **How Difficult Can This Be - Understanding Learning Disabilities** - Look at the world through the eyes of a learning disabled child. Join in a series of classroom activities that cause frustration, anxiety, and tension -- emotions all too familiar to students with learning disabilities. A "must view for parents and teachers." (Rick Lavoie, 1 Hour)   49.95 _____

* = New Addition

• • • • • • • The International Dyslexia Association • • • • • • •
Readings *in* DYSLEXIA

✓
**indicate
quantity
ordering**

"Annals of Dyslexia"
IDA's scholarly journal contains updates on current research and selected proceedings from talks given at IDA International Conferences. <u>Annals</u> are available from 1982 through the present year. Costs vary depending on the issue:

2001 ....**$18.50 per book**   1986-1987 *(1984 & 1985 out-of-print)*...............**$12.00 per book**
1996 through 2000 ....**$18.00 per book**   1983...**$9.00 per book**
1991 through 1995 *(1992 out-of-print)* ....**$16.00 per book**   1956, 1963, 1968, 1969, 1970, 1978, 1980 -1 Bulletin..**$5.00 per book**
1988-1990 *(1989 out-of-print)* ....**$14.00 per book**

"Language and the Developing Child" *by Katrina deHirsch,*   **$15.00**   *(1984, paper, 308 pages)*
This collection of papers introduces a new generation of teachers, clinicians, and parents to the work of one of the key figures in the search for the causes and treatment of dyslexia, autism, stuttering, and other language disorders. Ms. deHirsch pioneered research which demonstrates the implications of childhood language acquisition on school success and opened doors to the practice of early language screening and intervention.

"Intimacy with Language: A Forgotten Basic in Teacher Education"   **$9.00**   *(1988, paper, 80 pages)*
"Dyslexia and Evolving Educational Patterns," symposium proceedings which tell what scholars and teachers are saying about the role of language in teacher education: designing thoughtful, demanding, teacher training programs; enforcing certification standards that encourage the best minds to become teachers; selecting, supervising, and evaluating teachers wisely; and lobbying for educational reform that is possible, humane, and cost effective.

"Reading, Writing, and Speech Problems in Children and Selected Papers" *by Samuel T. Orton*   **$22.00**   *(1989, hardcover, 359 pages)*
First published in 1937 and reprinted in 1989, this classic is a tribute to the man who aroused the attention of the scientific community and provided the sound educational principles on which much teaching of individuals with dyslexia today is based.

"All Language and the Creation of Literacy"   **$12.00**   *(1991, paper, 93 pages)*
A selection of papers presented at two symposia, "Whole Language and Phonics" and "Literacy and Language." These papers present two opposing philosophies in the teaching of reading. The scope of concern is placed into the larger context of literacy, meaning all aspects of language, not reading alone.

"Many Faces of Dyslexia" *by Margaret Byrd Rawson*   **$18.50**   *(1992, paper, 270 pages)*
A selection of the writings of Margaret Rawson, a 98-year-old pioneer in the field of dyslexia, and editor emeritus of IDA. Mrs. Rawson has inspired several generations of professionals, parents, and students through her lectures, papers, and teacher-training sessions dealing with language and its meaning in our lives.

* "Dyslexia Over the Lifespan: A Fifty-Five Year Longitudinal Study" *by Margaret Byrd Rawson*   **$12.00**   *(1995 , paper, 197 pages)*
Margaret Rawson extended her study of 56 dyslexic and non-dyslexic boys, and has brought to a close the report of a longitudinal account spanning 55 years in the lives of its subjects, together with reflections on the connections of that history with the broader field of dyslexia.

* "Bridges to Reading" *by the Parents' Educational Resource Center*   **$21.00**   *(1995)*
A kit of first step strategies, puzzles, and games for parents to use when they suspect their child has a reading problem.

"Dyslexia: Finding the Answers"   **$6.95 plus** *$3.20 shipping*
IDA's new video provides basic up-to-date information. This video is perfect for the parent who has just learned their child may have dyslexia or the teacher who has students with reading problems.

(please print)

Name _____

Address _____

City _____ State _____ Zip _____-_____

Phone _____ Fax _____

Total Amount of Order _____
Less 20% IDA member discount
*member discount does not apply to
"Bridges to Reading," "Dyslexia Over the Lifespan,"
or bulk order of The Emeritus Series* _____

Shipping   Subtotal _____

(10% of total order for U.S. and 20% for international) _____
(Maryland residents add 5% sales tax)
Enclosed is check for $ _____

OR Please charge my ☐ VISA   ☐ MasterCard   ☐ AMERICAN EXPRESS   ☐ DISCOVER

Account #

☐☐☐☐ ☐☐☐☐ ☐☐☐☐ ☐☐☐☐ ☐☐☐☐

Exp. Date _____

Signature (required for ID purposes)   Please allow 3 to 5 weeks for delivery. Sorry, no billings or C.O.D.s

To place your order, please send this form to:

THE INTERNATIONAL DYSLEXIA ASSOCIATION®
8600 LaSalle Road • Chester Building, Suite 382 • Baltimore, MD 21286-2044
Phone: (410) 296-0232 • Fax: (410) 321-5069
or order on-line at *http://www.interdys.org*

READINGS IN DYSLEXIA (continued)

**indicate
quantity
ordering**

REPRINTS FROM <u>ANNALS</u>

To order reprints, place a check next to each title. $3.00 each

No. TITLE

_____ 156 **Individual Differences in Word Recognition Skills of ESL Children** *by Ester Geva, Zoreh Yaghoubzadeh & Barbara Schuster (2000)*

_____ 155 **Schools as Host Environments: Toward a School-Wide Reading Improvement Model** *by Ed Kamé enui, Deborah Simmons & Michael Coyne (2000)*

_____ 154 **The Neural Basis of Developmental Dyslexia** *by Thomas Zeffiro & Guinevere Eden (2000)*

_____ 153 **Repeated Reading to Enhance Fluency: Old Approaches and New Directions** *by Marianne Meyer & Rebecca Felton (1999)*

_____ 152 **It's Never Too Late to Remediate: Teaching Word Recognition to Students with Reading Disabilities in Grades 4-7** *by Sylvia Abbott & Virginia Berninger (1999)*

_____ 151 **Rapid Serial Naming and the Double Deficit Hypothesis** *by Maryanne Wolf, Martha Bridge Denckla, M.D. & Laurie Cutting, Ph.D. (1999)*

_____ 150 **Benefits of Multisensory Structured Language Instruction for At-Risk Foreign Language Learners: A Comparison Study of High School Spanish Students** *by Richard L. Sparks, Marjorie Artzer, Jon Patton, Leonore Ganschow, Karen Miller, Dorothy Hordubay, Geri Walsh (1998)*

_____ 149 **Predicting the Future Achievement of Second Graders with Reading Disabilities: Contributions of Phonemic Awareness, Verbal Memory, Rapid Naming, and IQ** *by Hollis S. Scarborough (1998)*

_____ 148 **Longitudinal Course of Rapid Naming in Disabled and Nondisabled Readers** *by Marianne S. Meyer, Frank B. Wood, Lesley A. Hart, Rebecca H. Felton (1998)*

_____ 147 **Structured, Sequential, Multisensory Teaching: The Orton Legacy** *by Marcia K. Henry, Ph.D. (1998)*

_____ 146 **The Great Debate: Then and Now** *by Marilyn Jager Adams, Ph.D. (1997 Annals)* (1998)

_____ 145 **Are Reading Methods Changing Again?** *by Jeanne Chall, Ph.D. (1997 Annals)*

_____ 144 **The Samuel T. Orton Award for 1996 to Jeanne S. Chall, Ph.D.** *by Roselmina Indrisano (1997 Annals)*

_____ 143 **Coping with Dyslexia in the Regular Classroom: Inclusion or Exclusion?** *by Sylvia O. Richardson, M.D. (1996 Annals)*

_____ 142 **Handwriting: A Neglected Cornerstone of Literacy** *by Betty Sheffield (1996 Annals)*

_____ 141 **How Children Learn to Read and Why They Fail** *by Philip B. Gough, Ph.D. (1996 Annals)*

_____ 140 **Middle and High School Students: Effects of an Individualized Structured Language Curriculum** *by Jane Fell Greene, Ed.D. (1996 Annals)*

_____ 139 **Toward a Definition of Dyslexia** *by G. Reid Lyon, Ph.D. (1995 Annals)*

_____ 138 **Instructional Strategies for Long-Term Success** *by Henry B. Reiff, Paul J. Gerber, and Rick Gensberg (1994 Annals)*

_____ 137 **The Missing Foundation in Teacher Education: Knowledge of the Structure of Spoken and Written Language** *by Louisa Cook Moats (1994 Annals)*

_____ 136 **Training Phonological Awareness: A Study with Inner-City Kindergarten Children** *by Susan Brady, Ph.D., Anne Fowler, Ph.D., Brenda Stone, and Nancy Winbury (1994 Annals)*

_____ 135 **Dyslexia in the Workplace: Implications of the Americans with Disabilities Act** *by Diana L. Sauter, Ph.D., and Donna McPeek (1993 Annals)*

_____ 134 **Attention Deficits: Current Concepts, Controversies, Management, and Approaches to a Classroom Instruction** *by Betsy Busch, M.D. (1993 Annals)*

_____ 133 **Familial Patterns of Learning Disabilities** *by Sandra Smith (1992 Annals)*

_____ 132 **A Future of Reversals-Dyslexic Talents in a World of Computer Visualization** *by Thomas G. West (1992 Annals)*

_____ 131 **The Impact of an Intensive Multisensory Reading Program on a Population of Learning Disabled Delinquents** *by Stephen B. Simpson, James A. Swanson, and Ken Kunkel (1992 Annals)*

_____ 130 **The Effects of Multisensory Structured Language Instruction on Native Language and Foreign Language Aptitude Skills of At-Risk High School Foreign Language Learners** *by Richard Sparks, Leonore Ganschow, Jane Sue Skinner, and Marjorie Artzer (1992 Annals)*

_____ 129 **Spelling Errors and Reading Fluency in Compensated Adult Dyslexics** *by Dianne L. Lefly and Bruce F. Pennington, Ph.D. (1991 Annals)*

_____ 128 **Nonverbal Learning Disabilities and Remedial Interventions** *by Jean M. Foss (1991 Annals)*

_____ 127 **Early Language Intervention: A Deterrent to Reading Disability** *by Diane J. Sawyer and Katharine Butler, Ph.D. (1991 Annals)*

_____ 126 **The Structured Flexibility of Orton-Gillingham** *by Betty B. Sheffield (1991 Annals)*

_____ 125 **Gender Differences in Cognitive Abilities of Reading-Disabled Twins** *by J.C. DeFries, Sally J.Wadsworth and Jacquelyn J. Gillis (1990 Annals)*

_____ 124 **Whole Language vs. Code Emphasis: Underlying Assumptions and Their Implications for Reading Instruction** *by I.Y. and A.M. Liberman (1990 Annals)*

_____ 123 **Written Narratives of Normal and Learning Disabled Students** *by Doris J. Johnson and James O. Grant, Ph.D. (1989 Annals)*

_____ 122 **Using Genetics to Understand Dyslexia** *by Bruce F. Pennington, Ph.D. (1989 Annals)*

READINGS IN DYSLEXIA (continued)

indicate quantity ordering

_____ 121 Ordinary and Extraordinary Brain Development: Anatomical Variation in Developmental Dyslexia *by Albert M. Galaburda, M.D.* (1989 Annals)

_____ 120 Gifts, Talents, and the Dyslexias: Wellsprings, Springboards, and Finding Foley's Rocks *by Priscilla L. Vail* (1990 Annals)

_____ 119 Genetic and Environmental Etiologies of Reading Disability: A Twin Study *by Michele C. La Buda and J.C. Defries* (1988 Annals)

_____ 118 Phonics: Integrated Decoding and Spelling Instruction Based on Word Origin and Structure *by Marcia K. Henry, Ph.D.* (1988 Annals)

_____ 117 Phoneme Segmentation Training: Effect on Reading Readiness *by Eileen W. Ball, Ph.D. and Benita A. Blachman, Ph.D.* (1988 Annals)

_____ 116 The Quest for Literacy *by Mary Lee Enfield, Ph.D.* (1988 Annals)

_____ 115 Specific Developmental Dyslexia: Retrospective and Prospective Views *by Sylvia O. Richardson, M.D.* (1989 Annals)

_____ 114 A New Look at Reading Comprehension Instruction for Disabled Readers *by Katherine Maria* (1987 Annals)

_____ 113 Dyslexia: Especially for Parents *by Regina Cicci, Ph.D.* (1987 Annals)

_____ 112 The Use of Morphological Knowledge in Spelling Derived Forms *by Learning Disabled and Normal Students* *by Joanne F. Carlisle, Ph.D.* (1987 Annals)

_____ 111 Learning Disabilities and Psychological Development in Childhood and Adolescence *by Jonathan Cohen, Ph.D.* (1986 Annals)

_____ 110 Language and the Developing Child: Pivotal Ideas of Katrina de Hirsch *by Jeannette Jefferson Jansky, Ph.D.* (1986 Annals)

_____ 109 The Many Faces of Dyslexia *by Margaret Byrd Rawson.* Response to "The Many Faces of Dyslexia" *by Albert M. Galaburda, M.D.* (1986 Annals)

_____ 108 A Developmental Framework for Developmental Dyslexia *by Uta Frith* (1986 Annals)

_____ 107 The School and the Dyslexic-Mutually Exclusive? *by William Ellis* (1986 Annals)

_____ 106 A Rescue Service for All Dyslexic Children *by Elaine Miles* (1985 Annals)

_____ 105 Developmental Dyslexia: A Review of Biological Interactions *by Albert Galaburda, M.D.* (1985)

_____ 104 Personal Perspectives (with an introduction by Regina Cicci, Ph.D.) Dyslexia-My Invisible Handicap *by Thomas S. Mautner,* One Parent's Experience with Dyslexia *by Leonard J. Hartwig,* The Brain of a Learning-Disabled Individual *by Norman Geschwind, M.D.* (1984 Annals)

_____ 101 Adapting a College Preparatory Curriculum for Dyslexic Adolescents *by Julia Ann Greenwood, Gita H. Morris and Charlotte G. Morgan* (1983 Annals)

_____ 100 Memory as a Factor in the Contemporary Efficiency of Dyslexic Children with High Abstract Reasoning Ability *by K. Joyce Steeves* (1983 Annals)

_____ 99 Developmental Dyslexia: Current Anatomical Research *by Albert Galaburda. M.D.* (1983 Annals)

_____ 98 Why Orton Was Right *by Norman Geschwind M.D.* (1982 Annals)

_____ 97 Strategies for Initial Reading Instruction *by Linda W. Camp, Nancy E. Winbury and Danielle Zinna* (1981 Bulletin)

_____ 95 A Diversity Model for Dyslexia *by Margaret Byrd Rawson*

_____ 94 Persistent Auditory Disorders in Young Dyslexic Adults *by Doris J. Johnson, Ph.D.* (1980 Bulletin)

_____ 93 Written Language Disorders *by Regina Cicci, Ph.D.* (1980 Bulletin)

_____ 92 Patterning and Organizational Deficits in Children with Language and Learning Disabilities *by Katrina de Hirsch, F.C.S.T. and Jeannette J. Jansky, Ph.D.* (1980 Bulletin)

_____ 88 Two School Principals Speak: Program Planning for Dyslexic Children in the General Classroom *by Genevieve Oliphant, Ph.D. and* The School Principal as Advocate for the Child with Learning Differences *by William Ellis* (1979 Bulletin)

_____ 76 Dyslexia and Learning Disabilities: Their Relationship *by Margaret Byrd Rawson* (1978 Bulletin)

_____ 72 The Advantages of Being Dyslexic *by Richard L. Masland, M.D.* (1976 Bulletin)

_____ 61 A Neurologic Overview of Specific Language Disability for the Non-Neurologist *by Drake D. Duane, M.D.* (1974 Bulletin)

_____ 57 The Language Therapist as a Basic Mathematics Tutor for Adolescents *by Alice Ansara* (1973)

_____ 55 Early Prediction of Reading Problems *by Jeanette J. Jansky, Ph.D. and* A Kindergarten Screening Index to Predict Reading Failure *by Dorothy M. Tower* (1973 Bulletin)

_____ 48 Language Therapy to Salvage the Potential of Dyslexic Adolescents *by Alice Ansara* (1972)

_____ 43 Auditory Perception and Reading Disability *by Genevieve Oliphant, Ph.D.* (1972 Bulletin)

_____ 35 The Structure of English: The Language to be Learned *by Margaret Byrd Rawson* (1972 Bulletin)

_____ 27 Language Disability in Men of Eminence *by L.J. Thompson, M.D.* (1969 Bulletin)

_____ 22 Dyslexics as Adults: The Possibilities and the Challenge *by Margaret Byrd Rawson* (1977 Bulletin)

_____ 11 The Orton-Gillingham Approach *by June Lyday Orton*

_____ 2 "Can't Spell, Can't Read" *by J. Roswell Gallagher, M.D.*

The International Dyslexia Association

● ● ● ● ● ● ● ● ● ● ●

The Orton Emeritus Series when completed will consist of 26 monographs each dedicated to a specific topic related to dyslexia. **$5.00 each.** The following are now available:

The "A" Book - "Adults With Dyslexia: Aspiring and Achieving" by Joan R. Knight was written to help the adult with dyslexia to better understand themselves, and also to assist families of adults with learning problems in understanding their needs.

The "B" Book - "Basic Facts About Dyslexia, Part I: What Every Layperson Ought to Know" by Angela Wilkins and Alice Garside is a thorough look at the "basics" of dyslexia. This is an excellent initial book for parents or individuals who have just learned that they or their child may have dyslexia. (Second Edition)

The "B" Book Part II - "Basic Facts About Dyslexia: What Professionals Ought To Know" by Louisa Cook Moats, Ed.D. is a version of the original "B" book which was written with the parent in mind. This monograph is written primarily for the educator, who already knows "the basics" about dyslexia but wishes to further their understanding.

The "C" Book - "College: How Students with Dyslexia Can Maximize the Experience" by Joan Stoner, Ed.D., Mary Farrell, Ph.D., Barbara Priddy Guyer, Ph.D., with a forword by Barbara Cordoni, Ed.D. This is a valuable resource and guide for choosing a college or university for those with dyslexia.

The "D" Book - "Doctors Ask Questions About Dyslexia: A Review of Medical Research" by Sylvia O. Richardson, M.D., past-president of IDA. This book reviews current research and provides a comprehensive look at dyslexia from the medical perspective. (Second Edition)

The "E" Book - "Early Childhood Education" by Carole Hill, Educational Consultant, Dallas, Texas and Pam Quarterman, Director, Oak Hill Academy, Dallas, Texas addresses the importance of early identification and appropriate intervention.

The "J" Book - "Justice for All" by Stanley J. Antonoff, James Olivier, and Karen Norlander explains how certain federal laws can help individuals with learning difficulties.

The "K" Book - "Kids Who Learn Differently: Strategies for Successful Studying" by Nancy E. Hennessy and Lois H. Rothschild provides an understanding of how children learn, and how to help them to study more efficiently.

The "L" Book - "Listening Comprehension and Attention: Basic Facts" by Doris J. Johnson, Ph.D., will help readers understand the complex issues of listening comprehension, identification of symptoms, the evaluation process, and how to find help.

The "O" Book - "The Other Sixteen Hours: The Social and Emotional Problems of Dyslexia," by Michael Ryan, Ph.D., is an in-depth and sensitive perspective on the many frustrations faced by people with dyslexia.

The "P" Book - "Phonological Awareness: A Critical Factor in Dyslexia" by Joseph Torgesen, Ph.D., Professor of Psychology, Florida State University, explains phonological awareness and why it is an essential primary diagnostic criterion in learning to read.

The "R" Book - "Reading, Writing and Spelling: The Multisensory Structured Language Approach" by Helaine Schupack and Barbara A. Wilson gives information on the methods of instruction used to assist individuals with dyslexia with reading, writing, and spelling problems.

The "S" Book (Part I) - "Independent Schools and Programs for Individuals with Dyslexia: What are the Questions" by Jean M. Foss and Diana Hanbury King will answer the questions most frequently asked by parents of children with learning problems when considering independent schooling.

The "T" Book - "Testing: Critical Components in the Identification of Dyslexia" by Jane Fell Greene, Ed.D. and Louisa Cook Moats, Ed.D., answers the many questions that parents ask when having their child tested.

Glossary of Learning Disabilities Terms

This glossary is a compilation of terms and definitions adapted from a number of sources, which are duly noted. All definitions not otherwise attributed have been written by the Learning Disabilities Council.

Academic Classes - Classes in basic subjects such as reading, arithmetic, science, and social studies at elementary level; and English, history, science and math at secondary level.[1]

Accommodation – Adaptations and modifications of printed materials, teaching approaches and techniques, etc., designed to enable students with learning disabilities to accomplish school work with greater ease and effectiveness. The accommodations also help students participate in and benefit from classroom activities.

Achievement Test - A test that measures the extent to which a person has acquired certain information or mastered certain skills, usually as a result of planned instruction or training. These tests are often called educational tests.

ADA - Americans with Disabilities Act – A law which applies to persons with a physical or mental impairment that substantially limits one or more of life's activities. Such persons are protected from discrimination by the ADA and Section 504. ADA prohibits discrimination solely on the basis of a disability.

Adaptive Physical Education - A special physical education program developed to fit the limits and disabilities of persons with handicaps.[2]

ADD - Attention Deficit Disorder - A term frequently used to describe the academic and behavioral problems of children who have difficulty focusing and maintaining attention.

ADHD - Attention Deficit Hyperactivity Disorder – Characterized by difficulty sitting still, paying attention, or controlling impulsive behavior. For some people, the problem is so pervasive and persistent that it interferes with their daily lives, including home, academic, social, and work settings.[3] Some people use "ADD" when they are referring to this condition.

Age of Eligibility - All eligible children with disabilities, who have not graduated from high school, who are in need of special education and related services, and who are between the ages two to 21, inclusive.[4]

Amphetamines - A group of drugs used to stimulate the cerebral cortex of the brain. Sometimes used to treat hyperactivity. (See also Dexedrine and Ritalin.)[2]

Anoxia - Deficient amount of oxygen in the tissues of a part of the body or in the bloodstream supplying such part.[5]

Aptitude Test - A test designed to measure a person's ability to learn and the likelihood of success in future school work or in a specific career.

Articulation (Speech) - Refers to the production of speech sounds resulting from the movements of the lips, jaw, and tongue as they modify the flow of air.[1]

Assistive Technology - Equipment that enhances the ability of students and employees to be more efficient or successful. For individuals with learning disabilities, computer grammar checkers, an overhead projector used by a teacher, or the audiovisual information delivered through a CD-ROM would be typical examples.[6]

Association - Ability to relate concepts presented through the senses (visual, auditory, tactile, or kinesthetic).[7]

Attention Span - The length of time an individual can concentrate on a task without being distracted or losing interest. (See also Distractibility.)[2]

Auditory Discrimination - Ability to detect differences in sounds; may be gross ability, such as detecting the differences between the noises made by a cat and dog, or fine ability, such as detecting the differences made by the sounds of the letters m and n.

Auditory Figure-Ground - Ability to attend to one sound against a background of sounds (e.g., hearing the teacher's voice against classroom noise).[8]

Auditory Memory - Ability to retain information which has been presented orally; may be short term memory, such as recalling information presented several seconds before; long term memory, such as recalling information presented more than a minute before; or sequential memory, such as recalling a series of information in proper order.

Basic Skill Area - Includes such subjects as reading, writing, spelling, and mathematics.[1]

Behavior Modification - A technique intended to change behavior by rewarding desirable actions and ignoring or "negatively rewarding" undesirable actions.[2]

Benchmarks - The measurements that are taken at equal increments of time during the year and provide a marker or gauge that tells how well the student is doing in relation to the annual goal. Is same as short-term objectives.

Binocular Fusion - The blending of separate images from each eye into a single meaningful image.[2]

BIP - Behavioral Intervention Plan - A plan that utilizes positive behavioral interventions and supports to address behaviors that interfere with the learning of students with disabilities or with the learning of others, or behaviors that require disciplinary action.[4]

Blending - See Sound Blending.

Body Image - The concept and awareness of one's own body as it relates to space, movement, and other objects.[8]

Brain Damage - Any actual structural (tissue) damage due to any cause or causes. This means verifiable damage, not neurological performance that is indicative of damage.

Catastrophic Reaction - Extreme terror, grief, frustration, or anger without apparent cause. May be triggered by changes in routine, unexpected events, or over-stimulation. Children reacting in this manner may throw or break things, scream uncontrollably, or burst into tears.[2]

CEC - Council for Exceptional Children; an organization of professionals and parents working to help those with disabilities.

Central Auditory Processing Problem - The inability to understand spoken language in a meaningful way in the absence of what is commonly considered a hearing loss.[9]

Central Nervous System (CNS) - The brain and the spinal cord.[2]

Cerebral Cortex - The outer layer of the brain; controls thinking, feeling, and voluntary movement.[2]

Channel - The routes through which the content of communication flows. It includes both the modalities through which impression is received and the form of expression through which the response is made. Ex: Auditory - Vocal Channel.[7]

Child Study Committee - Is located in each school building to receive and act upon referrals of students suspected of being handicapped. The membership of this committee usually consists of at least three persons, including the school principal or a person chosen by the principal, the teacher or teachers, specialists, and the referring source if appropriate. (Note: Some school districts call this by other names.)

CNS - See Central Nervous System.

Cognition - The act or process of knowing; the various thinking skills and processes are considered cognitive skills.[10]

Cognitive Ability - Intellectual ability; thinking and reasoning skills.

Cognitive Style - A person's typical approach to learning activities and problem solving. For example, some people carefully analyze each task, deciding what must be done and in what order. Others react impulsively to situations.[2]

Collaborative Consultation - The student participates in the general education classroom. The special educator serves as consultant to general education teachers, collaborating with them in planning and implementing instructional accommodations in regular classrooms.

Compensation - Process in which a person is taught how to cope with his learning problems, how to "work around" skills or abilities which may be lacking; emphasis is placed on using the individual's strengths. (See Remediation.)

Conceptualization - The process of forming a general idea from what is observed. For example, seeing apples, bananas, and oranges and recognizing that they are all fruit.[2]

Conceptual Disorder - Disturbances in thinking, reasoning, generalizing, memorizing.

Configuration - The visual shape or form of words; may be used as a cue in word-attack skills.[11]

Congenital - A condition existing at birth or before birth. Congenital does not imply that a condition is hereditary.[2]

Contingency Self-Management - A student manages his or her own behavior with checklists or other cues and is rewarded or not based on his or her performance.

Continuum - A graded series of program options to serve students with differing levels of need of special education and related services.[12]

Coordination - The harmonious functioning of the muscles in the body to perform complex movements.[2]

Co-Teaching - The student participates in the general education classroom. The special educator and general educator teach the class together, both planning and delivering instruction.

Criterion Referenced Test - Designed to provide information on specific knowledge or skills possessed by a student. Such tests usually cover relatively small units of content and are closely related to instruction. Their scores have meaning in terms of what the student knows or can do, rather than their relation to the scores made by some external reference group.

Cross-Categorical - Refers to a system in which a teacher addresses more than one handicapping condition within one instructional period (for example, a student with learning disabilities may receive instruction in the same special education classroom as a student with an emotional/behavioral disorder). Also called multi-categorical.

Cross Dominance - A condition in which the preferred eye, hand, or foot is not on the same side of the body. For example, a person may be right-footed and right-eyed but left-handed. Also called Mixed Dominance.[2]

Decoding - The process of getting meaning from written or spoken symbols. (See Receptive Language.)[2]

Developmental Lag - A delay in some aspect of physical or mental development.[2]

Dexedrine - Trade name for one of several stimulant drugs often given to modify hyperactivity in children.[2]

Directionality - The ability to know right from left, up from down, forward from backward and direction and orientation.[13]

Disability - Any physical and/or mental problem that causes a person to have difficulty in doing certain tasks such as walking, seeing, hearing, speaking, learning, or working.

Discrepancy - Significant difference; defined differently by different school districts.

Discrimination - Process of detecting differences between and/or among stimuli.[1]

Disinhibition - Lack of restraint in responding to a situation. A child exhibiting disinhibition reacts impulsively and often inappropriately.[2]

Distractibility - The shifting of attention from the task at hand to sounds, sights, and other stimuli that normally occur in the environment.[2]

Due Process - The application of law to ensure that an individual's rights are protected. When applied to children with learning disabilities, Due Process means that parents have the right to request a full review of any educational program developed for their child. A Due Process hearing may be requested to ensure that all requirements of IDEA have been met.[2]

Dysarthria - A disorder of the speech muscles that affects the ability to pronounce words.[2]

Dyscalculia - Difficulty in understanding or using mathematical symbols or functions. A child with dyscalculia may be able to read and write but have difficulty performing mathematical calculations.

Dysfunction - Any disturbance or impairment in the normal functioning of an organ or body part.[2]

Dysgraphia - Difficulty in producing legible handwriting with age-appropriate speed.

Dyslexia - Impairment of the ability to deal with language (speaking, reading, spelling, writing).

Dysnomia - Difficulty in remembering names or recalling appropriate words to use in a given context.

Dyspraxia - Difficulty in performing fine motor acts such as drawing, buttoning, etc. A person with dyspraxia has difficulty producing and sequencing the movements necessary to perform these kinds of tasks.

Early Intervention Program - A program specially designed to assist developmentally delayed infants and preschool children. The purpose of this type of program is to help prevent or reduce problems as the child matures.[2]

Educational Consultant/Diagnostician - An individual who may be familiar with school curriculum and requirements at various grade levels; may or may not have a background in learning disabilities; may conduct educational evaluations.

Educational Evaluation - The evaluation generally consists of a battery of educational tests, along with an analysis of class work designed to determine the current levels of achievement in areas such as reading, math, spelling, etc.

Educational Psychologist - See School Psychologist.

EEG - Electroencephalogram - A graphic recording of electrical currents developed in the cerebral cortex during brain functioning. Sometimes called a "brain wave test." A machine called an electroencephalograph records the pattern of these electrical currents on paper.[2]

Eligibility - A team determines (1) whether a child has a handicapping condition which requires special education and, in some cases, related services such as speech and language therapy; (2) whether the child needs special education.

Encoding - The process of expressing language (i.e., selecting words; formulating them into ideas; producing them through speaking or writing). (See Expressive Language.)[1]

ESY - Extended School Year Services - Special Education and Related Services that are provided to a child with a disability beyond the normal school year, in accordance with the child's IEP, and at no cost to the parents of the child. ESY services must meet standards established by the LEA or SEA.[4]

Etiology - The study of the cause or origin of a condition or disease.[2]

Expressive Language - Communication through writing, speaking, and/or gestures.[2]

Eye-Hand Coordination - The ability of the eyes and hands to work together to complete a task. Examples are drawing and writing.[2]

FAPE – See Free Appropriate Public Education.

Far Point Copying - Writing while copying from a model some distance away, e.g. copying from a chalkboard.

FBA - Functional Behavioral Assessment - A process to determine the underlying cause or functions of a child's behavior that impede the learning of a child with a disability or the learning of the child's peers.[4]

FCLD - Foundation for Children with Learning Disabilities. (Now known as NCLD - The National Center for Learning Disabilities.)

Figure - Ground Discrimination - The ability to sort out important information from the surrounding environment. For example, hearing a teacher's voice while ignoring other classroom noises (air conditioners, heaters, etc.), or seeing a word among others on a crowded page.[2]

Fine Motor - The use of small muscles for precision tasks such as writing, tying bows, zipping a zipper, typing, doing puzzles.[2]

Free Appropriate Public Education (FAPE) - A guarantee given by IDEA to all eligible students with disabilities. It refers to specialized instruction, provided to a student at no cost to the parents, that addresses the student's needs and provides educational benefit.

Full-time Special Class (Self-Contained) - The student spends the majority of his or her day in a separate classroom with a smaller group of students who receive intensive instruction from a special educator in areas of need. The students may spend a portion of their day in regular classrooms but most of their instruction occurs in this special class.

General Education - All education not included under Special Education. (See Regular Education.)

Gross Motor - The use of large muscles for activities requiring strength and balance. Examples are walking, running, and jumping.[2]

Haptic Sense - Combined kinesthetic and tactile senses.[1]

Homebound Instruction - Homebound instruction is usually used for short, temporary periods of time when a student cannot attend school. In this situation, a teacher comes to the home and provides instruction there.

Hyperkinesis - Another term for hyperactivity.[1]

Hyperactivity (or Hyperkinesis) - Disorganized and disruptive behavior characterized by constant and excessive movement. A hyperactive child usually has difficulty sticking to one task for an extended period and may react more intensely to a situation than a child who is not hyperactive.[2]

Hypoactivity - Underactivity; child may appear to be in a daze, lacking energy.

IAES - Interim Alternative Educational Setting - An assignment which may be used for a maximum of 45 days when disciplinary action is needed.

IDEA - See Individuals with Disabilities Education Act.

IEP - See Individualized Education Plan (or Program).

Impulsivity - Reacting to a situation without considering the consequences.[2]

Inclusion - The idea that students with disabilities should be included in the general education program at their school. Can be partial inclusion (the student is in general education classes for some subjects) or full inclusion (the student is in all general education classes).

Individuals with Disabilities Education Act (IDEA) – Public Law 101-476, the Individuals with Disabilities Education Act. This law strengthens the rights of children with disabilities – and their parents. It builds upon the achievements gained under Public Law 94-142. Further clarification was provided in 1997 with Public Law 105-17.

Individualized Education Plan (IEP) - A written education prescription developed for each student with a disability. Sometimes called an Individualized Education Program. School districts are required by law to develop these plans, in cooperation with parents.[2]

Informal Tests - Task-oriented tests to provide information concerning specific skills. Are not standardized.[1]

Insertions - In reading, spelling, or math, the addition of letters or numbers which do not belong in a word or numeral, e.g. sinceare for sincere.

International Dyslexia Association - Formerly The Orton Dyslexia Society. An organization of professionals, scientists, and parents in the field of LD.

Inversions - In reading, spelling, or math, confusion of up-down directionality of letters or numbers, e.g. m for w, 6 for 9, etc.

I.Q. (Intelligence Quotient) - A standard score which usually has a mean of 100 and a standard deviation of 15. Such a score is obtained from an individual's performance on a standardized test of intelligence, such as the Wechsler Intelligence Scale for Children (WISC).

Itinerant Teacher - Special Education teacher who moves from school to school for instruction and consultation.[11]

Kinesthetic - Pertaining to the muscles.[2]

Kinesthetic Method - A way of teaching words by using the muscles. For example, a student might trace the outline of a word with a finger while looking at the word and saying aloud the word or its letters, in sequence.[2]

Laterality - The tendency to prefer the hand, foot, eye, and ear on a particular side of the body. For example, many people use their right hand when eating and their right foot when kicking.[2]

LD - Learning disability, learning disabled, learning disabilities.

LDA - Learning Disabilities Association of America.

LEA - Local Education Agency (a school district).

Learning Disabilities (LD) - Disorders of the basic psychological processes that affect the way a child learns. Many children with learning disabilities have average or above average intelligence. Learning disabilities may cause difficulties in listening, thinking, talking, reading, writing, spelling, or arithmetic. Included are perceptual handicaps, dyslexia, and developmental aphasia. Excluded are learning difficulties caused by visual, hearing, or motor handicaps, mental retardation, emotional disturbances, or environmental disadvantage.[2]

Learning Disorder - Damage or impairment to the nervous system that results in a learning disability.[2]

Learning Style - The channels through which a person best understands and retains learning. All individuals learn best through one or more channels: vision, hearing, movement, touching, or a combination of these.

Lesion - Abnormal change in body tissue due to injury or disease.[2]

Licensed Clinical Psychologist - A psychologist who is competent to apply the principles and techniques of psychological evaluation and psychotherapy to individual clients for the purpose of ameliorating problems of behavioral and/or emotional maladjustment.[14]

Licensed Clinical Social Worker - A social worker who, by education and experience, is professionally qualified to provide direct diagnostic, preventive and treatment services where functioning is threatened or affected by social and psychological stress or health impairment.[14]

Licensed Professional Counselor - A person trained in counseling and guidance services with emphasis on individual and group guidance and counseling; assists individuals in achieving more effective personal, social, educational, and career development and adjustment.[14]

Linguistic Approach - Method for teaching reading (decoding skills) which emphasizes use of word families. For example, the child is taught to read at and then subsequently is taught to decode words such as cat, bat, sat, mat, etc. Early stories adhere strictly to the words which have been taught previously and so may sometimes seem nonsensical, e.g., Sam sat on a mat. The cat sat on a mat. The cat is fat, etc.

Location - This term indicates where the special education and related services included in the IEP will be provided – such as the regular classroom, resource room, a combination of locations. Location is a general description; it does not need to be specific such as Mr. Smith's class or Virginia Elementary School.[12]

Mainstreaming - The practice of placing handicapped children with special educational needs into regular classrooms for at least a part of the child's school programs.[2]

Manifestation Determination - In all suspension or expulsion cases over 10 days, the school must conduct an IEP team meeting (with other qualified personnel) to determine if the behavior was a manifestation of the student's disability.

Maturation Lag - Delayed maturity in one or several skills or areas of development.[2]

Mediation - Mediation is a process by which you or the school invite a third, impartial party to hear both sides of your argument in an informal fashion.

Mental Age - The age for which a given score on a mental ability test is average or normal. The term is most appropriately used at the early age levels where mental growth is rapid.

Milieu Therapy - A clinical technique designed to control a child's environment and minimize conflicting and confusing information.[2]

Minimal Brain Dysfunction (MBD) - A broad and non-specific term formerly used to describe learning disabilities.[2]

Mixed Dominance - See Cross Dominance.

Mixed Laterality or Lateral Confusion - Tendency to perform some tasks with a right side preference and others with a left, or the shifting from right to left for certain activities.[15]

Modality - The sensory channel used to acquire information. Visual, auditory, tactile, kinesthetic, olfactory (sense of smell), and gustatory (taste) are the most common modalities.[2]

Motor - Pertaining to the origin or execution of muscular activity.[5]

Multi-Categorical - A special education classroom model in which students with more than one handicapping condition are assigned to a special education teacher. (Also called Cross-Categorical.)[1]

Multisensory - Involving most or all of the senses.[2]

NCLD - National Center for Learning Disabilities.

Near Point Copying - Writing while copying from a model close at hand, e.g., copying from a textbook.

Neurological Examination - Testing of the sensory or motor responses to determine if there is impairment of the nervous system.[2]

Noncategorical - Refers to a system of grouping handicapped children together without reference to a particular label or category of exceptionality.[10]

Norm-Referenced Test - (See Standardized Test.)

Norms - Statistics that provide a frame of reference by which meaning may be given to test scores. Norms are based upon the actual performance of pupils of various grades or ages in the standardization group for the test. Since they represent average or typical performance, they should not be regarded as standards or universally desirable levels of attainment. The most common types of norms are standard scores such as stanines or deviation IQ, percentile rank, grade or age equivalents.

Ombudsman - An official appointed to investigate complaints and speak for individuals with grievances.[2]

Oral Language - Those verbal communication skills needed to understand (listen) and to use (speak) language.

Organicity - A disorder of the central nervous system; brain damage.[2]

Orton Dyslexia Society - See International Dyslexia Association.

Orton-Gillingham Approach - An approach to teaching individuals with learning disabilities. The technique, devised by Dr. Samuel Orton, Anna Gilllingham, and Bessie Stillman, stresses a multisensory, phonetic, structured, sequential approach to learning.

Part-time Special Class (Resource) - The special educator takes students needing special education services into a special class for instruction only in specific areas in which they have difficulties.

Perceptual Abilities - The abilities to process, organize, and interpret the information obtained by the five senses; a function of the brain.

Perceptual Handicap - Difficulty in ability to process and organize as well as interpret information through the senses.

Perceptual Speed - Specific meaning of this term varies, depending upon the manner in which a given test measures this ability. May refer to motor speed (how fast something is copied or manipulated) or to visual discrimination (how quickly identical items in a given series are identified).

Perseveration - The repeating of words, motions, or tasks. A child who perseverates often has difficulty shifting to a new task and continues working on an old task long after classmates have stopped.[2]

Phonics Approach - Method for teaching reading and spelling in which emphasis is placed on learning the sounds which individual and various

combinations of letters make in a word. In decoding a word, the child sounds out individual letters or letter combinations and then blends them to form a word.

Phonological Awareness - The awareness of the sounds of speech and how they relate to print, including sequence of sounds within words, awareness of word boundaries, discrimination, blending, segmentation, deletion, rhyming.[16]

Procedural Safeguards - Section 1415 of IDEA which includes the rules of procedure that attempt to level the playing field between schools and parents. These safeguards include the opportunity to examine the child's records, to have advance notice before any significant actions are taken, the right to pursue mediation and litigation, the right to view exhibits and to know the names of witnesses in advance of a hearing, the right to confront and cross-examine witnesses, the right to a fair hearing and, for parents, the right to possible reimbursement of reasonable attorney's fees.[12]

Program - The special education and related services, including accommodations, modifications, supplementary aids and services, as determined by a child's IEP.[17]

Program Modifications - Included in this term are any modifications needed by the student in order (1) to advance appropriately toward attaining each of the annual goals; (2) to be involved and progress in the general curriculum, and to participate in extracurricular and other nonacademic activities; and (3) to be educated and participate with other students with and without disabilities.[12]

Psychiatrist - An individual who treats behavioral or emotional problems. Is a licensed medical doctor (M.D.), so is permitted to use medications in treating a problem.

Psychological Examination - An evaluation by a certified school or clinical psychologist of the intellectual and behavioral characteristics of a person.[1]

Psychomotor - Pertaining to the motor effects of psychological processes. Psychomotor tests are tests of motor skill which depend upon sensory or perceptual motor coordination.[5]

Public Law (P.L.) 94-142 - The federal Education for All Handicapped Children Act that became law in 1975. P.L. 94-142 requires each state to provide free and appropriate public education to all handicapped children from birth through age 21. The law also requires that an Individualized Education Plan be prepared for each handicapped child, that parents must have access to their child's school records, and are entitled to a Due Process hearing if they are dissatisfied with the educational plan. Reauthorized as IDEA. (See IDEA.)[2]

Readiness - Acquisition of skills considered prerequisite for academic learning.[11]

Reasoning Ability - Specific meaning of this term varies, depending upon the manner in which a given test measures this ability; generally refers to nonverbal, deductive, inductive, analytical thinking.

Receptive Language (Decoding) - Language that is spoken or written by others and received by the individual. The receptive language skills are listening and reading.[10]

Referral - A request made for special education evaluation to the school principal or special education coordinator.

Regrouping - In arithmetic, the processes traditionally known as carrying in addition or borrowing in subtraction.

Regular Education - All education not included under Special Education (same as General Education).

Rehabilitation Act of 1973 - The Civil Rights Act for the Handicapped. The act prohibits discrimination on the basis of physical or mental handicap in all federally-assisted programs. Section 504 of the act provides further guarantees.

Related Services - Services including transportation and such developmental, corrective, and other supportive services as may be required to assist a child with a disability to benefit from special education. These services may include speech-language pathology and audiology services, physical and occupational therapy, psychological services, recreation (including therapeutic recreation), social work services, counseling services (including rehabilitation and psychological counseling), medical services for diagnostic and evaluation purposes, and parent counseling and training. Included may be developmental, corrective, or supportive services such as artistic and cultural programs, and art, music and dance therapy if they are required to assist a child with a disability to benefit from special education.[4]

Remediation - Process in which an individual is provided instruction and practice in skills which are weak or nonexistent in an effort to develop/strengthen these skills.

Resource Teacher - A specialist who works with students with disabilities; may also act as a consultant to other teachers.[1]

Reversals - Difficulty in reading or reproducing letters alone, letters in words, or words in sentences in their proper position in space or in proper order. May also refer to reversal of mathematical concepts (add/subtract, multiple/divide) and symbols (< > x +). See also Transposition.[1]

Ritalin - Trade name for one of several stimulant drugs often given to modify hyperactivity in children.[2]

Scatter - Variability in an individual's test scores.[18]

School Psychologist - A person who specializes in problems manifested in and associated with educational systems and who uses psychological concepts and methods in programs which attempt to improve learning conditions for students.[14]

SEA - State Education Agency (the state Department of Education).

Section 504 - See Rehabilitation Act of 1973.[12]

Self-Concept - How a person feels and thinks about himself or herself. Sometimes called self-image or self-esteem.[2]

Self-Contained – See Full-time Special Class.

Semantics - The meaning or understanding given to oral or written language.

Sensorimotor - Relationship between sensation and movement. Sometimes spelled sensory-motor.[2]

Sensory Acuity - The ability to respond to sensation at normal levels of intensity.[5]

Sequence - The detail of information in its accustomed order (for example, days of the week, the alphabet, etc.).[1]

Service Plan - An individualized educational plan designed for students with special needs who are enrolled in a private school setting.

Short Term Objectives - See Benchmarks.

Sight Words - Words a child can recognize on sight without aid of phonics or other word-attack skills.[11]

Sight Word Approach - Also known as "whole word" approach; method for teaching reading which relies heavily upon a child's visual memory skills, with minimal emphasis on sounding out a word; child memorizes the word based on its overall configuration.

SLD - Specific Learning Disability. Difficulty in certain areas of learning as contrasted with a general learning disability, (i.e., difficulty in all areas of learning). Also sometimes refers to Specific Language Disability.

Slingerland Method - A highly structured, multisensory teaching method designed for group instruction of persons with specific learning disabilities. Named for its developer, Beth Slingerland.[2]

Social Perceptions - The ability to interpret stimuli in the social environment and appropriately relate such interpretations to social situations.

Socio-Cultural - Combined social and cultural factors as they affect the development of a child in all areas of life.[1]

Soft Neurological Signs - Neurological abnormalities that are mild or slight and difficult to detect, as contrasted with the gross or obvious neurological abnormalities.[10]

Sound Blending - The ability to combine smoothly all the sounds or parts of a word into the whole.[11]

Spatial Orientation - Awareness of space around the person in terms of distance, form, direction, and position.[5]

Spatial Relationships - The ability to perceive the relationships between self and two or more objects and the relationships of the objects to each other.[5]

Special Education - Specially-designed instruction to meet the needs of students with disabilities.

Specific Language Disability (SLD) - Difficulty in some aspect of learning how to read, write, spell, or speak. Is also called Specific Language Learning Disability (SLD sometimes refers to Specific Learning Disability.)

Standardized Test - A test that compares a child's performance with the performance of a large group of similar children (usually children of the same age). Also called a norm-referenced test. IQ tests and most achievement tests are standardized.[2]

Structure - Consistent use of rules, limits, and routines. The use of structure reassures a child with learning disabilities that the environment is somewhat predictable and stable.[2]

Structural Analysis - Using syllabication, prefix, suffix, and root word clues, etc. to read or spell a word.

Substitution - In reading, spelling or math, interchanging a given letter, number, or word for another, e.g. <u>sereal</u> for <u>cereal</u>.

Supplementary Aids and Services - Aids, services, and other supports that are provided in regular education classes or other education-related settings to enable a child with disabilities to be educated with children without disabilities to the maximum extent appropriate.[4]

Supports for School Personnel - This refers to any needed support for the regular education teacher in order for the student with L.D. to be able to participate in and progress in the general education curriculum. This may include assistance in providing program modifications as well as specific training in strategies and skills that will assist the teacher in working with the student in the classroom.[12]

Survival Skills - Minimal skills needed for a student to cope with everyday society.[1]

Syntax - Grammar, sentence structure, and word order in oral or written language.

Syndrome - A set of symptoms that indicates a specific disorder.[2]

Tactile - Having to do with the sense of touch.[2]

Task Analysis - The technique of carefully examining a particular task to discover the elements it comprises and the processes required to perform it.[10]

Thematic Maturity - Ability to write in a logical, organized manner that easily and efficiently conveys meaning.

Thinking Skills - Refers to the manner in which humans acquire, interpret, organize, store, retrieve, and employ knowledge.[1]

Transition Plan - The part of the IEP that outlines what transition services are necessary to help the student move from school to the next step in their life.

Transition Services - Component of the IEP, beginning by the time a student with a disability reaches age 14. The term identifies a coordinated set of activities for the student, designed within an outcome-oriented process, that promotes movement from school to post-school activities. Transition goals may include post-secondary education, vocational training, integrated employment (including supported employment), continuing and adult education, adult services, independent living, or community participation.[4]

Transposition - In reading, spelling, or math, confusion in the order of letters in a word or numbers in a numeral, e.g., <u>sliver</u> for <u>silver</u>, <u>432</u> for <u>423</u>, etc.

VAKT - Acronym for visual-auditory-kinesthetic-tactile; multisensory teaching approach which emphasizes using all of the senses to teach skills and concepts.

Verbal Ability - Specific meaning of this term varies, depending upon the manner in which a given test measures this ability. Generally refers to oral or spoken language abilities.

Visual Association - Ability to relate concepts which are presented visually, through pictures or written words. For example, given a picture of a dog, house, flower and bone, the child is able to indicate that the dog and bone go together.

Visual Closure - Ability to see only the outline of an item or picture, or a partially completed picture, and still be able to indicate what it is.

Visual Discrimination - Ability to detect similarities and/or differences in materials which are presented visually, e.g., ability to discriminate <u>h</u> from <u>n</u>, <u>o</u> from <u>c</u>, <u>b</u> from <u>d</u>, etc.

Visual Figure-Ground - Ability to focus on the foreground of material presented visually, rather than background. Those who have difficulty with this may find it hard to keep their place while copying or reading, may find a crowded page of print or illustrations confusing, etc.

Visual Memory - Ability to retain information which is presented visually; may be short-term memory, such as recalling information presented several seconds before; long-term memory, such as recalling

information presented more than a minute before; or sequential memory, such as recalling a series of information in proper order.

Visual Motor - Ability to translate information received visually into a motor response. Difficulties are often characterized by poor handwriting, etc.

Visual Perception - Ability to correctly interpret what is seen. For example, a child sees a triangle and identifies it as a triangle.[2]

Word Attack Skills - Ability to analyze unfamiliar words visually and phonetically.[2]

Word recognition - Ability to read or pronounce a word; usually implies that the word is recognized immediately by sight and that the child does not need to apply word analysis skills. Does not imply understanding of the word.

Written Language - Encompasses all facets of written expression, e.g. handwriting, capitalization, punctuation, spelling, format, ability to express one's thoughts in sentences and paragraphs, etc.

The following sources were used in the development of this glossary:

[1] Virginia Department of Education. *Guidelines for Programs for Students with Specific Learning Disabilities in Virginia's Public Schools.* 1980.

[2] Foundation for Children with Learning Disabilities. *The FCLD Learning Disabilities Resource Guide.* 1985.

[3] www.CHADD.org

[4] Virginia Department of Education. *Regulations Governing Special Education Programs for Children with Disabilities in Virginia.* 2000.

[5] Myers, P., and D. Hammill. *Methods for Learning Disorders.* 2d ed. New York: John Wiley and Sons, Inc., 1976.

[6] www.ldanatl.org

[7] Kirk, S. A., and W. D. Kirk. *Psycholinguistic Learning Disabilities: Diagnosis and Remediation.* Urbana, Ill.: University of Illinois Press, 1971.

[8] *SLD Gazette*. Massachusetts Association for Children and Adults with Learning Disabilities. March 1977.

[9] Learning Disabilities Association of America, *Fact Sheet*, Jan. 1996.

[10] Lerner, J. W. *Children with Learning Disabilities*. 2ᵈ ed. Boston: Houghton Mifflin Co., 1976.

[11] Wallace, G. *Characteristics of Learning Disabilities: A Television Series. Richmond, Va.: The Learning Disabilities Council, 1975.*

[12] Tomey, H.A., III. *Individualized Education Program: The Process*. Richmond, Va.: Virginia Department of Education, 2000.

[13] Valett, R. E. *The Remediation of Learning Disabilities*. Palo Alto, Calif.: Fearon Publishers, 1967.

[14] Virginia Department of Health Regulatory Boards. *Code of Virginia, Chapter 28 – Behavioral Science Professions.*

[15] Lerner, J. W. *Learning Disabilities: Theories, Diagnosis and Teaching Strategies*. Boston: Houghton Mifflin Co., 1971.

[16] Cicci, R. Pre-Conference Symposium Handout, "Language, Learning, and Literacy." Virginia Department of Education, Arlington, Va., April 19, 1991.

[17] Wright, P.W.D., and P.D. Wright. *Wrightslaw: Special Education Law.* Hartsfield, Va.: Harbor House Law Press, 1999.

[18] Bryan, T., and J. Bryan. *Understanding Learning Disabilities*. 2ᵈ ed. Sherman Oaks, Calif.: Alfred Publishing Co., 1978.

ENDNOTES

Chapter 1. Learning Disabilities: The Hidden Disability

1.   Several sources have been used in this book's attempt to delineate what learning disabilities are: American Psychiatric Association: *Diagnostic and Statistical Manual of Mental Disorders* (4th ed.), 1994, 78; W. N. Bender, *Learning Disabilities: Characteristics, Identification, and Teaching Strategies* (3d ed.), Boston: Allyn & Bacon, 1998; and D. P. Hallahan and J. M. Kauffman, *Exceptional Learners: An Introduction to Special Education* (8th ed.), Boston: Allyn & Bacon, 2000, 210.

2.   Virginia Association for Children and Adults with Learning Disabilities, *I'm Not Lazy...I Want To; I'm Not Dumb...I Try To; I'm Not Naughty...I Need Help. Maybe It's a Learning Disability.*

3.   The discussion concerning the difference between ADD and ADHD continues. The differences in points of view are represented by three sources: American Psychiatric Association (see note 1); R. A. Barkley, *Attention-Deficit Hyperactivity Disorder: A Handbook for Diagnosis and Treatment*, New York: Guilford Press, 1998; and D. P. Hallahan and J. M. Kauffman (see note 1).

4.   Rebecca Chapman Booth, "What Does ADD 'Look' Like?" [Electronic Data Base] 2001, prepared by Rebecca Chapman Booth © 1998, all rights reserved, [www.add.org, National ADDA]. Used with permission of the author.

5.   Peter Jaksa, "Fact Sheet on Attention Deficit Hyperactivity Disorder (ADHD/ADD)," [Electronic Data Base] 2001, © 1998, Peter Jaksa, [www.add.org, National ADDA]. Used with permission of the author.

6.   See note 4.

7.   Ibid.

8.   See note 5.

9.   See note 5.

10.   Virginia Department of Education, "School-Based Interventions," *Attention-Deficit Hyperactivity Disorder and the Schools*, 1995, 20.

11.   See note 4.

12.   See note 4.

13.   The two sources used to develop this information are: George Bright, M.D., and M. L. Trusdell, "Characteristics of Learning Disabilities," Paper developed for the Learning Disabilities Council, Richmond, Va.; and C. Nissenbaum, *The Problem of Learning Disabilities—Dyslexia*, 2d ed., 1985, used with permission of the National Institute of Dyslexia.

Chapter 2. Coping as a Parent

1.   H. Fried, *Plain Talk About Children with Learning Disabilities*, Washington, D.C.: U. S. Department of Health, Education and Welfare, 1979, 3.

Chapter 3. Helping Your Child at Home

1. R. Frank, "Self-Esteem Building," *Interact*, April 1985, 4-5.
2. S. Stevens, *The Learning Disabled Child: Ways That Parents Can Help*, Winston-Salem, N.C.: John F. Blair Publishers, 1980, 84-85.
3. See note 1.
4. B. Osman, "Spotting Problems and Setting a Course," *New York Times Fall Survey*, Nov. 11, 1984: Section 12, 46.
5. _____, "Learning Disabilities: A Family Affair," *Their World*, New York: Foundation for Children with Learning Disabilities, 1987.
6. P. Rozantes, "Hints for a Happier Home," *The Observer*, February 1981, 7.
7. Ibid.
8. Ibid.
9. See note 5.
10. See note 6.
11. M. Brutten, S. O. Richardson, and C. Mangel, *Something's Wrong with My Child*, New York: Harcourt Brace Jovanovich, 1973, 136.
12. Ibid., 137-138.
13. See note 6.
14. Brutten, Richardson, and Mangel, *Something's Wrong with My Child*, 127.
15. See note 2.
16. Ibid., 96.
17. Ibid., 98.
18. D. Pastor, "Self-Control Therapy with Learning Disabled Children," *ACLD Newsbriefs*, Pittsburgh, Pa.: Association for Children and Adults with Learning Disabilities, January/February 1986.
19. Ibid.
20. Brutten, Richardson, and Mangel, *Something's Wrong with My Child*, 134.
21. Ibid., 131.
22. Ibid., 132.
23. W. Sternberg, "Self-Esteem and Your Learning Disabled Child," *HELP, Arkansas ACLD Newsletter*.
24. See note 2.
25. S. White, "Building Social Skills and Self-Esteem: How Parents Can Help," *Minnesota ACLD Newsletter*.
26. Ibid.
27. Ibid.
28. Brutten, Richardson, and Mangel, *Something's Wrong with My Child*, 141-142.
29. M. Guhsey, "Behavior Management Tips," adapted from a paper developed for *Weekday Early Education*, Richmond, Va.
30. U. S. Department of Health, Education, and Welfare, adapted from *Plain Talk About Dealing with an Angry Child*, 1978.

Chapter 4. The Student with Learning Disabilities at School

1.   The interpretations given in this chapter to Public Law 101-476, the Individuals with Disabilities Education Act (IDEA); to Section 504 of the Rehabilitation Act of 1973; and to the Americans with Disabilities Act (ADA) would not have been possible without the knowledgeable guidance of Harley A. Tomey, III, Educational Specialist in Learning Disabilities with the Virginia Department of Education, and of Robin L. Hegner, Esq. The primary sources were *The Individualized Education Program: The Process* by Mr. Tomey, published by the Virginia Department of Education; and the *Federal Register*, vol. 64, no. 48, March 12, 1999.

2.   The graphic appearing on page 2 of this chapter is printed with permission of the Parent Educational Advocacy Training Center (PEATC), 6320 Augusta Dr., Suite 1200, Springfield, VA 22150. PEATC has Parent Training Centers in Virginia, Maryland, and West Virginia. (Appendix B-3, No. 4, has further information.)

3.   D. Lillie and P. Place, *Partners—A Guide to Working with Schools for Parents of Children with Special Instructional Needs*, Glenview, Ill.: Scott Foresman & Co., 1982.

4.   National Information Center for Handicapped Children and Youth, *NICHCY News Digest*, 1984.

5.   National Information Center for Handicapped Children and Youth, *Closer Look*, 1977.

6.   Ibid.

7.   See note 3.

8.   See note 5.

9.   T. Craig, "Especially For Parents—Don't Wait and See!" *Their World*, New York: Foundation for Children with Learning Disabilities, 1984.

10.   See note 3.

11.   See note 3.

12.   *Federal Register*, Section 504 of the Rehabilitation Act of 1973.

Chapter 5. The Young Adult

1.   Public Law 101-476, popularly called IDEA (Individuals with Disabilities Education Act), is the basis of the information given in this section of Chapter 5. More details about IDEA can be obtained through OSERS (202/205-5465) or through the internet (www.ed.gov/offices/OSERS/IDEA/index.html).

2.   Additional information about the legislation discussed in this section on ADA (Americans with Disabilities Act) is available through the ADA Information Line at the U.S. Department of Justice (800/514-0301).

3.   The Office of Civil Rights (202/205-5413) was the source of this information on Section 504 of the Rehabilitation Act of 1973.

4.   M. Dietz Meyer, "Get Ready for College, *Their World*, New York: Foundation for Children with Learning Disabilities, 1988, 62-63.

5.   Ibid.

6.   B. Scheiber and J. Talpin, *Campus Access for Learning Disabled Students*, Washington, D.C.: National Information Center for Handicapped Children and Youth, 1985.

7.   J. W. Blalock and D. J. Johnson, *Adults with Learning Disabilities*, New York: Harcourt Brace and Jovanovich, 1987.

8. Portions of this list have been provided by the National Center for Learning Disabilities, New York, by e-mail.

Chapter 6. Adults with Learning Disabilities

1. "National Resources for Adults with Learning Disabilities," *NCLD News*, vol. 7, no. 4, Fall 1997, 2. Information in this section of *Understanding Learning Disabilities...*was excerpted by *NCLD News* from publications of the National Adult Literacy and Learning Disabilities Center and HEATH Resource Center.
2. Ibid.
3. Ibid.
4. Dale S. Brown, "Job Accommodations for People with Dyslexia: Coping in the Workplace," *Perspectives*, Baltimore, Md.: International Dyslexia Association, 1996.
5. Ibid.
6. Sally L. Smith, "Self-Esteem: Issues for the Adult Learner," *Linkages*, Washington, D.C.: National Adult Literacy and Learning Disabilities Center, 1994. Sally L. Smith is the author of *Succeeding Against the Odds: Strategies and Insights from the Learning Disabled*.
7. Ibid.
8. Paul Gerber, R. Ginsberg, and H. B. Reiff, "Identifying Alterable Patterns in Employment Success for Highly Successful Adults with Learning Disabilities," *Journal of Learning Disabilities*, 1992, vol. 25, no. 8, 475-487.
9. Ibid., 484.
10. H. B. Reiff, P. J. Gerber, and R. Ginsberg, "Definitions of Learning Disabilities from Adults with Learning Disabilities: The Insiders' Perspectives," *Journal of Learning Disabilities*, 1993, 16:121.

Chapter 7. Assistive Technology

1. Much of the information for this chapter is from material provided by the National Adult Literacy and Learning Disabilities Center, a program of the National Institute for Literacy. Some of the most helpful information was found in their publication, *Assistive Technology*, Spring, 1996. It lists several additional sources of information and services, including Closing the Gap, a disabilities information center that produces a quarterly newsletter on disabilities technology and hosts a yearly hands-on assistive computer technology conference. They can be contacted at Closing the Gap, Inc., P. O. Box 68, 526 Main Street, Henderson, Minn. 56044, phone 507/248-3294 (www.closingthegap.com).
2. Adrienne Riviere, "Meeting the Needs of Adults with Learning Disabilities," *Assistive Technology*, Washington, D.C.: National Adult Literacy and Learning Disabilities Center, Summer 1996, 1-2.

Chapter 8. Gifted, with Learning Disabilities

1. *ERIC Digest*: Clearinghouse on Handicapped and Gifted Children, *Gifted but Learning Disabled: A Puzzling Paradox*, Digest #E479, EC-90, 6.
2. Priscilla L. Vail, *Smart Kids with School Problems*, New York: E. P. Dutton, 1987.
3. "Gifted and L.D.: A Puzzling Combination," *Outlook*, May-June 1991.

4. Bobbie H. Jones, "The Gifted Dyslexic," *Annals of Dyslexia*, Baltimore, Md.: The International Dyslexia Association, 1986, 36:305.

5. See note 1.

6. See note 1.

7. See note 3.

8. See note 3.

9. Priscilla L. Vail, "The Double Mask: Concealment, Power, and the Courage to Stand Revealed," *Perspectives*, Baltimore, Md.: International Dyslexia Association, 2000, 7.

10. See note 3 above. This source cites evidence provided by Dr. Candice Feiring (who was Assistant Professor of Pediatrics at Rutgers Medical School, New Brunswick, N.J.) and Dr. Laurence Taft (who was chairman of the Department of Pediatrics at Rutgers). In an article in *Pediatric Annals*, the two doctors theorized concerning the low incidence of the identification of gifted children with L.D.

11. See note 4, 307.

12. See note 9, 8.

13. See note 4, 316.

14. See note 3, 6.

BIBLIOGRAPHY

American Psychiatric Association. *Diagnostic and Statistical Manual of Mental Disorders.* 4th ed. (1994).

Americans with Disabilities Act of 1990 (ADA). P.L. 101-336. 42 USC 12101 note.

Barkley, R. A. *Attention-Deficit Hyperactivity Disorder: A Handbook for Diagnosis and Treatment.* New York: Guilford Press, 1998.

Bell, J. M. "The Lifelong Impact of a Label." Schwab Learning™. www.schwablearning.org (2001).

Bender, W. N. *Learning Disabilities: Characteristics, Identification, and Teaching Strategies.* 3rd ed. Boston: Allyn and Bacon, 1998.

Blalock, J. W., and D. J. Johnson. *Adults with Learning Disabilities.* New York: Harcourt Brace Jovanovich, 1987.

Booth, R. C. "What Does ADD 'Look' Like?" www.add.org/content/abc/basic.htm. Prepared by Rebecca Chapman Booth © 1998.

Bright, G., M.D., and M. L. Trusdell. "Characteristics of Learning Disabilities." Paper developed for the Learning Disabilities Council, Richmond, Va.

Brown, D. S. "Get Your Child Ready for Work." *Newsbriefs,* Learning Disabilities Association of America (September-October 1988).

_____. "Job Accommodations for People with Dyslexia: Coping in the Workplace." *Perspectives,* The International Dyslexia Association (1996).

Brutten, M., S. O. Richardson, and C. Mangel. *Something's Wrong with My Child.* New York: Harcourt Brace Jovanovich, 1973.

Bryan, T., and J. Bryan. *Understanding Learning Disabilities.* 2nd ed. Sherman Oaks, Calif.: Alfred Publishing Co., 1978.

Center on Technology and Learning Disabilities, The Frostig Center, Pasadena, Calif.

Cicci, R. Pre-Conference Symposium Handout. "Language Learning and Literacy." Virginia Department of Education, Arlington, Va. (April 19, 1991).

Craig, T. "Especially for Parents—Don't Wait and See!" *Their World* (1984).

Dietz Meyer, M. "Get Ready for College." *Their World* (1988): 62-63.

"Fact Sheet." Learning Disabilities Association of America (January 1996).

Federal Register 64 (March 12, 1999).

Forness, S. R., and K. A. Kavale. *Impact of ADHD on School Systems*. In P. Jensen and J. R. Cooper (eds.), NIH Consensus Conference in ADHD. In press.

Foundation for Children with Learning Disabilities. *The FCLD Learning Disabilities Resource Guide* (1985).

Frank, R. "Self-Esteem Building." *Interact* (April 1985): 4-5.

Fried, H. *Plain Talk About Children with Learning Disabilities*. Washington, D.C.: U. S. Department of Health, Education and Welfare, 1979.

Gerber, P., R. Ginsberg, and H. Reiff. "Indentifying Alterable Patterns in Employment Success for Highly Successful Adults with Learning Disabilities." *Journal of Learning Disabilities* 25 (1992): 475-487.

"Gifted and L.D.: A Puzzling Combination." *Outlook* (May-June 1991): 6.

"Gifted but Learning Disabled: A Puzzling Paradox." *ERIC Digest*, Clearinghouse on Handicapped and Gifted Children. Digest #E479, EC-90.

Gordon, S. *A Survival Guide for People Who Have Handicaps*. Syracuse, N.Y.: Institute for Family Research and Education.

Guhsey, M. "Behavior Management Tips." Adapted from a paper developed for Weekday Early Education, Richmond, Va.

Hallahan, D. P., and J. M. Kauffman. *Exceptional Learners: An Introduction to Special Education*. 8th ed. Boston: Allyn and Bacon, 2000.

Hallahan, D. P., J. M. Kauffman, and J. W. Lloyd. *Introduction to Learning Disabilities*. Boston: Allyn and Bacon, 2000.

Houck, C., and C. Geller. *Learning Disabilities: Understanding Concepts, Characteristics and Issues*. Englewood Cliffs: Prentice Hall, Inc., 1984.

Individuals with Disabilities Education Act of 1990 (IDEA). P.L. 101-476, Title 20, USC Sec. 1400 et seq.

International Dyslexia Association. *The Orton Emeritus Series* (1993-1999).

Jaksa, P. "Fact Sheet on Attention Deficit Hyperactivity Disorder (ADHD/ADD)." www.add.org/content/abc/factsheet/htm (1998).

Jones, B. H. "The Gifted Dyslexic." *Annals of Dyslexia* 36 (1986): 305.

Kirk, S. A., and W. D. Kirk. *Psycholinguistic Learning Disabilities: Diagnosis and Remediation.* Urbana, Ill.: Univ. of Illinois Press, 1971.

Lerner, J. W. *Learning Disabilities: Theories, Diagnosis, and Teaching Strategies.* Boston: Houghton Mifflin Co., 1971.

Lerner, J. W. *Children with Learning Disabilities.* 2nd ed. Boston: Houghton Mifflin Co., 1976.

Lillie, D., and P. Place. *Partners—A Guide to Working with Schools for Parents of Children with Special Instructional Needs.* Glenview, Ill.: Scott Foresman and Co., 1982.

"List of Appropriate School-Based Accommodations." www.add.org/content/school.htm.

Massachusetts Association for Children and Adults with Learning Disabilities. *SLD Gazette* (March 1977).

Myers, P., and D. Hammill. *Methods for Learning Disorders.* 2nd ed. New York: John Wiley and Sons, Inc., 1976.

National Adult Literacy and Learning Disabilities Center. *Assistive Technology* (1996).

National Information Center for Handicapped Children and Youth. *Closer Look* (1977).

_____. *NICHCY News Digest* (1984).

"National Resources for Adults with Learning Disabilities." *NCLD News* 7 (Fall 1997): 2.

"NCLD's Resource List." *Their World* (2000).

Nied, B., and K. Nied. "Jonathan's Story." *Their World* (2000).

Nissenbaum, C. *The Problem of Learning Disabilities-Dyslexia.* 2nd ed. Chevy Chase, Md.: Tri-Services, Inc., 1985.

Osman, B. "Spotting Problems and Setting a Course." *New York Times Fall Survey* (November 11, 1984): 46.

_____. "Learning Disabilities: A Family Affair." *Their World* (1987).

Parent Educational Advocacy Training Center (PEATC), Springfield, Va.

Pastor, D. "Self-Control Therapy with Learning Disabled Children." *ACLD Newsbriefs* (January/February 1986).

Payne, Nancie. "Tips for Workplace Success." *Linkages* 2 (Spring 1995).

Raskind, M. H., and E. L. Higgins. "Assistive Technology for Postsecondary Students with Learning Disabilities: An Overview." *Journal of Learning Disabilities* (1998).

Reiff, H. B., P. J. Gerber, and R. Ginsberg. "Definitions of Learning Disabilities from Adults with Learning Disabilities: The Insiders' Perspectives." *Journal of Learning Disabilities* 16 (Spring 1993): 121.

Riviere, A. "Meeting the Needs of Adults with Learning Disabilities." *Assistive Technology* (Summer 1996): 1-2.

Robins, Cynthia. "One Man's Battle Against Dyslexia." *San Francisco Examiner* (March 8, 1992).

Rozantes, P. "Hints for a Happier Home." *The Observer* (February 1981): 7.

Salvia, J., and J. E. Ysseldyke. *Assessment*. 7th ed. Boston: Houghton Mifflin, 1998.

Scheiber, B., and J. Talpin. *Campus Access for Learning Disabled Students*. Washington, D.C.: National Information Center for Handicapped Children and Youth, 1985.

Schwab Foundation for Learning. *Bridges to Reading: What to Do When You Suspect Your Child Has a Reading Problem* (1999).

Section 504, Rehabilitation Act of 1973, P. L. 112, Vol. 87: 355.

Smith, S. L. "Self-Esteem: Issues for the Adult Learner." *Linkages* (Summer 1994): 1.

Smith, T. E. C., C. A. Dowdy, E. A. Polloway, and G. E. Blalock. *Children and Adults with Learning Disabilities*. Boston: Allyn and Bacon, 1997.

Sternberg, W. "Self-Esteem and Your Learning Disabled Child." *HELP*. Arkansas ACLD Newsletter.

Stevens, S. *The Learning Disabled Child: Ways that Parents Can Help*. Winston-Salem, N.C.: John F. Blair Publishers, 1980.

Sturomski, Neil. "Taking the GED Tests: Accommodating Accommodations." *Newsbriefs* (January/February 2001).

Tomey, H. A., III. *Individualized Education Program: The Process*. Richmond, Va.: Virginia Department of Education, 2000.

U. S. Department of Education. Office of Special Education and Rehabilitation Services. "Clarification of Policy to Address the Needs of Children with Attention Deficit Disorders Within General and/or Special Education." Assistant Secretary Memorandum, September 16, 1991. www.add.org/content/legal/memo.htm.

_____. *Nineteenth Annual Report to Congress on the Implementation of the Individuals with Disabilities Education Act*, 1997.

_____. "Final Regulations for Assistance to States for the Education of Children with Disabilities and the Early Intervention Program for Infants and Toddlers with Disabilities." *Federal Register* 64 (March 12, 1999).

U. S. Department of Health, Education, and Welfare. *Plain Talk About Dealing with an Angry Child* (1978).

Uzielli, Alessandro. "A Brother's Perspective." Adaptation of a speech given at the 1999 NCLD Benefit. *Their World* (2000).

Vail, P. L. *Smart Kids with School Problems*. New York: E. P. Dutton, 1987.

_____. "The Double Mask: Concealment, Power, and the Courage to Stand Revealed." *Perspectives* (Spring 2000).

Valett, R. E. *The Remediation of Learning Disabilities*. Palo Alto, Calif.: Fearon Publishers, 1967.

Virginia Association for Children and Adults with Learning Disabilities. *I'm Not Lazy...I Want to; I'm Not Dumb ...I Try to; I'm Not Naughty ...I Need Help; Maybe It's a Learning Disability*.

Virginia Department of Education. *Program Guidelines for Students with Specific Learning Disabilities in Virginia's Public Schools*, 1980.

_____. "School-Based Interventions." *Attention-Deficit Hyperactivity Disorder and the Schools*, 1995.

_____. *Guide to Discipline Under IDEA '97 Amendments and Federal Regulations*, June 1999.

_____. *Regulations Governing Special Education Programs for Children with Disabilities in Virginia*, 2000.

_____. *The Virginia 2000 College Selection Guidebook for Students with Disabilities, Their Parents, and High School Staff*, 2000.

Virginia Department of Health Regulatory Boards. *Code of Virginia, Chapter 28— Behavioral Science Professions*.

Wallace, G. *Characteristics of Learning Disabilities: A Television Series*. Richmond, Va.: The Learning Disabilities Council, 1975.

Walter, P. "It's Never Too Late." *Their World* (1999).

Wanderman, R. "One Person's Path to Literacy." www.ldresources.com (2000).

Wehmeyer, M. L., M. Agran, and C. Hughes. *Teaching Self-Determination to Students with Disabilities: Basic Skills for Successful Transition*. Baltimore, Md.: Paul H. Brookes, 1998.

Westhead, E. "Post-Secondary Education for the L.D. Student—A Few Suggestions." Paper prepared for the Virginia Association for Children and Adults with Learning Disabilities, 1980.

White, S. "Building Social Skills and Self-Esteem: How Parents Can Help." *Minnesota ACLD Newsletter*.

Wright, P. W. D., and P. D. Wright. *Wrightslaw: Special Education Law*. Hartsfield, Va.: Harbor House Law Press, 1999.

Suggested Changes and Additions to This Book

Please mail this form to:

Learning Disabilities Council
P.O. Box 8451
Richmond, Virginia 23226

I suggest the following changes or additions to **Understanding Learning Disabilities: A Parent Guide and Workbook** (Third Edition, 2002):

_____

_____

_____

_____

_____

_____

_____

Submitted by:

_____
Name (Optional)

_____
Address

_____
                                                    Zip

Phone (____)_____

FAX   (____)_____

E-mail _____